"*Emptying the Nest* is a wonderful blend of valuable insights, innovative advice, and much needed 'loving accountability' for young adults and their families. This book is a 'must have' for every parent seeking to foster not only self pride and independence for their adolescent/emerging adult, but for themselves as well."

—Jeffrey Bernstein, Ph.D., child and family psychologist
and author of *10 Days to a Less Defiant Child*

"In *Emptying the Nest*, Brad Sachs maps out the challenging terrain of contemporary parenthood. Skillfully and gently, he leads readers through the complex choreography required not only to help young adults achieve the well-documented need for healthy separation and self-sufficiency, but also to help them cultivate what is often overlooked—that a life well-lived must have significance and meaning. Practical and compassionate, innovative and empathic, this book provides parents with the necessary tools to finish the job right."

—Madeline Levine, Ph.D, author of *The Price of Privilege*

"Finally a book with wise, clear and do-able advice for parents not only as their children emerge into adulthood, but also for the parents as they emerge from the responsibilities of the nest into a new stage of their own lives."   —Ruth Nemzoff, Ed.D., author of *Don't Bite Your Tongue*

"Brad Sachs has produced an excellent book that captures the obstacles, challenges, and joys of helping young adults achieve independence . . . a wonderful resource for parents and professionals alike."

—Robert Brooks, Ph.D., faculty, Harvard Medical School
and coauthor of *Raising Resilient Children*

"In *Emptying the Nest*, family psychologist Brad Sachs zeroes in on the parent/grown child issues which interfere with a healthy and self-assured departure. With piercing insight, compassion, and a measure of firmness, Sachs helps us to chart the course for the modern young adult's march towards independence and maturity. Beautifully written, informative, and filled with vivid real-life vignettes, it's a must read for all parents concerned about their child's lingering, and their own difficulty in letting go."

—Neil Bernstein, Ph.D., parenting expert and
author of *There When He Needs You*

"For almost three decades, family psychologist Brad Sachs has written about parents and children with wit, warmth, and wisdom. In *Emptying the Nest*, he offers us unique insight and realistic counsel when it comes to addressing the dilemmas and conflicts that arise when young adults have returned to their parents' home, or are having difficulty leaving. Sachs reassuringly guides readers through the last stage of hands-on parenthood with a generous helping of care, candor, and sensitivity."

—Jerrold Lee Shapiro, Ph.D.,
professor at Santa Clara University
and author of *The Measure of a Man*

"This wonderfully written book is chock full of concrete advice. With specific suggestions for defusing chronic family impasses, Sachs provides a roadmap to family resolution that will benefit parents and children. Therapists will find the numerous case examples especially helpful in understanding how to work with families whose offspring cannot quite make it out the door to adulthood."

—Geoffrey Greif, DSW, professor of social work,
University of Maryland

"This book is filled with sensible advice for parents of emerging adults. Drawing on his many years of experience treating young adults and their families, Sachs presents their stories with insights that will surely help others through this eventful and sometimes difficult time of life."

—Jeffrey Jensen Arnett, Ph.D., Clark University,
author of *Emerging Adulthood*

"Young adulthood has become a perilous journey of late, filled with detours and dead ends that leave all too many young people side-tracked. *Emptying the Nest* provides a compassionate, thoughtful roadmap toward a successful adulthood that is likely to be useful not only to parents, but to young adults themselves. It provides guidance not only for emptying the nest, but for sending our youth off on a successful flight toward a fulfilling adulthood."

—Joseph P. Allen, Ph.D., author of
Escaping the Endless Adolescence

EMPTYING THE NEST

LAUNCHING YOUR YOUNG ADULT
TOWARD SUCCESS AND SELF-RELIANCE

Brad E. Sachs, Ph.D.

palgrave
macmillan

EMPTYING THE NEST
Copyright © Brad E. Sachs, 2010.
All rights reserved.

First published in 2010 by PALGRAVE MACMILLAN® in the U.S.—a
division of St. Martin's Press LLC, 175 Fifth Avenue, New York, NY
10010.

Where this book is distributed in the UK, Europe and the rest of the world,
this is by Palgrave Macmillan, a division of Macmillan Publishers Limited,
registered in England, company number 785998, of Houndmills,
Basingstoke, Hampshire RG21 6XS.

Palgrave Macmillan is the global academic imprint of the above companies
and has companies and representatives throughout the world.

Palgrave® and Macmillan® are registered trademarks in the United States,
the United Kingdom, Europe and other countries.

ISBN: 978-0-230-62058-2

Library of Congress Cataloging-in-Publication Data
Sachs, Brad, 1956–
    Emptying the nest : launching your young adult toward success and self-
reliance / Brad E. Sachs.
        p.   cm.
    Includes index.
    ISBN 978-0-230-62058-2 (pbk.)
    1. Empty nesters—Psychology.   2. Parent and adult child.
3. Separation (Psychology)   4. Identity (Psychology)   I. Title.
HQ1059.4.S23   2010
306.874084'4—dc22

                                                              2010001490

A catalogue record of the book is available from the British Library.

Design by Letra Libre, Inc.

First edition: July 2010

10 9 8 7 6 5 4 3 2 1

Printed in the United States of America.

THIS BOOK IS DEDICATED
TO THE GENERATIONS . . .

L'dor v'dor

For my parents,
Herbert and Claire Sachs,
With love and gratitude

For my young adult children,
Matt and Jessica
With love and laughter

For two young adults who have
bravely launched themselves unto parenthood
Josh and Angela
With love and admiration

For my wife,
Karen Meckler, M.D.
With love and affection

And for Autumn
With love and wonder

Let the hearts of parents be turned to their children and the hearts of children turned to their parents.

Malachi 3:24

All journeys have secret destinations of which the traveler is unaware.

Martin Buber

CONTENTS

ACKNOWLEDGMENTS

I extend my deepest gratitude to . . .

My ever-adamantine agent, Sarah Jane Freymann, who for more than a decade now has thoughtfully helped me sort out the literary wheat from the chaff while remaining open-minded about my range of writing projects (some of which will thankfully never see the light of day).

My editor, Luba Ostashevsky, for her initial interest in my work with young adults and their families, and for gently but insistently helping me to brighten, sharpen, and burnish the manuscript.

My brother and sister-in-law, Drs. Paul and Janet Sachs (time-saving hint: look in Chapter Five).

My brother and sister-in-law, Lee Sachs and Deborah Pangle (thanks for having established a New York outpost to support the next generation).

My wonderful young adult nephews and niece, Dan, Rachel, Adam, and Anatole Sachs.

My mother-in-law, Selma Meckler, who has always treated me like one of her sons.

My uncle and aunt, Dr. Ken and Roberta Sachs.

Joe and Marie Freedman, for raising the delightful Angela, who has brought new life to our family.

The many, many friends who have helped us to navigate some of the up's and down's that we have encountered in the last several years—too numerous to name individually, but, in particular: Dr. Tom Burns, Norman Gross, David and Judy Gilberg, Heidi Praff and Robert

Schrier, Dr. Scott and Teri Strahlman, Scott and Susan Rosenthal, Eric and Helen Metzman, Dr. Andy Farb, and Roberta Israeloff.

Phyllis Stern, M.A., whose calm, wise, and caring voice stays with me, even after all of these years of being apart.

The Earles, for everything.

Cliff Rubin, webmaster extraordinaire.

Dr. Roger Lewin, for his penetrating and compassionate perspective as we struggle through hour after hour attempting to stake out, seek out, and sort out the sometimes elusive beauty of the human predicament.

Our redoubtable dogs, Dasia and Hunan, for helping to establish the right priorities (meals, naps, and walks, not necessarily in that order).

Finally, I want to express my appreciation to the many young adults and parents who have consulted with me, and who in the process have taught me so much about tenacity, courage, and the resilient power of family love.

A portion of the profits from the sale of this book will be donated to Grassroots Crisis Intervention Center, in Columbia, Maryland.

EMPTYING
THE NEST

INTRODUCTION

PULLING ANCHOR, SETTING SAIL

About ten years ago I began treating a young man named Richie who, despite being bright and engaging, was an abysmal high school student, struggling miserably through sophomore year. Richie had two main interests, video games and electric guitar, and everything else, including academic achievement, took a distant backseat to these two pursuits. How he ultimately graduated I will never know, but somehow he churned out enough credits to march down the aisle with the rest of his senior class one sunny June day and receive a diploma. Based on the number of phone calls and conferences I had been a part of during his high school years, though, I suspect that the school's administration and faculty were as happy to see Richie finally depart as he was to go.

Not surprisingly, however, even though he had left high school, he had not yet left *home,* and his first several years following graduation were inconsistent and difficult ones, both for him and his parents. He started a rock band but couldn't get it off the ground, possibly because the band members were smoking too much pot to get their rehearsal and marketing efforts together and move forward. He then decided to take some computer classes at the local community college, but quickly lost interest and withdrew without actually earning any credits. Then he started up another band, one that fell apart when his drummer (and best friend) was arrested for drug-dealing and sent to rehab. Following this debacle, Richie gamely enrolled in a technical institute to study computer repair, bankrolled by his parents, a nine-month program that he actually did complete. He abruptly quit his first job after three weeks, however, because he found the work intolerably boring.

At this point 20-year-old Richie and his family re-contacted me for family therapy and continued their treatment through this exasperatingly unproductive phase. Partially as a result of being in therapy, none of them ever quite gave up, despite many tense moments and complicated forks in the road. I helped Richie to understand how his behavior was actually eliciting the parental nagging that he so detested, and helped the parents to see that many of their efforts to "motivate" him, despite being well-intended, were backfiring. We worked on establishing more effective intergenerational communication, and clarifying the extent to which Richie's parents should be financially supporting him at this stage in his life, and what he should be responsible for at home in return for their support. I assisted him in exploring career possibilities and his parents in broadening their social network and taking up some new interests. All three of them commendably made the adjustments that resulted in a more livable family life.

Nevertheless, when Richie reached the age of 22 without substantial progress toward self-sufficiency, they all agreed that he would take an extended visit to a favorite aunt and uncle on the West Coast, at which point he and I lost touch with each other for a long time.

One day, just a few years ago, I received an email from him, completely out of the blue, which began with an apology for not having stayed in contact. I will never forget the next sentence, which began with the words, "I wanted to happily let you know that I am now a millionaire." Astonished, I continued reading and learned that while he was out West he had found friends who shared his passion for both video games and rock music, and they had invited him to collaborate with them on a rock-based video game that they'd been working on. They eventually designed a product that was becoming extremely popular and making all of them a good deal of money. The name of this game? Surely you've heard of it . . . the ubiquitous and inestimable *Guitar Hero*.

In other words, Richie, who barely graduated from high school and was not even close to a college degree, was now in the position of accruing more income in one year than most of his fellow high school students *combined*, and was doing so by pursuing something that he actually enjoyed.

The point of this story is not that the ultimate goal of human development is to strike it rich, nor that everyone is destined to be rewarded abundantly for following their passion. My point is simply that it's unwise to give up on young adults no matter how maddeningly uneven their developmental trajectory may be, and that the more empathy, patience, understanding, and faith we are able to summon on their behalf, the greater the likelihood that they will eventually find ways to forge ahead with their lives in positive ways, and, through so doing, not only pay tribute to their parents, but, more importantly, to themselves.

Back at the turn of the millennium, when I was speaking to audiences after the publication of my book *The Good Enough Child: How to Have an Imperfect Family and Be Perfectly Satisfied*, I was frequently asked, "This is all well and good, but when are you going to write a book about parenting *teens?*" Apparently, many readers were preparing their children (and themselves) for the transition into adolescence, or were already in the midst of raising adolescents.

After having encountered this question frequently enough, I decided to follow through and answered it by writing *The Good Enough Teen: Raising Adolescents with Love and Acceptance (Despite How Impossible They Can Be)* and *When No One Understands: Letters to a Teenager on Life, Loss, and the Hard Road to Adulthood*.

Interestingly enough, as I have been speaking to audiences after the publication of *The Good Enough Teen* and *When No One Understands*, I have frequently been asked, "This is all well and good, but when are you going to write a book about finally getting our kids to leave home and become independent, particularly when they don't appear to want to or be able to, or when the economy doesn't seem able to accommodate them?" Apparently many readers were struggling with young adults who were having difficulty leaving the nest and embracing the job of psychological liberation and financial self-sufficiency.

Around the same time, I began receiving requests from numerous schools and school systems to help them address the challenges of keeping students engaged and focused during their final year of high school. Educators nationwide seemed to be in agreement that many of their seniors had "pulled the plug" and begun "running out the clock" early in the year, particularly once college applications had been completed and sent in. The educators were concerned that the students' premature disengagement yielded months of bored and restless underachievement and resulted in academic, emotional, and behavioral problems as these students vacantly trudged their way toward graduation.

I also began to notice that in my practice I was working with many young adults who, although competent and talented, had been unable to successfully make the transition to independent life, and who, after having taken their first, tentative steps toward separation, by way of college, work, or the armed services, had quickly or eventually chosen to "fold their cards" and, with very mixed feelings (few of them positive ones), returned home.

Related to this, in my ongoing consultations with deans of student services and with student health clinic staff at various colleges and universities, I was hearing more and more about increasing numbers of freshmen and sophomores who seemed unable or unwilling to create an independent life and whose parents often remained surprisingly involved in their lives, even when they were hundreds or thousands of miles apart.

And of course, we cannot ignore the reality that since about 2007 and 2008 there has been a historic economic downturn that has completely transformed the prospects for independence and prosperity for legions of young adults. As of this writing, the American unemployment rate is 10.0 percent, which is a 35-year high. Our economic forecast remains bleak, predicting a very long, slow, and "jobless" recovery—in other words, unemployment will remain high for the foreseeable future.

This has already ratcheted up the "surface tension" in countless families as young adults desperately try to find ways to achieve financial solvency and sovereignty in the midst of what many writers are calling the Great Recession. Meanwhile their parents, feeling like their own backs are to the wall because of lost jobs, diminished income, or severely shrunken retirement and savings accounts, are being forced to wrestle with the excruciating dilemma of exactly how much fiscal and emotional underwriting they can afford to provide for their young adult children, and worrying about how long they will be effectively and productively able to do so. At the same time, many mothers and fathers are worrying about how they can afford to help pay for their own parents' elder care.

Finally, over the past several years, my eldest son graduated from college, my middle son commenced college, and my daughter is preparing to finish up high school and depart for college. In addition, my wife and I have recently become grandparents, providing us with the unique opportunity to empty one family nest while wondrously watching another one begin to fill. So, as with my previous books, I have been provided with the opportunity to explore a topic in the field of family psychology not only from a clinical perspective, but also from a personal point of view, which always produces a more practical and realistic approach.

With all of this in mind, a book that specifically addressed the needs and concerns of parents of children who are attempting to *complete* adolescence, but having difficulty doing so, gradually began to take shape. After all, the ultimate signpost of successful child-rearing is that the child eventually becomes an independent, functional young adult, able to take care of him- or herself, and others as well. No matter how much love and support was offered, no matter how many extracurricular activities were excelled in, no matter how high their GPAs or SATs or ACTs—or even their postgraduate GREs or LSATs or MCATs—no matter where they went to college or how they left home, one's tenure as a parent has not been fulfilled unless and until one's children can stand on their own feet.

Now, of course, when I talk about fulfilling your tenure as a parent, I do not mean no longer worrying about how your children are doing or being available to help and support them—after all, caring parents will always love their children and want the best for them. But it does mean no longer having to feel so *responsible* for young adult children—psychologically or financially—and trusting that they can manage life's inevitable ups and downs on their own, without permanently giving up or giving in.

Emptying the Nest, then, is a guide for parents who want to finish the job right, who want to launch their beloved young adults into their own uniquely successful orbit, rather than one that remains wobbly or stunted or too vulnerable to their family's gravitational field. It will describe the challenges and address the concerns of families whose young adult children appear not to be laying the groundwork for a healthy and successful departure from home, or who left home temporarily but returned for an indeterminate period of time because of their inability to function independently.

This book will provide you with practical guidance that will assist not only in emancipating your young adult, but in liberating you, the parent, as well, so that both generations can successfully evolve to the next stage of their development. At the same time, it will help you to build, rebuild, or maintain the family connections that sustain us all as we each discover and follow the pathways of our lives, together and as unique individuals.

True maturity is achieved when we take on the weight of our own decision-making and live with the consequences. We know that we do not suddenly become mature on a given date simply because we have reached a chronological milestone. We either mature step by step, with each passing day, or we do not. Our maturity is ultimately the result of our having encountered, with increasing independence, innumerable predicaments, dilemmas, and decisions throughout our development.

⁓ ⁓

There are universal challenges to the process of launching young adults toward maturity that families of every generation, and in every culture, have faced. But there are also some vexing challenges that contemporary families are confronted with that appear to be accounting for the recent upsurge in young adults who don't seem to be making regular progress on their passage from reliance to self-reliance, from immaturity to maturity.

Just to provide one example, Stephanie Coontz, an expert on contemporary families, notes that in 1960, two-thirds of all men and more than three-quarters of all women had already attained fiscal self-reliance and residential independence by age 30, whether by earning a living wage through employment or, for many of the females, by marrying a man who had secured such employment. Today, however, fewer than one-half of all women and less than one-third of men have achieved the marks of independence by age 30.

So, what are some of these challenges?

One is that present day mothers and fathers have been so closely involved with their children's lives in so many concrete ways from *before* birth and throughout childhood and adolescence—fostering the optimal prenatal environment; creating the most enriching intellectual climate at home; volunteering in classrooms; coaching teams; attending innumerable practices, performances, recitals, and contests; attempting to provide just the right mix of tutors, coaches, mentors, diagnosticians, and clinicians—that family connectedness can border on engulfment, making it more difficult to break free than in previous eras. "Helicopter" parents, "hothouse" or "teacup" children—our terminology suggests our uncertainty and ambivalence when it comes to striking the optimal balance between support and enabling, between care and overprotectiveness.

The fact that the size of the average American family continues to decrease, meaning that parents often have all their genetic eggs in just one or two baskets, can also make it more difficult for the young adult to find the right escape hatch, or the right time and way to leave. Raising fewer children more easily creates the possibility of focusing too intently on those children, which in turn makes their eventual emancipation more involved and emotionally fraught for everyone involved.

Modern technology is certainly a contributing factor as well—the proliferation of cell phones, wireless laptops, and assorted smartphones and PDAs enables parents and young adults to text, call, or Skype each other, often numerous times of day despite great distances and at a negligible cost, if any. (Many of us still can quaintly reminisce about the very brief long-distance, collect calls that we hurriedly made from dormitory rooms or hallways when we were in college, trying desperately to keep the time short and the cost down.)

Worried caregivers can now easily and inexpensively install global positioning systems in their children's cars or cell phones, allowing caregivers to track their children's movements 24 hours a day, or utilize cyber-monitoring devices that provide them with access to all of their children's instant messages, text messages, and emails. Or they can, with the click of a mouse, visit school-sponsored websites that provide up-to-date information on all tests, homework, and class work that may or may not have been completed. Many colleges have even set up computer stations where students can engage in a quick, webcam-based "Hi, Mom, hi, Dad" check-in. These perpetual electronic umbilical cords can work against the process of separation, however, particularly when the young adult is feeling insecure about his capacity to strike out on his own.

In addition, our unstable economy is leaving many young adults uncomfortably straddling dependence and independence, and remaining morosely mired in the former longer than they would like. It also requires many parents to provide various stipends to sustain their young adult's autonomy, which of course may simultaneously undercut the foundation and endurance of that autonomy and dramatically erode the parents' own standard of living.

Paying for college and other postsecondary education, providing financial subsidies, offering coresidence, taking over loan payments and credit card debt, cosigning leases, purchasing a car, helping with property taxes, extending health insurance coverage—any or all of these may at times be necessary if young adults are to have the flexibility to pursue the more extensive education and training required to survive in a frigid economic climate. But this means that the era of hardworking caregivers being easily able to boost their children to a higher standard of living than they themselves experienced, all while anticipating or savoring their retirement, is long gone. More and more often, emptying the nest sometimes seems to require saying good-bye to a hard earned nest egg.

For example, I currently see a skyrocketing number of students who are choosing to matriculate at community colleges not because they can't get into or survive a four-year college, but because four-year colleges are financially out of reach. While attending community college makes sense on many levels, it still often means living at home rather than in a dormitory, thus temporarily delaying the young adult's leave-taking, and keeping the original family constellation intact for at least one or two years longer than it might have otherwise.

Meanwhile, young scholars are completing their undergraduate degrees with an average of $20,000 in loans, in addition to possibly thousands more in credit card debt, strapping them financially before they even begin their professional life. Graduate school may add to the almost insurmountable insolvency that plagues even accomplished and high-achieving young adults. And entry-level and early-career salaries for both high school and college graduates, as well as for those who have completed graduate school, have not kept up with the cost of living, making it increasingly difficult for young adults to afford decent housing or medical insurance.

Tough economy or not, however, the reality is that many young adults have simply not been expected to practice financial self-sufficiency and restraint during their adolescence, which hobbles their capacity to do so as young adults. Many parents whom I work with seem to have protected their offspring from actively learning about possibly antiquated concepts such as "living within a budget" or "saving for a rainy day." Teenagers' summers are less frequently spent mowing lawns or babysitting, working as a lifeguard or a dishwasher—and in the process discovering exactly how hard you have to work to buy that five-dollar grande mocha latte or that ten-dollar movie ticket (or, on a larger scale, that several-hundred-dollar, app-laden iPhone). Instead, high school students are often encouraged, and sometimes forced, to participate in (usually quite pricy) enrichment programs during their summer breaks—camps, workshops, travel abroad, precollege institutes—that surely have social and educational *value*, but that teach them little about financial *values*.

As a result, many young adults have unrealistically come to expect that they should always be entitled to enjoy the standard of living that they have grown accustomed to during their "years of plenty," without understanding the basis for (or the impermanence of) their state of abundance, or how to manage in the face of real or relative scarcity.

There is also a swelling generation of students who are accustomed to having their parents conscientiously play the role of their educational advocate, because the students have experienced learning challenges, attention deficits, autism spectrum disorders, and other neurological and psychoeducational difficulties. For example, the ratio of students identified with learning disabilities who graduate from high school and matriculate at four-year colleges went from one in one hundred in 1987 to one in nine in 2007, while the number of learning-disabled students who proceeded on to *any* form of postsecondary education leaped from one-third to almost three-quarters by 2003. After a decade or more of having their education industriously sculpted by their parents, along with a veritable retinue of tutors, coaches, and other supportive professionals, it should come as no surprise that their capacity to function independently, both in college and beyond, is at times compromised.

A recent one-panel cartoon in the *New Yorker* by Roz Chast humorously and exquisitely captured this reality. Titled "The Grad-School Parent-Teacher Conference," the cartoon shows two parents sitting dutifully in front of their daughter's professor and being told, "Barbara is very mature for a 28-year-old . . . and she certainly isn't drinking as much as she used to." Even the parents of young adults who are intellectually capable enough to pursue their education beyond college may still not feel as if they are truly able to turn over the reins and release their children into an independent future.

From a sociocultural standpoint, we tend to do very little to conduct our children from adolescence to young adulthood. Anthropological literature abounds with accounts of how native cultures collectively usher their youth into adulthood through the use of traditional, deeply meaningful rituals (usually with separate rites for girls and for boys). Aside from a high school commencement ceremony, however, or eligibility for a driver's license, the right to buy cigarettes and alcohol, and to enlist in the army, American culture doesn't seem to believe that any form of symbolic initiation is necessary for its own youth.

And in this same sociocultural context, we often broadcast a very confusing array of mixed messages to young adults regarding the value of growing up and leaving youth behind. Many of my adolescent patients have told me that they plan *not* to work as hard as their exhausted parents, who seem unhappily incarcerated in an Alcatraz of professional duties and personal responsibilities. And, on the flip side, many parents expend great effort trying to appear young, hip, and fashionable. Surely adolescents must observe this and wonder what the appeal of adulthood could possibly be if adults themselves are backing away from maturity and trying to look, sound, and behave like their own children.

When we parents were growing up, adulthood was where "the action" was, so we couldn't wait until we were adults, too. We saw our parents as having acquired the knowledge, the savvy, and the worldliness that enabled them to instruct and guide us to become more adult in manners, attire, correct behavior in the workplace, and so on. Now, however, adults turn to their own offspring to seek instruction and guidance on how to use online search engines or download music onto their new and ever-more-bewildering MP3 players. It's as if our society is turning upside down, with an emphasis on adults devolving down toward youth rather than young people evolving up toward adulthood.

Finally, the revolution in psychopharmacology in recent decades may also be contributing to the number of lagging young adults. On the one hand, psychotropic medications have clearly relieved unnecessary suffering for numerous children and adolescents, and surely saved lives. On the other hand, being told for years by parents and clinicians that medication is necessary for optimal functioning may sometimes produce the paradoxical effect of interfering with that functioning, as the young adult slowly loses faith in her own interior strengths and becomes reliant on external aid and intervention.

But such deleterious side effects may not only be psychologically based. Recent neurobiological research conducted at various research institutes, and cited by Dr. Leonard Sax, has suggested that the regular use of psychostimulants may affect the part of the brain that is associated with (among other functions) the motivation to act on one's impulses, even when those impulses are positive, growth-promoting ones. Perhaps the ever-increasing numbers of young adults who have been medicated for attention deficit disorders and related psychoeducational unevenness over the years are actually straining against a neurological leash that is tethering them dejectedly in place.

All of these factors are surely conspiring to make the already daunting process of separation and differentiation even more daunting for both generations. It is usually at this point that a family psychologist, such as myslf, is brought into the picture. And while every family is one of a kind, I have learned to perceive certain regularly recognizable patterns when exasperated parents show up in my office, with or without a young adult in tow.

What I usually observe is what typically happens whenever the process of normal, spontaneous family development runs aground: resentment and hopelessness have set in, and the process of assigning blame has begun. The parents may blame their young adult child for not taking responsibility, for not being motivated, for being anything from "oafish" or "lazy" to "selfish." Young adults, for their part, are all too eager to return the favor, angrily faulting their parents for being too controlling or unable to let go, for being anything from "stingy" or "unsupportive" to "impossible."

Often, my first and most important task is to convince families to stop the blame game and to help *everyone*—parents and young adult alike—understand that no one person is to blame, but that each of them is responsible for contributing to the situation. Only then are we able to set about crafting a new plan for individual and family growth, one that simultaneously allows for more independence on the part of each family member and better relationships among all of them. This book will enable you to make the sometimes elusive dream of your young adult's "success and self-reliance," as the subtitle says, a more substantive reality.

To do so, I will address many of the questions that arise as contemporary families prepare to launch their young adult children toward productive lives. These questions include:

- What are the typical developmental tasks and challenges involved with young adults' separation from their parents?
- Why do some families successfully launch their young adult children forward, while others see their young adults return home after having departed, and what factors account for when or whether the young adult is "relaunched"?
- What kinds of young adult departures tend to endure and lead to self-reliance in the long run, and what kinds are destined, over time, to compromise growth or ultimately fail?
- What contemporary factors (economic, sociological, etc.) account for the growing number of young adults struggling to achieve independence?
- What are the changes that parents need to make to foster their young adult's self-reliance, as well as the parents' own adaptation to middle age and beyond?
- How can the relationship between parent and young adult evolve in healthy ways during the separation and liberation process?
- What, ultimately, constitutes a life of success and significance for young adults and their parents?

A friend of mine who recently took a business trip told me that, just after the plane landed, the flight attendant announced to all passengers, "And now that we've arrived at the terminal, I will tell you what my father told me when I turned 18—Get out!" I don't know how old that attendant was, but, based on my many conversations with the families I treat, and on what I hear from my fellow parents, I can assure you that "getting out" is not quite so easy to do these days, whether one has reached the magical threshold of 18, 21, or even 25 and beyond.

∼ ∽

There will, of course, always be children who have few difficulties departing from home, giddily (or level-headedly) plunging straight into the beckoning white surf of young adulthood. And their parents will be more than happy to have you believe that this has come about because of their parental wisdom and virtuosity. Or, the parents may modestly claim no credit and attribute it all to the child.

But the reality is that for many young adults—possibly for one or more of your own—there is more fear than fearlessness about this next stage of their life. The transition into adulthood seems more akin to one of those cartoon scenes in which a character dashes off a cliff, stares down in disbelief at the chasm below, and then falls, grasping at thin, shallow-rooted branches during the terrifying descent while trying to figure out what to do next.

In my work, I can loosely group struggling young adults into five different categories which, taken together, capture the immense variety and complexity of today's journey toward self-sufficiency. These categories—Progressing, Regrouping, Meandering, Recovering, and Floundering—represent the extent to which that journey can vary among different young adults, and from family to family, in our society.

PROGRESSING

Progressing young adults are moving ahead nicely with their lives and forging paths that are likely to lead to self-reliance in the near future, but still have some maturing to do and require a degree of parental support and guidance. While their parents sometimes become annoyed, the frustration is usually short-lived, and they tend to not experience great difficulty or conflict with their young adult, who is showing over-all signs of positive growth and development.

For example, 22-year-old Essie has just begun her second year as a graduate student in chemical engineering. While she is doing well aca-demically, she is often short on money and tends to run up credit card debts a couple of times a year, and then needs her parents to bail her out. They have lectured her repeatedly that she must learn to manage her money, but despite Essie's agreeing that she must be more careful, her credit card bills inevitably start to expand. The reality is that she never learned to budget because she was never expected to have a job in high school or college, or to save money, or to contribute to her ex-penses. Instead, her parents encouraged her to spend her high school summers attending science camps and programs that they proudly paid for. So it should come as no surprise that Essie still counts on her par-ents to rescue her. On the other hand, it is difficult for them to get ter-ribly upset with her, knowing that she is functioning well overall, and that once she finishes graduate school she is likely to find a solid job making good money.

REGROUPING

Young adults who are regrouping have left the nest and established some independence outside, but have returned home for a short (or long) period of time to lay the groundwork for their next foray toward self-reliance. They are taking a step backward, but it is probably with the intention of ultimately moving forward. They require some support from their parents during this phase, and there may be some tension as everyone adjusts to their return, but everyone is relatively easily able to adapt because there is still a concrete plan for advancement in place.

Shadonya, 21 years old, earned a certificate as a personal trainer after graduating high school and worked in a gym for a year, living in her own in an apartment with two friends, but recently decided that she would like to go to college and earn a degree in physical therapy. She has picked out a program that she would like to attend, but can't afford it at this point in her life. With this in mind, she has asked her parents if she can move back home for at least a year, and probably two, to save money while continuing to work part-time at the gym and attending school, a plan that they have all agreed to.

Arguments between Shadonya and her parents occur fairly frequently, as her parents had grown accustomed to not having any children at home. Shadonya often has her boyfriend over in the evening, and he tends to stay fairly late, and while she likes to cook, she does not always clean up after herself very thoroughly. But, overall, they are pleased that she's working hard and toward a definite, legitimate goal, and she is happy that she has been given a chance to live rent-free for a while in order to achieve that goal, so all three of them are generally able to share the house without an excessive amount of friction.

MEANDERING

Meandering young adults are also moving ahead with their lives, but are not doing so in as direct a fashion as those who are Progressing or Regrouping. Meanderers' growth is more wayward, more often proceeding sideways, or sometimes even in reverse, rather than forward. Because of this, they need regular support and guidance from their parents. Their parents generally feel some hope and optimism regarding their child's academic or professional endeavors, but are also starting to wonder when true self-sufficiency will emerge, fearing that they will have to continue to provide emotional and financial subsidies for much longer than they had originally anticipated.

Ramin, 24, was a business student in college, but by his junior year he had been seriously bitten by the acting bug and decided that he wanted to make a career of it. He moved to Brooklyn, sublet an apartment, got a job as a server at a midscale restaurant, and started auditioning in New York City—but with little success. His parents then agreed to sponsor his participation in a two-year acting institute that supposedly had excellent connections in the film and drama industry, but despite completing the program, Ramin was still unable to get any regular gigs.

While he continues to work at the restaurant and diligently pounds the pavement in search of acting jobs, Ramin still requires monthly infusions of cash to make ends meet, and there is no clear point at which he will be close to having established financial independence. His parents are thinking about setting some sort of deadline for him to begin managing things on his own without any regular support from them, but they understand that even modest success in the entertainment industry is a gamble even under the best of economic circumstances. They want to give their son every chance to make his dream a reality, but they know that at some point they may have to pull the plug, and they don't know exactly how and when to do so. Meanwhile, they postpone the possibility that one or both of them could retire as they agonize over their decision.

RECOVERING

Young adults who are recovering have also left and established some independence outside of the home, but are returning under different circumstances than Regroupers: they have come back home with their tail between their legs to recover from an experience that did not work out well, and there is not yet any clear plan or time frame for their next departure. Because of this, significant support may be necessary, and tension can run high due to the uncertainty of the situation.

Nineteen-year-old Kelvin graduated from high school and got an apartment with his buddy Thad (the one-year lease was cosigned by all four of their parents), while they both got jobs at a local restaurant. The apartment worked out disastrously; Thad's girlfriend basically moved in just a few weeks after they signed the lease, and mooched off of the two of them constantly. After hosting a few get-togethers for their friends, word quickly spread through social networking sites, and many local (and not so local) teens and young adults began showing up uninvited and partying well into the morning hours. The festivities prompted difficulties with the landlord, who was being regularly besieged by complaints from the neighboring tenants. The apartment quickly took on a bombed-out look from the reckless nightly revelry.

Meanwhile, the restaurant where they both worked fell on hard times in the shrinking economy, and cut both Kelvin and Thad's hours in half in an effort to reduce costs. No longer able to make rent and cover their expenses, Kelvin and Thad concocted a drug-dealing scheme that quickly collapsed when an irate and inebriated customer showed up at their apartment with a gun, pointing it at them and demanding that they turn over their cash and their stash. Terrified, and now in a deep financial hole, Kelvin was forced to return home, furious with himself, but taking it out on his parents and blaming them for not covering his rent for a few more months while he tried to find a new job.

This naturally created a charged atmosphere, with Kelvin thrashing about, frantically trying to find a way to move out again, and his parents enraged at him now that they were on the hook not only for the last six months of his lease, but also for the blown security deposit as a result of all of the party-related damage to the apartment.

FLOUNDERING

Those who are floundering have not yet summoned the capacity to leave their parents' house and remain developmentally marooned, frustrating both themselves and their parents with their perplexing state of suspended animation. They remain adolescent in behavior and outlook, and thus they bring on themselves the kind of parenting that adolescents require, leading to a strained climate and high-octane clashes because the parents no longer want to raise an adolescent, and the floundering young adult is tired of being treated like an adolescent.

Twenty-year old Denise, who works part-time shampooing clients in a local hair salon, displays no interest in any paths she'd like to follow toward self-sufficiency. Her parents are at their wit's end, having had all of their suggestions spurned by their psychologically and financially dependent daughter. They resort to nagging her to do something—anything—but to no avail. The parents' nagging does nothing more than precipitate a belligerent tirade in which Denise blames all of her difficulties on their constant hectoring, while they crossly counter that they wouldn't have to ride her if she'd simply get off the couch and get moving with her life.

❧ ❧

These five categories, like any groupings that attempt to classify people, cannot rigidly define your young adult, and it's certainly possible that he or she has inhabited more than one of them at various points in their development. Most likely, though, you picked up this book because at least one of these categories—Progressing, Regrouping, Recovering, Meandering, or Floundering—looks familiar to you. These are the categories on which we will be focusing most of our attention, because they are the ones that tend to be breeding grounds for the anger, agitation, and disappointment that can corrode family love and life and turn caring parents and young adults into exasperated adversaries.

As an individual parent, you are unlikely to be able to exert any significant influence over the immense economic, sociocultural, and technological forces that we have been discussing. But you are certainly able to exert a significant influence over how you and your child respond to those forces, much as we prepare for inclement weather so that we are as safe and comfortable as possible, even though we can't stop the rain. It is this influence—what is truly within your power as the parent of a young adult—that we will be considering in the coming pages.

CHAPTER ONE

THE RITES AND WRONGS OF PASSAGE

DEVELOPMENTAL TASKS FOR YOUNG ADULTS

The transition into young adulthood is ultimately an "inside job." One of the challenges for parents of young adults is understanding what is going on inside of their children, what they are privately building in the secret workshop of their soul.

We know that personal liberation at this stage of life requires a new assertion of self, an original and inventive taking stock and staking out of the individual's needs and objectives in contrast to what others (parents, peers, and previous mentors and role models) have expected, or still expect, of them. In order to achieve independence, they need to define and make good on their obligation to themselves, which requires that they acknowledge their strengths, weaknesses, conflicts, and struggles.

Sometimes young adults' efforts toward this end are evident to us, and we are gratified when we witness their growth. Other times the issues that they are grappling with are mostly invisible—to us, and, just as often, to them—and if we recognize the struggles at all we underestimate their difficulty, or don't realize how hard our child is working to tackle them.

In this chapter, we will examine some of the subtler developmental tasks that young adults must attend to so that their launch results in true psychological liberation and the ability to stand on their own feet.

GRIEVING

To eventually leave the nest, young adults must first come to terms with and mourn for the end of their childhood and adolescence, the stages of life when they were able to count on other people—usually their parents—to be responsible for them and to nurture them. The grieving process entails considerable feelings of loss, longing, and heartbreak, yet unless it is completed, growth is always stymied.

Grieving is difficult but necessary work, and, when done wholeheartedly, it can be liberating work. Only when we grieve are we able to come to terms with what we have lost, to let go of it and prepare for the next important developmental phase. When we don't grieve, we remain stuck, halfway in the cocoon and halfway out. Overcoming grief propels us forth toward an enlarged sense of self. That is one of the reasons why I am not surprised when parents complain to me about their children "giving them grief": young adults often project their grief onto others, particularly those whom they are closest to, because what they are going through can be so hard for them to bear.

Grief does not exist to return us comfortably to our previous status quo, but rather toward an expanded sense of oneself. I find it helpful to visualize the psychological tomb as the psychological womb: when we properly bury what needs to be left behind, heartbreaking as that burial may be, we can then allow new parts of our self to be conceived, to gestate, and to eventually be born. Without such grieving, our present and future will forever be haunted by the restless ghosts of the past. (By the way, it is healthier to acknowledge and accept the grief than to pretend it's not there. This is not a time to be "macho.")

Because we don't speak the language of grief to our children and tend to exclusively train our parenting attention on their achievements, accomplishments, and acquisitions, we don't provide them with the opportunity to sort through the pain of loss in a way that enables them to grow. And when young adults don't grieve, it is not just that they miss out on growth—they also leave themselves open to what I refer to as anguish, a state of hopelessness which can express itself in many forms, such as depression, rage, underachievement, addictions, relational instability, psychosomatic distress, and self-destructive behavior. Many of the young adult patients I treat display these symptoms, but, to my way of thinking, these are indications of unresolved grief rather than of emotional disturbance.

The young adult's capacity to say good-bye to her childhood—and to the belief that she will always be taken care of by others—becomes the psychological foundation for her ability to welcome and cultivate the responsibilities and privileges of adulthood.

COMPOSING A DECLARATION OF INTERDEPENDENCE

Young adults have to learn to nimbly navigate between being an "I" and a "we," becoming self-assured enough that they can trust their instincts, but still be able to turn to trusted family members and other adults for support and perspective when necessary. They also need to be depended upon by others, to manifest or "act out" their altruistic nature. Adulthood requires establishing a balance between when we care and when we are cared for. Psychologists refer to this as healthy "interdependence," which straddles independence and dependence and synthesizes the best of both.

Interdependence might mean that a young adult can still count on her parents for workable doses of emotional sustenance without feeling like she has completely compromised her pride and self-reliance. But interdependence also might mean that her parents can begin to turn to *her* for help or support without engulfing or derailing her.

Twenty-three-year-old Katie needed some extra money for a down payment on a condo she had found, but she was hesitant to ask her parents for financial assistance. "Once I ask them, it's like I'm admitting that I can't manage things on my own, and I'm back to feeling like a little girl again." Her fear of losing her independence ignored the many steps toward self-reliance she had already taken, including living on her own for two years after college without having to ask her parents for any significant financial subsidies.

In fact, the extent to which Katie's parents had been lauding her for having been so self-reliant was what convinced her that any state other than absolute self-reliance would disappoint and anger them. I encouraged her to talk with her parents more about how they achieved independence when they were her age, and she was surprised to learn that they had actually relied on her mother's parents quite a bit in their early years of marriage. It was Katie's maternal grandparents who had taken care of her parents' medical bills, purchased a car for them, and provided a "bridge loan" when they bought their first house. This realization helped her to soften the hard distinction she had made between financial independence and dependence and to consider asking them for help. When she finally made her request, she was surprised at how willing her parents were to assist, precisely because they had been so impressed with her efforts to establish financial autonomy over the past couple of years, and because they remembered their own parents' generosity years before.

Katie's taking the risk of asking her parents for assistance also opened the door for some intergenerational reciprocity. When her widowed 85-year-old grandmother broke her hip, she needed someone to be available to her for several weeks until she could regain her mobility. Katie, who worked nights as a nurse's aide, offered to let her grandmother stay with her during the day in her new condo until her parents, who both worked nine-to-five jobs, picked the grandmother up in the evening and brought her back to their house during the initial phase of her recovery.

IDENTIFY WITHOUT BECOMING IDENTICAL

Young adults must learn to trust that they can identify with their parents in positive or negative ways without feeling that they have to be identical to their parents. The goal is to emulate the qualities of their parents that they value and that will serve as solid guideposts, while feeling free to disentangle themselves from those that won't—in other words, to "take what's best and leave the rest."

Twenty-two-year-old Carmen confessed, "I realize now that I'm very similar to my mom in that we both get worked up over little things. But I also seem to get a grip more quickly than she does. She's completely obsessed with exercise. I like to exercise, too, but I don't think it's the end of the world if I don't get a workout in."

Ben, 20, admitted, "I'd like to have my father's work habits, and in some ways I come close. I'm a harder worker than my brother and sister, I think. But I'm not as hard a worker as he is; he just has an unbelievable amount of energy. The thing is, though, he doesn't know how not to work hard, and that's something that I'm trying to figure out, because even though he's been very successful, he doesn't always seem happy. If your success doesn't lead to happiness, then what exactly is the point of being so successful?"

DEVELOPING A PERSONAL PHILOSOPHY

Alexander Hamilton wrote, "Those who stand for nothing fall for anything." An important aspect of young adulthood is making explicit the self that the person has been sculpting and discovering since childhood. He must construct a psychic engine composed of desire and vision that will be strong enough to carry the freight of his soul forward in the face of life's challenges. As part of this process, he has to learn to:

- struggle with the collapse of certain beliefs which may have helped to stabilize and comfort him during the preceding years, but that no longer hold true or have relevance in the crucible of adult life;
- come to terms with his limitations, yet continue to find ways to progress forward and prove that he can withstand pressure, disappointment, and unhappiness; and

- shift his focus from external validation to internal validation, and expand the definition of self beyond simply "doing" (achieving, accomplishing, acquiring) and into the realm of "being" (loving, creating, contemplating).

As I often remind young adults as well as their parents, the most meaningful objective is not to *perform* but to *transform*.

Dominic, 20, had always dreamed of a career in geology, but found the college curriculum to be less compelling than he had hoped. Not only was he earning mediocre grades, but he simply wasn't enjoying his course work. He did find himself very excited, however, by an elective course he took on learning styles, which rekindled one of his earliest professional fantasies, that of becoming a teacher. Over the course of his final two years of college he shifted gears, acquired enough education credits to become a secondary school science teacher, completed his student teaching, and eventually got a job teaching high school science.

"It was difficult to give up the fantasy of going into geology—there's a long history of that in my family: my father and one of my grandfathers are both geologists. But there was something missing there for me. I wasn't connecting well with the other students and the professors. Once I took that education course, though, it was like a lightbulb went off and I knew I belonged. So I guess I had to be willing to get to know myself a bit better and figure out what I really wanted to do."

OVERCOMING THE FEAR OF LEAVING HOME

During the launching phase, parents like to imagine their children at the prow of the USS Adulthood, confidently surveying the calm seas ahead, but even the most confident young adults feel some trepidation about separation. When these fears get the best of them, they often try to manage them in unproductive ways, such as by:

- not leaving, or not displaying any evidence of concretely preparing to leave. ("I'll get a job when I need to, but right now I just don't need a whole lot of money, I'm fine the way things are, I can skateboard everywhere and bum cigarettes off my friends.")

- acting like they've already left when they may not have fully done so yet. ("Your stupid rules don't apply to me anymore. I'm outta here as soon as I turn 18 and have enough money, so in the meantime, I don't have to follow any curfews, treat you with respect, or do any chores.")

- forcing themselves to leave on questionable or dangerous terms, often guaranteeing their return. ("I'm going to ditch senior year of high school and hitchhike up to Canada with my friend Maurice—I've heard there are lots of good jobs there. I'm sure we'll meet up with some people we can crash with.")

The elemental fear of leaving home needs to be acknowledged and come to terms with, however frustrating its outward manifestations.

Seventeen-year-old Philip was being recruited by numerous colleges because of his wrestling prowess. By the beginning of his junior year, coaches were contacting him to invite him for campus visits and workouts with their teams. But he started off his senior year by getting a DUI on the way home from a party, and things quickly went into a tailspin from there. By November, he was academically ineligible to wrestle and frequently binge-drinking, at which point his parents contacted me.

In my conversations with Philip, it became clear that he was much more anxious about going away to college than he had been acknowledging to anyone. While he was flattered by the college recruiters, he had little academic self-confidence, and his few experiences away from home (assorted weeklong wrestling camps over the past few summers) had been suffused with homesickness that he had worked hard to suppress. "I'm afraid I'm going to get to college and blow it. Everyone has all of these expectations for me and what I'm supposed to be able to accomplish, and I just know that I'm going to wind up disappointing everyone."

So while his parents (and prospective coaches) were becoming increasingly excited about his college prospects, Philip was growing more and more frightened about the vertiginous cliff that he was feeling shoved toward. Self-sabotage seemed to be the only way to both manage and convey his fears of leaving the nest.

However, as he began the difficult process of disclosing his fears, first (and most importantly) to himself, then to his parents, and eventually to the recruiting coaches, his behavior righted itself and he was able to finish his senior year on decent terms and without any further calamities. His family arranged for him to spend a "thirteenth year" at a boarding school, which gave him some extra time to mature, and the following year he decided to attend college, where he became a successful student while also participating on the wrestling team.

CREATING A TEMPORARILY TOXIC HOME ENVIRONMENT

Many young adults feel the need to "spoil the nest" so that it becomes a little easier for them spread their wings and fly away from it, and easier for the family members whom they need to fly away from. There is always a part of us that needs to degrade the people whom we are leaving behind, no matter how important they have been to us. (In fact, often the intensity of the need to degrade is directly correlated with the intensity of their importance.)

One of the surest ways to do this is to create enough conflict and tension that a leave-taking feels more like a relief than a loss for both parent and child. While it is easy to simply be annoyed and irritable, it is essential to look beneath the surface and try to determine what hidden meanings the provocation might conceal.

In the spring of her senior year of high school, 18-year-old Fumi suddenly began leaving the house without informing her mother, Rita.

Naturally this upset Rita, who continued to insist that "out of respect" Fumi should let her know when she was going out, where she was going, and when she was due back. "I'm generally going to say yes," Rita told me, "but she still needs to let me know what's going on. What if I have to get in touch with her for some sort of emergency?"

Fumi, however, refused to comply, insisting that she was "not a little girl" anymore and was old enough to come and go as she pleased. Rita reminded Fumi that she was still living under her roof and threatened to take away her use of the car if this pattern persisted. Fumi replied that that didn't matter, that she would still leave without asking and would simply arrange to be picked up by a friend. Argument after argument ensued over a period of weeks in a struggle of wills.

If Fumi was simply looking for more space, she would simply have continued going out with her friends after notifying her mother, especially since Rita had made it clear to her that she'd generally give permission for her daughter's plans. The fact that Fumi had suddenly begun (in Rita's view) "disrespecting" her mother suggested that the daughter was trying to create some sort of friction that had a message.

During one of our discussions, Fumi complained to me about how clingy her mother had been with her recently. "She's constantly hanging around my room these days, sitting on my bed, won't give me any privacy at all. Don't get me wrong, we've had a good relationship all these years. I love her, but I'm really feeling suffocated by her. And she gets so sad when I am busy with other things. But it's my senior year, it's my last chance to be with my friends, and I don't want to spend my time hanging out with my mom."

During one of my discussions with Rita, she shed further light on this situation. "I had Fumi when I was 21 and her dad was never really in the picture, so it's just been the two of us for a long time. And she's been the greatest, she's just a wonderful daughter. But between raising her and working, I never really had time to date. And I know that I should be looking forward to my freedom when she leaves, but I don't know what I'll do and who I'll be without her."

Recognizing Rita's clinging as a sign that her mother wouldn't be functioning well without her devoted daughter in the day-to-day picture anymore, Fumi had subconsciously decided that she could best prepare her mother for the next stage of her life by being more difficult and challenging, making their ultimate separation from each other a little easier for Rita to bear. And not only was Fumi creating some distance between herself and her mother in order to prepare them both for the succeeding interval in their lives, but she was also "modeling" for her mother, that is, going out spontaneously, "without permission," in the face of Rita's refusal to give herself permission to go out more.

I suggested this hypothesis to Rita, and she responded positively. "I guess I'm not making it very easy on either of us by being such a stick-in-the-mud. It didn't occur to me that Fumi was all that worried about me and how I will do without her. She seems so self-centered."

"But what looks like self-centeredness to you may actually be her effort to try to get things moving in a more positive direction for you," I explained.

Once the conflict between this mother and daughter was examined in a different light, it began to resolve itself. Fumi agreed that she would go back to requesting permission to go out, and Rita agreed to meet with me a few times on her own to map out some ways to prepare more effectively for her adjustment to life after Fumi's departure.

ASKING QUESTIONS OF ONESELF RATHER THAN OTHERS

As I have heard the life stories of thousands of patients over the years, it has become clear to me that psychological growth occurs not so much as a result of the decisions we make, but more as a result of the questions we ask. Up until middle and late adolescence, many of the questions that teens ask of themselves concern what others think of them. In effect, they are asking:

- "What image do I want to project to the world that others will come to know me by?"

- "Whose approval is most important to me and how can I best earn it?"
- "Who must I differentiate from, and how should I do so without it working to my disadvantage?"
- "What achievements and accomplishments will enable me to look most successful to others?"

To chart a new and more self-directed route toward autonomy, these interior inquiries have to become more self-involved than concerned with the perceptions of others, resulting in the ability to frame queries such as:

- "Why do I do what I do?"
- "Who was I, who am I, and who do I want to become?"
- "What do I feel called upon to do with my life?"
- "Am I ever completely honest with myself?"
- "Am I comfortable simply being myself, and if not, why not?"
- "Do I need to work at seeing myself as more grand or more humble?"
- "Who is running the show here: me, or someone else?"
- "Should I focus on constructing my life or discovering my life?"

These are questions that can only be asked of and answered by oneself, and it is through asking and reflecting upon questions like this that we ultimately discover the paths that will lead toward a life of independence and meaning.

LOOSENING THE BORDER PATROL

During early and middle adolescence, teens will naturally reject and repudiate the advice and suggestions that caring adults are offering them, even (and especially) when it is meant to be helpful. They do this because they are struggling so hard to build out and bolster the fragile eggshell of their nascent identity, and taking in the recommendations offered by others threatens to crack the shell. In essence, they are like developing crustaceans who have shed their outgrown armor and then disappear for a time, hiding out in safety until a new, more capacious casing hardens enough to once again be truly protective. But in order to grow, young adults must be a little less closed off, and must practice taking in what others have to offer without feeling as though they are surrendering their hard-won, slowly coalescing selfhood.

Twenty-year-old Bruce was having a difficult time making it through his sophomore year of college. Psychological testing in seventh grade had identified him as having an attention deficit disorder, and at that point he began working with an organizational tutor and taking psychostimulant medication, both of which he used throughout middle school and the beginning of high school, with positive results. But by junior year he had decided that he didn't need tutoring or medication anymore, and withdrew completely from both. His performance declined noticeably, but he attributed this to "laziness."

Fortunately, he had achieved at a high enough level through the first half of high school that even though his grades dwindled during his junior and senior years, he was admitted into several colleges. But though his freshman year had gone decently, he was now floundering badly in three out of his four higher-level courses.

When his parents heard the extent to which Bruce felt that he was swimming upstream, they proposed that he go back on medication or reconsider some tutoring, but he forcefully refused, saying that he wanted to manage this on his own. During our initial session, I proposed to him that while it didn't matter to me whether or not he pursued tutoring or medication, they were best seen simply as tools, and that he would still be succeeding "on his own" even if he used a tool. After all, he certainly used other tools, such as a computer and a calculator, without compromising his belief that he was ultimately responsible for the results.

"But I should be able to do all of this without medication or outside help. I got through high school that way, and I got through last year, as well. "

"You did, and you're to be commended for this. But from what I've heard from your folks, you tended to do a lot better when you were on medication and working with a tutor than when you weren't."

"But as long as I depend on those things, then I'm never going to feel like my achievements are my own."

"Whose would they be if not yours?"

"I don't know, it just wouldn't feel the same. Look, I just don't want other people telling me how to study and I don't want any little pill controlling my brain."

"It isn't really controlling your brain. We're not absolutely sure about this, but in the case of psychostimulant medication, it seems to activate a part of the brain that is under-functioning a bit, which then helps you to filter out distractions and concentrate better. In other words, it just enables your brain to do what it's already capable of doing without getting sidetracked so easily. And the study strategies that educators have come up with basically do the same thing, jump-start that same part of your brain, the part that needs a bit of a boost. It's entirely up to you whether or not you take medicine or use a tutor, but I just want to be sure you understood how they both work."

Conceiving of medication and tutoring not as alien, outside forces that were abducting him, but as psychological instruments that he could choose when to implement and how to operate gave Bruce room to consider them differently. He decided that he would give some tutoring another try. Realizing that accepting help did not have to be equated with being helpless meant that he didn't have to patrol his personal borders quite so vigilantly and turn away resources that could be useful.

REEVALUATING OLD SURVIVAL TACTICS, DEVELOPING NEW ONES

Each of us created an arsenal of survival tactics early in life that helped us through the adversity we faced then, and many of these tactics retain their value over time and are worth carrying with us into adulthood. But sometimes the strategies that worked during our early years have to be reevaluated because they lose their relevance over time, becoming vestigial or even going against our essential goals and ambitions.

Seventeen-year-old Nicholas had to undergo numerous surgeries during the first dozen years of his life due to a congenital skeletal malformation, and he had wisely developed a one-day-at-a-time outlook that was exactly what was needed to make it through the endless medical ordeals he was constantly subjected to. But this one-day-at-a-time approach had ultimately begun interfering with his capacity to plan for life beyond high school—he was so understandably familiar with being "in the moment" that he had never learned how to think ahead and map out a future beyond the course of the next few days. This made necessary tasks such as filling out college applications and seeking out financial aid difficult to complete; for Nicholas, the formerly practical approach of living for today completely precluded the possibility of planning for tomorrow.

Being that Nicholas was a "gearhead" who enjoyed working on cars, I suggested an automotive analogy. Our work together involved inviting him to locate his personal "high beams" (or "brights") and practice looking a little farther down the road while reassuring him that he could still depend on his "low beams" and live for the moment, with his eyes on the ground close in front of him, when he needed to. This visualization helped him to begin thinking and acting more proactively when it came to planning his future while still being able to cultivate the "power of now" when necessary.

UNDERSTANDING THE IMPLICATIONS OF SUCCESS AS WELL AS FAILURE

Parents spend a good deal of time warning their children about the consequences of failure—of not doing well in school, cultivating good friendships, or participating in extracurricular activities—but insufficient time encouraging them to think about the implications of success. After all, success brings about complicated changes, too, and not all of them are entirely positive.

Many cultures share a similar folktale that explores the fluid nature of good fortune and bad fortune. In one version, a fine, stray horse randomly wanders into a poor family's barn, which they interpret as a blessing. But then their son goes for a ride on the horse, falls off, and breaks his leg, which they interpret as a curse. But after the village doctor sets his leg and the youth is being tended by a young nurse, they fall in love, and the injury enables him to escape being inducted into the army, which they interpret as a blessing. He marries the nurse, but unfortunately they are unable to conceive a child together, which they interpret as a curse. But then the young couple adopt a village orphan, who turns out to be of regal lineage, which they interpret as a blessing... and on and on. The point, of course, is that life is much too complicated for any one achievement or event to be understood in a purely positive or negative light.

Selena, 18, was resisting getting her driver's license, despite her parents' persistent efforts to mobilize her to do so. During a session, she confessed privately to me, "Once I start driving on my own, I doubt that I'll ever see my mom anymore." She went on to explain that family life was generally so busy that her car time with her mother was the only time when she could depend on relatively undivided attention from her. From Selena's perspective, the potential gains of having more independence appeared significantly outweighed by the loss of the closeness with her mother that she cherished and wasn't quite ready to relinquish.

Nineteen-year-old Quinn told me that he had learned to equate doing well with being unhappy by observing his overworked parents. "Most people would consider my mother and father to be very successful—they each make a lot of money, they each drive nice cars, and we live in a nice house in a nice neighborhood—but, to me, they're miserable. They moved here because they wanted my brother and me to be in a good school district, but that meant that that they each have ninety-minute commutes to work, so they've basically spent three hours a day in the car for the last fifteen years. And then my brother wound up having to go to a private school, anyway, because of his learning disabilities, so what was the point? They have to work even harder than before to pay his tuition.

"So now they're pushing me to do the same thing that they've done. 'You've gotta get a high-paying job—look how expensive it is to live,' they keep saying. Well, it's so expensive to live because that's how they've chosen to live! They're like those hamsters running around in circles without getting anywhere. Instead of my taking *their* advice, maybe they should take some of my advice."

"What would your advice be?" I inquired.

"I'd tell them to get off the treadmill. I'd tell them that I appreciate all that they've done, but that I'm not going to live the same life that they live. If that means I take things at a slower pace, so be it. If that means I'm not the best, not at the top of the heap, so be it. Looking at them, I'd rather be a happy failure than an unhappy success. I mean, what's the point of climbing a mountain if, when you get to the top, there's just another mountain that needs to be climbed?"

While his parents had surely tried to impress upon Quinn the importance of being successful, they had done so at such a great cost that the result was that he feared success—or at least his parents' definition of success—much more than he feared failure.

FORGING A CONNECTION BETWEEN FREEDOM AND RESPONSIBILITY

Children and young adolescents naturally associate growing older with having more freedom—liberty to be more on their own, to be out later at night, to drive a car, to drink, to date—but part of the young adult's developmental work is also to connect increased opportunity with a greater sense of responsibility. Responsibility can be best understood as behaving in a way that fosters the freedom and well-being of someone other than ourselves, whether or not it fosters our own. Stated briefly, to be responsible is to be altruistic. Unfortunately, in our culture, freedom and responsibility tend to be seen as opposites: freedom is associated with not having any responsibilities, as being excused from duty and accountability.

For true self-reliance to become a reality, the young adult has to learn to conceptualize freedom in a more mature way—to see it not as the absence of responsibility, but as the willingness to manage responsibility with efficacy, courage, and grace.

Stuart, 22, was used to enjoying a carefree life. Growing up, he had generally gotten everything he asked for—not just the basics, but also big-ticket items such as a BlackBerry and an expensive car—all without his having to contribute anything. His parents sent him to private schools from kindergarten all the way through high school, and completely paid for his private college education as well. He obtained a high-paying first job at a financial services firm right after graduating with a business degree, so he was able to continue living high on the hog, moving into his own apartment in a newly gentrified part of town.

Stuart continued to work hard to cultivate a life that was as free of obligations and as full of pleasure as possible—shopping for the finest clothes and high-tech gear, partying regularly with his friends and colleagues, frequent golf trips to first-class resorts, and numerous sexual liaisons with young women without making any serious commitment to any one of them... until one rainy night when, slightly inebriated, he was driving home from a party with a female friend, Fawn, and skidded into a telephone pole. He walked away from the accident with only minor scrapes and bruises, but Fawn incurred a serious spinal cord injury and was left paralyzed from the waist down.

At this point, Stuart had two choices. He could emotionally "walk away" from the accident, chalk it up to bad luck, and continue with his happy-go-lucky life. Or he could allow this catastrophe to shape him into a deeper, more mature, and noble human being. Fortunately, not only for Fawn but also for himself, he chose the latter.

Although he was not committed to Fawn or in love with her at the time of the accident (he admitted to me that, on that fateful night, he was simply taking her back to his apartment to have sex with her), he began to devote himself to her and to her family, making himself available to all of them as Fawn embarked on rehabilitation and the long, arduous adjustment to her permanent impairment. He struggled through the overpowering feelings of grief and remorse that he was shouldering, and we spoke about how to allow those feelings to mobilize rather than oppress him, how to use his grief and remorse to become more caring, more attentive, more compassionate.

Stuart got involved with a national organization supporting individuals with spinal cord injuries and their families, and convinced the CEO of his company to sponsor an annual golf tournament to raise money for research and rehabilitation. He remained close to Fawn, and eventually their relationship grew, with great courage from each, from one of guilt-based obligation to one of genuine affection, to the point that they eventually decided to get married.

In Stuart's case, what marked his transition into independent adulthood was not graduation from college or the establishment of financial self-sufficiency, all of which were achieved without tremendous sacrifice on his part, but his willingness to accept responsibility for his actions and rise to the painful occasion that he and Fawn had been confronted with.

FORGING RESPONSIBILITY TO YOUR OWN IDENTITY

Adulthood places numerous expectations on all of us, and while part of a young adult's job is to learn how to take on those responsibilities, another part of the job necessitates maintaining a strong and supple sense of personal identity while managing those responsibilities. We need to find ways to be accountable and dependable without becoming psychologically moribund and losing our soul in the process.

The development of our character is what makes it possible for us to separate and become our own individual selves, and an essential part of adulthood is strengthening our character so that it maintains its unique structure throughout our lives, despite what influences and events we are exposed to. As we shall see throughout this book, the challenge of forging a distinct identity is often the most daunting in family relationships: it is here where the young adult needs to find a way to navigate successfully between his loyalty to his family and his loyalty to himself. As a colleague once reminded me, the two most aggressive words in the English language are: "I am."

Nineteen-year-old Laila had been born to a drug-dependent mother and an incarcerated father, and at the age of two was taken from her mother by Child Protective Services due to neglect and was introduced into the foster care system. She spent the next four years in a series of foster homes, some organized and caring, some chaotic and neglectful. At the age of six she was adopted by a middle-class family in the suburbs, and her life changed dramatically for the better—she now had two loving parents, a kind older brother, and access to an excellent school system where she quickly began to thrive. She started second grade unable to read, and by the end of fourth grade she was already on her grade level. She continued to excel through middle school and into the beginning of high school, at which point her performance suddenly went into an inexplicable nosedive.

In my sessions with her, it gradually became clear that she was trying to make sense of her relationship with her birth mother while still trying to express gratitude to her adoptive parents.

"I lost track of my birth mother once I was taken from her. I'm told she visited me at the foster homes here and there, but by the time I was adopted, I don't think I'd seen her for years. I'm not even sure I'd want to now."

"Why not?"

"I don't know . . . too painful, I guess. My life is so different now, probably so different from hers. I know that she was a drug addict, that she was probably doing the sex-for-drugs thing, and that her life must have been awful. And look at me, look at my life! Nice clothes, good school, great home . . . I feel awful."

"Does that mean that you're not entitled to take advantage of what your life has to offer, because her life has been so difficult?"

"In a way, yes. It feels like a slap in the face for me to leave her behind and have such a fine life, with so many opportunities. But it would feel like a slap in the face for me to not make good on what my parents have given me. I don't know, I feel stuck."

"How old was your mom when she gave birth to you?"

"She just turned 17; I know that because I saw my birth certificate."

"How old are you now?"

"I'll be 17 in a couple of months." She looked up at the ceiling for a moment. "Which, I guess, means that I'm now the age that she was at when she gave birth to me." Laila let out a long sigh. "What different paths our lives have taken, it's really unbelievable."

As Laila was approaching the age that her mother was when she was born, the struggle between her loyalty to her own ambitions and her loyalty to her birth mother was intensifying. Somehow, it was no longer okay for her to succeed, because it was, in her mind, an act of treason directed against her birth mother, a "slap in the face," as Laila put it.

As we teased out the complexity of this dilemma, it occurred to Laila that the sudden downturn in her academic performance may have been a nod to her mom, an acknowledgment that she wasn't going to completely leave her behind. If she stayed in some kind of trouble (in this case, scholastic), she could then stay close to her mother, since under-functioning was the only existent link between the two of them.

With this hypothesis in mind, we spent some time discussing how she might continue to be a faithful daughter to her birth mother while still capitalizing on her strengths and pursuing her ambitions, thus being a faithful daughter to her adoptive parents, as well.

Laila's solution was an ingenious one: she decided that she would resume her previous high level of academic performance, but begin volunteering as a tutor to students with reading difficulties at a nearby elementary school. In this way, she could "justify" her desire for further growth and success by committing herself to helping others. She would never be able to go back in time and rescue her mother, but by rescuing these younger students who represented her mother, she was able to do so symbolically, which freed her to rescue herself from the emotional ties that had begun to bind her.

In spite of her challenging circumstances, Laila found a way to be true to herself without being disloyal to either her birth or adoptive parents. While not every young adult will experience a loyalty bind as dramatic as Laila's, every individual will at some point face some tough choices regarding who she is going to be most faithful to—herself or those whom she has depended on. The intensity of this bind is often what accounts for the difficulties the young adult may be experiencing in her pursuit of success and self-reliance.

EMOTIONAL AND BEHAVIORAL REGULATION

To more fully feel in charge of our own lives, we must not only be able to manage and master our external environment—school, work, relationships—but also our internal environment, the inner psychological landscape that we need to survey and navigate with greater skill as we leave the nest. This process involves allowing our thoughts and our feelings to shake hands, so to speak, and become intimately acquainted with each other, to support and feed each other as we find healthy ways to get our needs satisfied.

When we succeed in doing so, our minds and hearts collaborate in such a way that we are able to experience our emotions fully and enjoy a range of options in expressing them. When we fail to connect our thoughts and feelings, we are consigned to either suppressing our emotions and losing out on what they have to teach us about ourselves, or to being overpowered by them in such a way that impulse, rather than thoughtful reflection, dictates how we engage with others.

Regulating one's emotional life is not something that happens overnight, and children and adolescents will find themselves at various stages on the learning curve during their development. What is important is to continue to make significant strides toward self-regulation in order to fully transition into mature adulthood.

Nineteen-year-old Meghan, who was about fifty pounds overweight, was extremely sensitive to any comments having to do with weight or eating. Her mother, Sheila, was very close to Meghan and supportive of her, but whenever she made reference to weight-related matters, Meghan sensed that her mother was criticizing her. Sheila might suggest that Meghan choose a different outfit because the one she had on wasn't particularly flattering, or wonder out loud if she might be better off having iced tea with Splenda rather than a mocha frappuccino when they went out for coffee together.

Sheila may not have meant for these remarks to be taken too seriously, but Meghan was clearly predisposed to interpret them as disapproving. And when she felt disapproved of, she tended to binge on high-fat, high-sugar treats like ice cream and brownies. The more she binged, of course, the more weight she gained, and the more weight she gained, the angrier she got at her mother. When her anger reached the "red zone," Meghan would blow up at her mother, accusing her of constantly harping on her being overweight. Sheila would be astonished by how Meghan could misconstrue such innocuous statements, and she would try to reassure her that she loved her and was not criticizing her, just offering some advice on a take-it-or-leave-it basis. Her mother's befuddled reaction would enrage Meghan even more, and she'd find herself back at the grocery store, stuffing herself with more junk food.

The goal in this situation was to help Meghan learn how to regulate her emotions. Whether or not her mother intended to be disparaging was impossible to determine and, more importantly, beside the point—that was Meghan's interpretation, and, in response, she had fallen into the pattern of both suppressing and expressing her upset emotions through compulsive eating, which only kept the cycle going.

I asked Meghan to keep a log of every time her mother said something to her that was oriented around weight or eating, and to note the intensity of her emotional response to her mother's comment on a scale of 1 to 10. When Meghan came to our next appointment with her log, we noted that her response wasn't always a 10; sometimes it was as low as 3 or 4, just a passing ripple on her emotional pond. We spent some time discussing why her response varied (it often depended on such variables as how she was feeling about herself, what she was in the midst of at the time of the remark, whether she felt like she was doing well with her schoolwork, etc.) and how to keep it at the 3–4 rather than the 9–10 level. With this goal in mind, she agreed to make sure that she exercised regularly, and also to borrow a meditation DVD from the library and learn how to breathe in a calming manner.

We also explored what to do when her emotions, for whatever reasons, spiked up to the 9–10 level. We were looking for something that wouldn't entangle her any further with her mother, since these interactions were consistently infuriating, and inevitably seemed to fuel the cycle that she was desperately trying to break. We decided that she would refrain from talking to her mother about her feelings directly, even when she felt maligned by her, but instead write about them in a journal or email them to me.

Once Meghan figured out how to modulate her reactions to her mother and conceive of some ways to avoid her previous programmed response—a response that invariably made things worse—she found herself less troubled by Sheila's comments and better able to regulate her eating and weight.

One of the major challenges to emotional regulation that I have noticed with many young adults stems from their belief that *happiness* should be the goal of their existence. Having been told for years that they should be happy, and with so many parental resources devoted to keeping them happy (not to mention all the "shiny happy people" in TV commercials), their lives become singular quests for a state of perpetual euphoria that is not only impossible to maintain but that ultimately undermines their emotional development. The focus on happiness can block all the other "colors" of feeling that comprise a healthy human being's complete emotional spectrum. Unless we are familiar and on good terms with all of our feelings—sorrow as well as joy, despair as well as optimism—we not only lose out on many of life's most meaningful experiences, but we also deprive ourselves of the capacity to learn how to monitor our emotions, and instead wind up being governed by them. Part of Meghan's emotional reactivity probably derived from her belief that her mother should always be happy with her, so anything that Sheila said that made her *un*happy naturally aroused her ire.

CREATING A NEW NARRATIVE

All of us look for patterns that both explain and construct our identities—the story of who we have been, who we now are, and who we are destined to become. This story—the personal narrative that we create, cherish, and carry with us—is important because it imbues us with our unique sense of selfhood, the essence of who we are. But this story can also be limiting, a caricature that prevents us from more fully exploring and capitalizing on our potential.

An essential part of leaving adolescence behind is the expansion of our personal narrative in such a way that it still helps us to identify ourselves, but no longer inadvertently restricts our possibilities. The powerful forces that have been exerted on the developing child by family life, schools, and society at large all can combine to impress on him a false or oversimplified sense of who he is. To become a competent young adult, he must integrate the diverse aspects of his personality in a new and more sophisticated way that will allow him to live his life with enhanced resilience and authenticity.

Twenty-two-year-old Russell was unemployed and living at home with his mother, Dina, and his younger sister. When Russell was seven, his father began sexually molesting him and told the boy that if he disclosed this to anyone, his father would leave the family. This experience had psychologically handcuffed Russell, leaving him without any conceivable alternatives. As he explained it to me:

"If I told my mom what was happening, then my parents divorce, and I didn't want that. So I basically decided I would just put up with it all, you know, 'take one for the team,' as they say. And this went on for years until I was around thirteen, I guess, and then all of a sudden I couldn't stand it anymore—I mean I was getting interested in girls and this just felt too weird, too strange. And so I hemmed and hawed and finally told my mother what had been going on, and of course she went crazy, screaming at my dad and throwing his stuff out into the yard and calling the police, telling him to leave and never come back . . . and that's exactly what happened. She didn't want him involved anymore and he didn't want to be involved anymore, and that's still where things stand."

It was not a surprise that Russell composed a narrative built on the themes of having been victimized and abandoned, and he clung to this narrative like a drowning man clings to a piece of driftwood. But while he obviously had legitimate reasons to rely on these themes, his story was limiting him because he insisted (as we always do with our personal narrative) that it explained the significance of all his experience.

From his perspective, for example, young women were somehow always "abandoning" him. The possibility that he was contributing to the breakup, even though he rarely initiated it, never seemed to cross his mind. Somehow, every story he told about an abortive love affair ended with his being suddenly jilted without good reason.

When it came to his disappointing work life, he was always the victim of someone else's unfairness, inefficiency, or poor judgment. When he didn't get a job that he was applying for, it was because the interviewer hadn't taken enough time to get to know him. When he got fired, it was because his boss wanted to hire her nephew for the position, and Russell was the one she released "because she doesn't like men," even though some other male employees had been kept on.

He absolved himself of responsibility for every disappointment that occurred, because that was what it took to maintain the consistency of his narrative. For Russell to imagine that he actually had some influence or control over his relationships or his work life (this was clearly not the case while he was being abused by his father) was something that would force him to radically rewrite his life's script.

During our work together, we applied ourselves to reviewing his personal narrative so that he could begin reading from a more interesting, less limiting script. We acknowledged that he had in fact been victimized and abandoned, but that as long as that experience was the basis for his identity, he would have no choice but to spend the rest of his life deliberately seeking out new people to victimize and abandon him in order to maintain his fidelity to the narrative. And there would always be plenty of people willing to play the role of victimizer and abandoner.

We also looked for other important threads that needed to be woven into his narrative to make it more flexible, accurate, and relevant. For example, while his father had mistreated him, his mother had not, nor had her father, his beloved grandfather with whom he still had a close relationship.

Also, when he was sharing his painful history, I recalled that Russell had admitted that he had "taken one for the team" by silently absorbing his father's sexual molestation for the good of his family, which suggested that he had great courage and strength, qualities that he was probably stifling in an effort to prevent them from interfering with the safety of his victimized and abandoned mentality. While the work of rediscovering and embodying his inner strength and courage would certainly take away from the familiar confines of his initial narrative, it would also make it less likely that he would be victimized and abandoned—the sacrifice of that familiarity would be well worth what he would receive in return.

As Russell broadened his narrative and began to tell himself and others a richer, more variegated story, he began to live a richer life. He approached dating with new confidence and resolve, and started to experience longer-lasting and more satisfying relationships. And, as he approached his professional life with more optimistic expectations, rather than expecting to always "get the shaft," this naturally led him to examine his approach to job-seeking and employment with more objectivity, and to take note of the many ways in which he had been alienating his employers.

"I think I was giving off this chip-on-the-shoulder vibe, just waiting for someone to turn on me so that I could say, 'See, there's another person who doesn't appreciate me.' I was very testy, very temperamental, and I suspect that's one of the main reasons that I never seemed able to hold a job for very long. People probably get tired of that.

"But now I try to focus on that inner strength and resilience that we've talked about . . . just like I 'took one for the team' when it came to my family, I also try to 'take one for the team' at work, and it makes a big difference. People really respond well to that."

❧ ❧

We have been examining some of the important developmental tasks that young adults must take on to crystallize a self-sufficient, autonomous identity. But young adults are not alone when it comes to developmental tasks. You, the parent, have your work cut out for you, as well, and your tasks will be explored in our next chapters.

CHAPTER TWO

FAILURE TO LAUNCH

FAMILY DYNAMICS AND
THE EMERGING ADULT

"There are few situations in life more difficult to cope with than an adolescent son or daughter during the attempt to liberate themselves."

—*Anna Freud*

Liberation is an essential developmental task that depends on a healthy separation from the family unit, one that summons the past, gathers up the present, and surges into the future. Liberation reveals itself as a gradually expanding spiral of growth, maturation, and individuation on the part of both generations, increasingly leading all parties toward a healthy balance of self-reliance and interdependence.

For the young adult, liberation manifests itself through leaving home and establishing self-sufficiency. This is not so much a "day of reckoning" for young adults and their families, but an ongoing "phase of reckoning," a transitional period that will challenge every member of the family to grow. There will be intense periods of mutual hurt and reconciliation, anger and forgiveness, anguish and joy, loss and discovery, grief and healing, a "joint venture" of the struggles and dilemmas of all family members.

In every generation and in every culture, this fateful drama is played out on a unique stage for the highest stakes, for it illuminates the most elemental aspects of human development: the nature of love, loyalty, connection, freedom, responsibility, and selfhood. And, as with any turning point in human development, this process can easily go awry.

Over the course of my many years as a family psychologist, I have become enduringly acquainted with the ways in which the separation process can proceed in ways that either promote or inhibit growth. Establishing a healthy differentiation between parent and child is one of the most daunting of family challenges, and thus is often impeded and disturbed by various forces. Instead of the even, continuous, irreversible evolution that we'd like to enjoy, we often encounter distressing detours and frustrating regressions. Instead of ceaseless, observable development, we may face long periods of stalemate, a developmental deadlock in which growth appears to be completely stymied.

While it is easy to blame one generation or the other for a troubled separation, it has become clear to me that difficulties are fed by both parent and child. I have seen the ways in which each party, through acts of omission and commission, adds to the push and pull, the swirls and eddies, of intricate family forces. Parents cannot help but draw their young adult children into their own matrix of conflicts and problems, just as their young adult children cannot help but draw parents into theirs.

Parents at every stage of development convey to me their desire for their child's ultimate autonomy. In fact, their anxious response to their offspring's behavior, or misbehavior, is often rooted in a fear that the child's journey toward autonomy is somehow going to be thwarted. They ask questions such as:

- "When will he be able to sleep in his own bed?"
- "When will he be able to wake up in the morning and get his own bowl of cereal without waking me up?"
- "When will she and her brother figure out how to play together nicely without getting me involved in their fights?"

- "All of his friends go to sleepaway camp each summer—why won't he?"
- "Will she ever learn to organize her schoolwork, or will she always need me to go through her backpack for her?"
- "Will he ever be motivated to get a driver's license so I don't have to drive him everywhere?"
- "Is she ever going to apply to college?"
- "I told him to get a job because he's going to have to pay for his own cell phone, but he won't get off his butt and find one."
- "Will he ever, just, you know, *grow up?*"

The achievement of autonomy is one of life's great triumphs, but it is not easily won. While individual children will always become autonomous at different speeds, what I have noticed after carefully observing thousands of families is that the family climate has much more to do with how quickly autonomy is achieved than does the child's temperament. Parents are often surprised to learn of the many ways in which they are actually supplying the very chains that tether their child to the family's orbit, creating an environment in which it is inordinately difficult, if not impossible, for a young adult to launch herself into a new and distinct trajectory.

One way to understand this is to imagine that every family is balanced on the fulcrum of centripetal forces (seeking the center, or pointing inward) and centrifugal forces (fleeing the center, or pointing outward). *Centripetal* forces imbue the new generation with a sense of connectedness, loyalty, and tradition; they function as the glue that holds the family together and accounts for its ongoing continuity. *Centrifugal* forces, on the other hand, instill in the new generation a sense of freedom, initiative, and innovation; they function as the lubrication that enables the family to remain a family while allowing its members to leave the nest so that they can then enter and productively adapt to a changing world.

Though both centripetal and centrifugal forces are necessary for healthy functioning and growth, often a family will teeter back and forth between too much inwardness (or introversion) and too much outwardness (or extroversion), or some sort of conflicted combination of the two. As long as the imbalance is temporary and alterable, significant and lasting difficulties tend not to arise. However, when an imbalance between centripetal and centrifugal forces takes root and begins to establish residency within a family, healthy functioning and growth are invariably compromised.

With this framework in mind, when young adults display hesitancy in striking out on their own, it can be understood not as a flaw or defect in them or in their parents, but as a symptom of an imbalance or conflict between these centripetal and centrifugal forces.

In my experience, families in which young adult development seems to be hobbled or hindered belong to one or more of the following three categories:

1. When *centripetal* forces dominate, young adults feel overwhelmed by their loyalty to their family. They are not able to successfully leave home because leaving would be tantamount to a betrayal of their parents, and they see any significant life that is lived outside of the family's structure as a violation of love and trust. The guilt that these young adults feel as they consider growing beyond their family is so powerful that they regularly, and sometimes inventively, find ways to sabotage their own development.

2. When *centrifugal* forces dominate, young adults feel as if they have been, or are being, prematurely ejected from the family orbit. They are not able to successfully leave home because they don't believe that they have absorbed enough of the psychological nutrients of love, nurturance, and support necessary to make the daunting journey toward self-reliance.

3. When centripetal and centrifugal forces are misaligned, young adults find themselves in conflict—they are not able to successfully leave home because they are being asked to fulfill divergent missions for their parents. And not being

able to navigate effectively between these incongruous assignments stops them in their tracks. I call these "mission impossible" families.

One of the realities of child development that I find most fascinating, and most relevant during the launching phase, is that children are innate problem solvers, and that what we define as a child's "problem" is actually and invariably a child's attempt to *solve* a problem. As adults, we often think of children in problem-based modes, whereas children are generally thinking in solution-based modes.

So when we look at a young adult whose reluctance to leave the nest is a problem (from a parental perspective), it is, from her perspective, a solution. In these cases, reluctance becomes an unproductive solution to the imbalance of inward and outward forces, though often working at the expense of her future growth and happiness.

Let's take a look at brief examples of these three categories: the dominance of centripetal forces, of centrifugal forces, or a misalignment of the two. In each scenario below, the problem is the same—a college education that appears to be running aground early on—but the origin of the problem falls into one of these groups.

A CENTRIPETAL FAMILY

Denise and Ahmed were not entirely pleased that Lani, their bright and self-sufficient 18-year-old daughter, had chosen to attend a college out of state. This was because much of Lani's childhood had been devoted to tending to her overanxious mother. From a very early age she learned to calm her mother down when she became agitated, distract her with entertaining stories from school and the playground when she was depressed, and keep her company when she seemed lonely.

When Lani was 13 and planning on going to summer sleepaway camp with some friends for the first time, Denise got into a car accident and broke her pelvis two weeks before Lani's planned departure date, confining her to bed rest for a month. Denise and Ahmed agreed at that time that it would be best if Lani stayed home, rather than attend camp, so that she would be able to provide nursing support for her mother while her father continued working. Lani, who was a little anxious herself about her initial experience away from home, ambivalently agreed to forgo the camp experience.

A couple of years later, when Lani was 15, her science project won an award, and she and her fellow group members were invited to participate in an out-of-state national science fair competition, one that would entail several days of travel. A week before Lani was to leave, Denise went in for a mammogram, which displayed a growth that her doctor thought deserved a biopsy. Lani's parents both asked her to not attend the science program so that she could be available if the news was bad, and, once again, she capitulated.

Lani's parents also assigned her to keep an eye on her rebellious sister, Gena, who was three years younger. Lani's job was to report back to her parents if there was any evidence that Gena was getting into trouble or making bad decisions, and to counsel Gena when necessary. Not surprisingly, Lani's monitoring duties created significant friction between the two girls and interfered with their ability to develop a close relationship.

With all of the responsibilities that she had been shouldering, it was somewhat surprising to me that Lani eventually liberated herself to the extent that she was able to push off and go to college. But even though she finally departed, she appeared to be kept on a very long leash. Denise texted her several times a day, sometimes just to "touch base," sometimes to ask her to call Gena and see how she was doing, sometimes for moral support.

Lani did well academically her first semester, but by the second semester she seemed to have hit a wall. Her grades were declining, she withdrew from the community outreach program that had so enthused her in the fall, and she was spending more and more of her time in contact with her old high school boyfriend, Lao. The two of them had started dating at the end of junior year, but had agreed to break it off after graduation, partly because Lao was going to continue living at home and attend community college. Now, however, they were growing close again, and she was spending more time texting and talking to him than she was with her new college friends.

By the middle of her second semester, she had already decided not to return to college and informed her parents that she was going to move back home, get a job, and think about how she wanted to continue her education at another college. Denise and Ahmed were both supportive of Lani's decision, but, interestingly enough, Lani herself didn't seem to be. Instead of finding work and beginning the process of transferring to another college—and instead of resuming her supervision of Gena, not to mention her chronic caregiving toward her mother—she spent most of her time hanging out at her boyfriend's house. This infuriated Denise, who had been looking forward to Lani's slavish resumption of her previous responsibilities. The more she pushed Lani to stay at home and "be a part of the family," the more time Lani spent at Lao's, and the less time she spent considering her future. It was at this point that the family came to consult with me.

Lani, despite somehow having been able to set sail, was unable to avoid being pulled back to shore by the undertow of her family's centripetal forces. She was clearly not happy about this turn of events, revealed by her unwillingness to cheerily resume her old roles—in other words, she had returned home but "under protest." And yet, home is where she wound up, and without any apparent motivation to undertake another departure in the near future.

Our work together did not initially focus on Lani, but instead addressed the necessity for Denise and Ahmed to work together both as a married couple supporting each other, as well as coparents supporting the worrisome Gena, so that Lani was emancipated from feeling so responsible for everyone. Once this family's centripetal forces were realigned, Lani, now liberated, began to naturally take care of her own future rather than the rest of her family. She decided to reapply to her original college and returned there to earn her degree.

A CENTRIFUGAL FAMILY

Unlike Lani's parents, Richard and Julia were very eager for their off-spring to leave home. Darren was the youngest of four, with three highly successful siblings, all of whom were either self-sufficient or moving quickly in that direction. But Darren was less driven and ambitious, and seemed to reserve most of his energy and intellect for his favorite hobby, fishing.

His parents, however, seemed unable to adjust to his slower pace—with three out the door, Richard and Julia were eagerly looking forward to retiring from their tiresome government jobs and moving to West Virginia, where they had bought some lakefront property and were in the process of renovating a house. Darren's graduation from high school and subsequent departure for college were the final ingredients necessary to affirm their freedom.

In fact, as I listened to their history, it seemed as if this mother and father, although warm and pleasant individuals, had essentially tossed in the towel on parenting three years before, when Darren's next oldest sister had left home for college. For example, it was fine with them if Darren joined them every weekend to help rebuild the lake house, but it was clear that he was there to be put to work. It seemed equally fine, if not better, from his parents' perspective, for him to hang back and stay with his best friend, Pete, also an avid fisherman. The problem with this solution, however, was that Darren began to quietly resent his parents' nonparental priorities, and spent most of his weekends while they were away fishing and drinking vodka shots with friends. His level of academic focus and achievement fell more and more precipitously during his final two years of high school, his GPA plummeting as his alcohol use rose. He did not take the college search process seriously, and completed only two applications, both at the last minute. However, they were pleased that he eventually received one acceptance, and celebrated by hiring a real estate agent to help them put their house on the market so that they could finally make their move.

Unfortunately, within weeks of starting school he was hit by a car while drunkenly running across a busy intersection from one fraternity party to another, and suffered a broken arm and a ruptured spleen. Naturally, he was sent—where else?—back home to recuperate, much to his parents' dismay.

When they came to meet with me, Darren forthrightly admitted that he felt like he had been a "third wheel" in the family for several years. "They just wanna get on with their lives, I know that, but the problem is, I'm just not ready yet . . . that's why I didn't apply to colleges very seriously. I knew in my heart I wasn't ready, it wasn't going to work . . . and it didn't."

It seemed that just as Richard and Julia were unwaveringly determined to pry Darren out of the house so that they could finally move on with their lives, he countered with an equal determination to thwart their efforts until he received what he felt was his due.

In this family, the work consisted of helping Richard and Julia to "slow things down" and not expect Darren to leave home simply because he was 18, or because they were ready to retire. Once they adjusted their schedule and made it clear that they could be patient, Darren slowly moved himself back into forward gear, and eventually cut back on his drinking and became a successful college student.

A MISSION IMPOSSIBLE FAMILY

Unlike Lani and Darren, Janelle was blessed with two parents who were supportive when it came to finishing high school and going to college, neither rushing her through childhood prematurely nor possessively holding her back. So it wasn't surprising that her college application process went relatively smoothly and that she was admitted to an excellent liberal arts institution.

The challenge that Janelle had to meet was that each of her parents had very different agendas for her college experience. Her father, Marcus, was a moderately successful attorney who felt that he had been strongarmed into a legal career by his own father, who was also an attorney. He still looked back with regret on his choice of a career and wistfully wondered what his life would have been like if he had allowed himself a wider range of academic and social experiences in college and afterward, rather than having channeled all of his energy into law. Twenty years after having passed the bar, he still often fantasized about leaving the field and returning to graduate school in history or becoming a social studies teacher at a high school or community college.

Janelle's mother, Daphne, was a paralegal who lamented *not* having gone to law school, and constantly chafed at working under lawyers to whom she considered herself intellectually superior. However, an undergraduate experience mostly devoted to field hockey, a marriage that took place right after graduation, and her commitment to supporting her husband through law school had convinced her to lower her professional sights. Paralegal studies became a less than satisfactory auxiliary plan that she took up in her late thirties, but the dull work only reminded her of her restlessness and regrets.

Not surprisingly, Janelle got caught in the nostalgic crossfire of her parents' longings. Marcus strongly encouraged her to take a wide range of courses and to get involved in campus activities, which he had never done. Daphne, meanwhile, wanted Janelle to focus strictly on the courses that would lay the groundwork for a career in law, and strongly discouraged her from cultivating an active social life or from any other endeavors that might distract her from this ultimate aim.

Janelle somehow managed to reconcile her parents' conflicting master plans for her during her first semester, and found a workable middle ground, earning a GPA of 2.75 while getting involved with an intramural volleyball team, writing for the school newspaper, and beginning the process of pledging at a sorority. During winter break, however, there were several flare-ups at home. Daphne strongly suggested that they weren't going to continue subsidizing an education costing more than $50,000 a year for her to have only a 2.75 GPA, while her father countered by proudly affirming what a positive adjustment he believed Janelle had made, doing as well as she did academically while maintaining a range of extracurricular interests.

By the middle of her second semester, however, Janelle found herself unable to maintain an adequate balance. She joined an indoor lacrosse team, the newspaper editors were so pleased with her work that they began assigning her a story every week, and pledging the sorority took up more time than she had thought it would. All these activities basically annihilated her capacity to catch up on work and sleep on the weekend. She completed the semester with a B, two Cs, and an incomplete, and was placed on academic probation by the dean.

The summer after freshman year was a miserable one, as her parents battled over whether or not she should be allowed to return to school. Daphne insisted that Janelle should live at home under their watchful eye and attend community college for a year, while Marcus argued that she be allowed to return for one more semester to see if she could work her way off of probation. As a compromise, they agreed that Janelle would take a summer course at the community college and, based on her performance, a decision would be made regarding whether or not she'd be given another chance.

Janelle, however, was so upset by the high level of tension at home, and so envious of her carefree friends who returned home from college for school-free summers and hung out together every night, that she was unable to concentrate well. When she earned a C in the summer class, her mother (angrily) and father (ambivalently) decided to have her stay home until she "proves to us that she's ready to go back."

In this family's case, our energy was devoted to trying to align Marcus and Daphne's expectations for Janelle, and, ultimately, to leave it up to her to define how she could best invest her time and energy during her college years, rather than place her in the impossible position of straining to keep both of them satisfied. Once the parents understood that Janelle's priority needed to be living her *own* life, rather than reliving theirs for them, they were able to take a step back and allow her to move forward on her own, which of course she did.

~ ~

It is important to remember, as we discuss this trio of family "force fields," that variations on all three of them play significant roles in healthy child development. We often hear about parents needing to provide "roots and wings" for their children, and what I'm describing isn't really all that different. Centripetal forces are the "roots" that help children to feel anchored and safe as they grow, and centrifugal forces are the "wings" that help children leave the nest and soar away to distant and exciting horizons.

Of course, all of us have expectations for our children, which sometimes include wanting them to make good on promises to ourselves that we may have defaulted on over the years. With this in mind, the fact that we sometimes give our children mixed messages about what we expect of them isn't really avoidable.

So, please don't think that a successful family is characterized by the complete absence of any of these forces. What we want to take a careful look at, however, is the way these forces are balanced and counterbalanced, and whether, over time, we are calibrating and recalibrating these forces in response to our child's temperament and developmental stage.

Early on in family life, for example, it is legitimate for parents to allow centripetal forces to hold sway, since children are small and need to be protected, both physically and emotionally. Obviously it would not make much sense to expect a three-year-old to make her own meals, select her own clothes, and set her own alarm clock to be up in time for preschool.

But later on in family life, parents should allow centrifugal forces to take hold, because when children are older they need space and support as they prepare to break away. It obviously would not make much sense, for example, to expect a 19-year-old to regularly be home by 8 P.M. on weekends so that she can finish off the night playing board games with her family.

We also have to acknowledge that while solid parental consistency is optimal, there will always be differences between parents when it comes to wishes and expectations for our children at any stage of development. One of the major advantages of a child having two parents is that she can experience two sets of regrets and two sets of hopes, and, ultimately, integrate and synthesize them into a balanced and satisfying whole. In Janelle's family, for example, it wasn't entirely problematic that Marcus and Daphne had differing expectations for her as she embarked for college—their differences provided her with two different angles of entry into college life, which ultimately can be a good thing.

The point is that when these forces are misapplied, the young adult's liberation process begins to buckle. Roots and wings are the essential parental nutriments, but if they are consistently not being offered in the right ratios, or they are imposed with too much intensity, a child will begin to make choices that may compromise her growth, and, as a result, mortgage her future. And this mortgage always comes due as she struggles to cross the threshold into young adulthood.

With this perspective in place, let's take a closer look at each of these three types of families, to see what we can learn about their inner workings and how, ultimately, to improve them.

THE CENTRIPETAL FAMILY

In the centripetal, inward-looking family, the young adult is encouraged to believe that leaving home creates more problems than it solves. Age-appropriate movement toward relative autonomy and efforts to find joy and meaning outside the family can unnerve the parents to such an extent that they (often unknowingly) redouble their efforts to tether the young adult as close to them as possible. Both generations operate under the (usually unspoken) assumption that the family should be the ultimate source of gratification, and that seeking it outside of the family is a violation of the family code. In this context, members feel like they are either totally "in" the family or totally "out of" the family—there appears to be no comfortable middle ground.

Parents keep these centripetal forces in place in many different ways. Sometimes they do this by ignoring or invalidating their child's ideas and imposing their own, resulting in a child who never learns to trust in his own perceptions and insights. In these situations, the child is never really seen as a separate person, but instead as a continuation of one or both of the parents. Boundaries between parent and child are blurry, and the child is discouraged from seeking independence in thought or action while the parents are impervious to the reality that their child has desires and beliefs of his own.

Other parents create self-fulfilling prophecies that are built on the premise that the child is not capable of autonomy—he is "sick" or "weak" or "disabled." These prophecies and critical diagnoses block the child from learning to compensate for whatever weaknesses he does have or from summoning his strengths in the service of self-reliance. As a result, the child can become functionally helpless, ruling out any possibility of eventual escape.

There are yet other parents who, by avoiding direct conflicts with their child, use centripetal forces to prevent him from learning how to articulate a separate and distinct position, which is a pivotal step in the direction of autonomy. Disagreements are generally ignored, suppressed, or too quickly defused by beating a retreat into a fraudulent state of consensual agreement and harmony.

Sometimes parents simply induce fear in the child, creating an image of the world as hostile, dangerous, and forbidding, and portraying the family as the only safe and reliable haven in which to hunker down.

Sometimes parents do this by promoting their child's dependence, unknowingly convincing him that he cannot survive without the parents. Through constant coddling, they ensure that their child never develops the skills and self-confidence to make it on his own. He may be spoiled and infantile in outlook, but, insatiably demanding as he becomes, at least he never pulls out of the station and heads down the tracks. He remains loyal to his family.

And sometimes parents maintain centripetal supremacy by overtly or covertly noting how much they have sacrificed for their child, making it clear not only that they live for him, but also that they live *through* him. This guilt-inducing enterprise can turn the child into a lifelong victim of self-sacrifice, with his own success and self-reliance the personal commodities that are likely to be given up.

No matter how centripetal forces establish dominance, however, the potential for the young adult's growth and eventual separation decreases in direct proportion to their strength—in other words, the centripetal forces beat down the impulse to leave the nest. Struggling to find freedom from the unholy alliances that characterize a relentlessly centripetal family is generally limited to the following developmental options:

SELF-SABOTAGE

Reluctant to displease his parents or make them unhappy, he will prune back his initiatives and sacrifice his ambitions, caving in to the family's ceaseless gravitational pull and becoming submissive and compliant. Self-determination will evaporate in the face of his efforts to maintain family fidelity. Some young adults will manage to maneuver themselves forward anyway, but as they do so they will engage in regular self-disruptive or self-destructive behavior in an effort to assuage the guilt of having broken the family mandate.

SUBSTANCE ABUSE

Consumed by the constant conflict between his own desires and those of his parents, he will try to numb the pain resulting from this inner torque, often relying on drugs and alcohol to numb the pain.

THE RETREAT TO ALTERNATE WORLDS

Desperate to find some niche that feels like it's his own, even though he's still compelled to remain physically close to his tangled family, he will retreat into a fantasy world that replaces the real world of living peers and potentially useful adults (mentors, teachers, etc.), often becoming immersed in the cyberworld (such as electronic entertainment and social networking).

THE DRAMATIC ESCAPE

Feeling completely caged in, he will eject himself in a desperate effort to break the centripetal deadlock. Because the ejection tends to be impulsive and explosive, however, it is usually not well thought out, resulting in an eventual return to the original stalemate. This is often seen when suffocated young adults exuberantly dream up half-baked plans for departure, schemes that eventually fall through precisely because they are poorly designed. In extreme cases, he may even arrange for a force stronger than his own family to facilitate his leave-taking, such as by enlisting in the armed services or by breaking the law seriously enough that his living situation winds up in the hands of the justice system rather than in his own or his family's.

Any of these developmental options can also take a toll on the young adult's growth-promoting peer relationships outside the family. For example, if a child grows up indulged and held back from socializing with others outside the nest, he is going to have difficulty finding friends or romantic partners his age who are likely to put up with his childish demands for very long, making a rueful return to the safety of home all the more compelling.

Or, without having been given the opportunity to learn to hold his ground and advocate for himself, he will be much more vulnerable to being manipulated or exploited. The limited skills that he learned in his family's stultifying culture will be useless in his peer culture, and the resultant "culture shock" will become overwhelming, prompting a flight from the inhospitable foreign land of independence back to the familiar province of dependence.

It should also be noted that after many years of unrelenting centripetal force, it often becomes completely unclear to the family who is binding whom. The young adult will complain that his parents won't let him breathe, while the parents complain that he is asphyxiating them. The cycle can become so entrenched and habitual over time that there is no longer any observable beginning or end, no longer any distinct actor or reactor, and the reactive chain that links them to each other begins to seem permanent, unbreakable.

Centripetal families can still effectively empty their nest, but to make progress on this front, they need to break this cycle and begin to examine, acknowledge, and alter the ways in which they have been curbing and detaining their young adults.

THE CENTRIFUGAL FAMILY

In the centrifugal family, the child is neglected in important ways by his parents and shoved toward autonomy, regardless of whether or not he feels ready. Sometimes this neglect is long-standing—meeting his needs was never a priority for his parents. Sometimes, as in the case of Darren, whose parents couldn't wait to move into their lake house, the neglect has commenced relatively recently, often when the parents decide that they want to make a fresh start in life—ending a marriage, starting a new professional direction, or simply living differently. Either way, centrifugal parents get to a point where they care less and less if their child is bound to them, and, in the process, fail to establish the foundation that may be necessary to support him as he pursues autonomy.

They come to envision their young adult as a hindrance, and adopt an attitude of "the sooner, the better" to leave-taking: parenthood feels burdensome and dependent children are expendable nuisances. So the child is forced to leave home feeling "underdone," undervalued, psychologically empty-handed and lacking the sense of being important enough to his parents that they committed to finishing the job of raising him.

Since young adults in centrifugal families are not freighted by the loyalty burdens assumed by children in the centripetal family, they are not always prone to being slowed in the same way. In fact, from the outside, they may appear to be footloose and fancy free, sometimes easily able to move out and move on. However, the apparent ease with which they separate can become a problem, because they know that, having dived (or been pushed) off the deck of the family ship, they must now sink or swim. Either they make it on their own out in the roiling currents of the real world, or they drown: there is no detectable life raft in which they can row back to shore in case they encounter turbulence.

This push toward premature autonomy—the sense that his parents have everything to gain and nothing to lose from his exit—actually prevents him from growing through and resolving the normal family conflicts that need to be sorted out to establish the basis for mature intimacy in young adult life. His early dismissal from the family will then lead him to enact with others—friends, romantic partners, colleagues, employers—the unsatisfied needs that haven't been met, which usually overwhelms and alienates them, leaving him feeling angry, confused, and lonely.

Parents often keep centrifugal forces in place by exaggerating their child's self-sufficiency, proudly (if not smugly) defining him as precocious and independent so as to justify the early ejection. They may also rationalize their neglect as teaching him to be independent, toughening him up, or not wanting to make him dependent. This helps them to ease whatever guilt they might feel about not providing him with the psychological shelter and guidance that he still needs before he'll be able to survive exposure to life's harsh winds.

Centrifugal forces are also maintained or heightened when parents conclude—often under the influence of professionals—that they are ineffective parents and that others with more experience and expertise need to take over, absolving them of responsibility. I often see this when families are told by educational and therapeutic "consultants" to discharge their struggling young adult to a wilderness program or therapeutic boot camp. Eager to do right by their offspring, and without being helped to understand the complexity of their family's plight, they naturally conclude that expelling him so that strangers with dubious training and qualifications can take over is really the best thing for him. Though these parents usually mean well, sometimes the results are disastrous.

No matter how these centrifugal forces are maintained, however, the potential for growth and eventual separation are imperiled. The young adult struggling to survive an untimely displacement will typically travel one or more of the following paths.

THE SELF-FULFILLING PROPHECY

He will behave in some bad way that provokes the very dismissal he fears, thus providing him with a sense of having some control over this process, rather than remaining a passive victim of it.

THE SELF-EXPULSION

He will preemptively expel himself, which also gives him a feeling of control over the ejection process.

THE DRIFTER

Unable to get what he needs at home but unable to make it on his own, he will just bump along, leaving his parents uncertain about whether or not they can "close the book" on parenthood.

THE ENTRENCHER

He will doggedly dig in his heels and either actively or passively resist any efforts to dislodge him until he feels his importance has been recognized and his needs for nurturance and support have been granted. There will be no departure unless he feels that he is departing with a "full tank."

Centrifugal families can still effectively empty their nest, but to do so effectively they need to realize that their young adult, no matter how old he is, still requires some parenting. Rather than getting angry and resentful about this, they must set their minds to more comprehensively complete childrearing—in whatever way their family situation requires—so that their offspring feels self-assured enough to depart.

THE MISSION IMPOSSIBLE FAMILY

The mission impossible family occupies an intermediate position between the centripetal and the centrifugal family, with some similarities and differences. Unlike the centripetal family, the young adult is entitled and encouraged to leave the parental orbit, and unlike the centrifugal family, the young adult is still viewed as someone who is loved and valued, deserving of being cared for as he propels himself forward.

Mission impossible families tend not to centripetally suffocate nor centrifugally exile, which leaves the young adult room to develop a wider and more integrated range of skills and ambitions. He is usually able to move successfully into the interpersonal world outside of his family, unlike the young adult from a centripetal family, and carries with him a reasonable set of expectations for these relationships, unlike the young adult from a centrifugal family. These realities combine to raise the odds of a successful embarkation.

What is uniquely complicated about the mission impossible family is that the young adult is both sent out and held on to at the same time, allowed to leave but still shackled to the family because he is entrusted with a mission that cannot ever be successfully accomplished. Often not seen as truly independent, he must report back to his parents on a regular basis, and the report that he provides needs to be an acceptable one: he is allowed to depart but only with very specific "marching orders."

It is completely natural for parents to ask their offspring to honor and expand the family's legacy and bring joy and pride to the entire family. However, these dreams and wishes are appropriate only up to a developmental point. At a certain juncture, parents have to release their child from being expected to belatedly live out unfulfilled aspects of their own unlived life, or to carry the burden of aspirations that they cannot realize themselves.

So the young adult from a mission impossible family, like his counterparts in centripetal and centrifugal families, suffers great turmoil when he attempts to separate. He is essentially called upon either to resolve the individual conflicts that one or both of his parents experience, or to help reconcile the interpersonal conflicts between the two of them. He may tackle this Sisyphean task, which can be completely incompatible with his strengths and temperament, with boundless ingenuity and determination, but it will be at the expense of his own liberation.

This is often seen when parents find themselves face-to-face with their own limitations and disillusionment, and then turn to their child to do what they have not done, as though seeking a kind of psychological salvation. It puts the child in an impossible position. He must embody all that the parents feel is lacking in themselves, must fulfill foregone pursuits, and become extraordinary in a futile effort to bolster his parent's sagging ego. Particularly when the child, like most mere mortals, is not incandescently talented, brilliant, or virtuosic, it is natural for him to give up trying, knowing that no matter what he does, he can never scale the dizzying heights that his parents have placed before him.

Some of the impossible missions that young adults tend to be burdened with include:

- making unfulfilled parental fantasies into realities, or providing parents with experiences that they missed when they were younger;
- fighting a battle for one parent against another, or, like a lightning rod, diverting one parent's anger away from the other by creating difficulties;
- attempting to bring embattled parents together by either attempting to be absolutely perfect, or, conversely, by becoming a serious problem;
- vigilantly guarding a fearful family secret for one or more family members;
- fulfilling dire parental prophecies for how things will ultimately play out.

It also must be emphasized that it is not always the number or intensity of expectations that are foisted onto young adults, but the extent to which these expectations conflict with each other that shreds them psychologically and impedes their development.

The missions that many conflicted young adults struggle to execute may also be impossible because they involve conflicts of loyalty. We might remember that Shakespeare's Prince Hamlet was bound by filial love to remain faithful to his dead father *and* compelled (almost) to destroy his own mother, which embroiled him in a tragic conflict of loyalties that brought him to the edge of a breakdown.

Some young adults struggle with mixed loyalties to their family and to themselves, while others have competing loyalties to different members within the family—any of these can break them down, like poor Hamlet, and lead to inner turmoil. For example, he may feel most loyal to the parent or family members whom he perceives as the strongest, hoping to absorb and benefit from that strength, or he may feel most loyal to the parent or family members whom he perceives as the weakest, in an effort to support and buttress the downtrodden, the underdog.

While young adults in mission impossible families are often better able to sow the seeds of departure than are young adults from centripetal or centrifugal families, they also have a hard time being true to themselves as they make their way forward, because they may be doing battle for one or both of their parents.

Twenty-three-year-old Donald was asked to leave medical school due to poor grades and unprofessional behavior with patients. I learned from him that his mother had always been contemptuous of his father for having been an inadequate breadwinner, and that his parents' marriage had consequently been a hostile one as far back as Donald could remember.

As he told his story, it occurred to me that Donald had been recruited by his mother to show up his father and ameliorate her disaffection—a successful son might compensate for her disappointment in her under-functioning husband. Therefore Donald was encouraged to study hard and be a success as a way of both surpassing his father and vicariously living out his mother's fantasy of leaving the husband behind.

He did this by decamping from home for a fine college and succeeding at a high enough level there to be admitted to medical school on his first try. But, as he confessed to me, his heart wasn't in it, and he realized early on that he never really had any interest in actually being a physician. Eventually this led to his academic underachievement and his inappropriate interactions in clinics and hospitals.

So, while Donald made strides toward a successful departure, the liftoff eventually ran out of steam because it was not driven by his own initiative and desire: a medical career was simply an assignment that he was completing for someone else. As he became increasingly aware that he was being induced to live out his mother's fantasy and, in the process, to make his own father—his fellow male and role model—look small, the loyalty bind in which he found himself made carrying out that mission truly impossible.

An additional facet of the mission impossible family that is often difficult to detect is that the impossible mission is often delegated covertly, perhaps not verbalized in so many words. Through countless little clues it becomes understood, though perhaps not consciously realized by the child. Parents will consistently and confidently assure me that they have no desire other than "wanting him to be happy" or "wanting her to be successful." Yet, as I slowly peel back the sometimes obscure and murky layers of family history and communication, it often becomes abundantly clear that there is a teeming matrix of confusing and conflicted expectations being conveyed by the parents, sometimes with astonishing tact and subtlety.

In Donald's case, his mother never explicitly told him that she wanted him to transcend his father, but her frequent and subtle put-downs of her husband, and her extravagant, gushing celebration of even the smallest of Donald's accomplishments, certainly got the point across to her son. And the fact that his father treated his mother callously, and never reached out to connect with his son and help deliver him to safety, made things just as impossible for Donald as did his mother's manipulation.

Perhaps the most potentially destructive impossible mission that a child is called upon by her parents to fulfill is the embodiment of the characteristics that the parents themselves are the least comfortable with and most conflicted about. Parents sometimes project their worst qualities onto one of their children, secretly convincing her to act out their own forbidden wishes and impulses, thus enabling them to self-righteously scold and punish her for behaving so badly and, in the process, feel better about themselves.

When parents attempt to quarantine the aspects of themselves that they most fear and are most troubled by, they delegate their child to enact those very aspects. This temporarily relieves them of the discomfort of inhabiting a guilty or hostile inner world, but puts the child in the position of having to live this out for them.

Because it is a subconscious process, parents are often not aware that they are actually goading their child into such activities as defying authority, sexual mischief, substance abuse, or acting with wanton disregard for the rights of others. In fact, they are understandably mystified that they—who may at this point in their lives be paragons of propriety and virtue—have raised a young adult who can behave so reprehensibly. Yet it is precisely because of their inability to come to terms with their own secret desires that they send their young adult on a doomed mission.

For example, Darius never forgave himself for the time during his late teens when he was dealing pot, an enterprise that resulted in the police coming to his house and arresting him, profoundly embarrassing his parents. From that point on he committed himself to becoming a good Christian and leading an unblemished life of ethical rectitude, telling no one—not even his wife—about his adolescent misdeeds. Naturally, he was both horrified and incensed when he learned that his 16-year-old son, Javon, had been apprehended trying to establish himself in the same illicit business. His initial reaction was to heap scorn on his son, as if he himself had never behaved similarly thirty years before.

What Darius didn't understand is that the shame that he still felt about his young adult transgressions, and his ongoing effort to simply erase them, actually set the stage for his son to repeat them. In our sessions, he courageously summoned the willingness to own up to his dishonorable past, which then gave him the opportunity to speak more candidly with Javon, rather than simply sitting in supercilious judgment of him. This brought father and son closer together, and served to steer Javon away from further trouble.

Interestingly, this process does not always have to play out problematically, despite the fact that it often does. For example, many non-

Jewish German students in the post-Holocaust era went to work in Israel, and acknowledged that they were doing so in order to help atone for Nazi crimes against the Jews, crimes to which their parents and grandparents were often working very hard not to admit. In this case, the younger generation was induced to step in and perform the redemptive work necessary to soften the guilt that their progenitors carried but were unwilling to acknowledge and expiate on their own.

Mission impossible families can still effectively empty their nest, but to do so they need to pay closer attention to the individual and marital conflicts that they have been assigning their young adult children to resolve for them. The parents must take the responsibility for resolving these conflicts themselves and stop expecting their children to do it for them.

Although I have roughly divided family dynamics into three categories, I have never met a family that falls neatly into just one. There are probably elements from all three that look familiar to you, and no one single category in which you feel that you fit.

Rather than attempt to artificially identify and pigeonhole your family, it is enough for now to simply note the characteristics of centripetal, centrifugal, and mission impossible systems that look familiar to you so that we can examine what motivates young adults and the ways in which parenting behaviors encourage or obstruct them. It is to these processes that our attention will now turn.

CHAPTER THREE

START YOUR ENGINES

FOSTERING AUTONOMY AND MOTIVATION

"The proverb warns that, 'You should not bite the hand that feeds you.' But maybe you should, if it prevents you from feeding yourself."

—*Thomas Szasz*

A healthy young adult's independence is fueled by four separate developmental forces, all of which can work together and, ideally, reinforce each other.

The first of these is an *intensifying desire for freedom*. President Franklin Delano Roosevelt wrote, "In the truest sense, freedom cannot be bestowed; it must be achieved." All human beings experience a desire to achieve personal freedom. In young adulthood this desire grows and deepens, and, as a result, any constraints on it are noticed more and challenged.

The second force is a *focusing of ambition and direction*. As adolescents become young men and young women, their thoughts about their future sharpen and clarify. Teenage wishes and fantasies that may have had varying degrees of realism congeal into actual, pursuable possibilities, and emerging adults map out with more precision the paths that will lead them to fulfill their personal and professional aspirations.

The third is an *intellectual maturation*. We know that brain growth continues well into our twenties, and that young adults display an evolving capacity to perform more sophisticated cognitive functions as they leave adolescence behind. For example, they are able to establish a more productive working relationship between their thoughts and their feelings; they can increasingly differentiate and reconcile (often conflicting) attitudes, intentions, and beliefs both within themselves and within others; and they display a better overall grasp and acceptance of life's complexity. These intellectual attainments enable them to summon and sustain the momentum necessary to unfasten themselves from their dependence on their parents and advance toward self-determination.

Finally, there is a *transfer of social loyalties*. Beginning in early adolescence, and with accelerating impetus, young adults gradually shift their relational energies away from their family of origin and toward people they choose—friends, significant others, or mentors. They now seek fulfillment and gratification in an expanding network of connections outside the family.

It is not difficult to see how these four forces can collaborate to promote separation and liberation, because once any single one is set into motion, it will inevitably yield the first "taste" of freedom. This taste, for almost everyone, is absolutely delicious and intoxicating, and promotes further movement toward expanded freedom.

For example, a transfer of loyalties away from the family will expose an individual to friends, advisers, role models, and sexual and romantic partners who present life experiences, principles, and ideas different from those she grew up with. As she begins to contemplate and relish these new realities, to step outside the family and look at her world through a wider lens, she will be motivated to harness her intellectual maturation and follow a course of action that leads to further separation and a more diligent pursuit of her now crystallizing goals.

As this happens, she can then view her parents, and her relationship with them, with more detachment and objectivity. No longer staring up at them as if they were omniscient and omnipotent, she can begin to take note of their own conflicts, dependencies, and vulnerabilities. She can start to see the demons that they struggle with and the pain that they feel.

As a result, she can understand more easily the force field of her family, and with this perspective in mind, make the adjustments necessary to gain some purchase on the foothills of Grownup Mountain. Having established a foothold in a world that feels more like her own rather than her family's (a world more of her own choosing), she can then take the risk of slowly turning back to her family from a position of more confident and tested autonomy, and begin relating to them in a more mature and independent manner.

Her parents, observing this growth, begin to feel less fearful and worried about her capacity to manage on her own, and interact with her more as "former parents" than as "active parents." They feel less compulsion to monitor and mandate, and more willingness to loosen their grip on Yesterday and sit back and enjoy her voyage from the realities of Today to the promise of Tomorrow, while turning their own attention to long-deferred interests and endeavors.

As a result, an intergenerational liberation is promoted. In fact, from my perspective, true liberation is one which creates *reciprocal* liberation. Rather than using as a model the all too common political revolutionary who ultimately achieves liberty for the oppressed and then quickly turns into a dictatorial oppressor himself, we want to conceive of liberation within the family as promoting the *mutual* acquisition of freedom.

For the most part, that is how things will play out—usually with a two-steps-up, one-step-back rhythm to it, but a rhythm that will eventually lead to independence. As we noted in the last chapter, however, sometimes when there is an incompatibility between a young adult's strengths and weaknesses and her family's influences, this developmental rhythm becomes interrupted and progress is slowed almost to a halt.

The young adult may feel overwhelmed by uncertainty regarding her ability to manage on her own while still being centrifugally thrust out of the nest before she feels ready. Or she feels guilty about leaving her centripetal family behind despite wanting to heed the call of the world beyond. Or she feels bound by her desire to leave home in a way that keeps everybody happy, and, in trying to fulfill mission impossible, she jettisons completely the prospects for her own happiness.

So how do we motivate young adults to capitalize on their inborn desire to separate and liberate, and counteract the forces that work against it? To answer this, we must first examine the very basis for motivation.

❧　❧

One of our main jobs as parents is to facilitate motivation so that our young adult children can achieve self-sufficiency through understanding both what they need, and how to go about getting it. Motivation is the psychological "stimulus package" that all of us require in order to succeed.

No matter what topic I am lecturing on to parents—whether it's academic achievement or preventing drug and alcohol abuse, building self-esteem or forging better peer relationships—I am generally asked the question, "How do I motivate my child?"

But the (sometimes distressing) reality is that you can't motivate *anyone* to do *anything*. The key to the motivational engine always lies *inside* an individual, not on the outside. Motivation is not something that you can do *to* someone else, but something that someone does *for oneself*. But what I often help parents realize is that while they cannot motivate their sons and daughters, they can certainly create a context in which their children are more likely to motivate themselves. And that, in the long run, is the only true motivation: an energy that derives from within rather than being dictated externally.

In fact, what I usually discover is that parents' well-intended efforts to motivate or activate their children have, over the years, actually had an *undermining* effect, making it less likely that, as young adults, they will be capable of motivating themselves. In other words, these efforts have not just been unproductive but truly counterproductive.

The parenting techniques that we come to rely on are the result of a complex interaction of several factors, which include the following:

- how we were raised by our own parents;
- our temperament and personality style;
- our child's temperament and personality style;
- our spouse's or fellow parent's approach to parenting;
- the overall context of our family life (sources of stress and support, such as physical health, extended family availability, financial status, and school and community resources).

In my work with parents, I attempt to integrate all of these factors and distinguish between Parental *Guidance* and Parental *Control*.

Parental Guidance is the effort parents make to:

- set rules and limits for their child's behavior;
- establish consequences, both positive and negative, to enforce these rules and limits;
- support her in learning about herself; and
- gradually "put down the reins" so that the child begins to pick them up and steer her life in her own direction, under her own power.

Parental Control is the effort—sometimes obvious and sometimes subtle—that parents make to govern and bridle children's behavior in such a way that their development as an individual apart from their parents is inhibited or interfered with in some way.

Parental Guidance reflects our understandable and necessary desire to regulate and socialize our child's behavior through affection, approval, and attentiveness, and through supervision, instruction and discipline, resulting in an *enhancement* of their sense of personal efficacy, autonomy, and authenticity. It is a more loving and trusting approach. Parental Control reflects our (sometimes subconscious) desire to bind and constrain our children, resulting in an *undermining* of their sense of personal efficacy, autonomy, and authenticity. This parental approach tends to be characterized more by fear than trust.

While appropriate Parental Guidance is absolutely essential when it comes to promoting healthy psychological growth, Parental Control is harmful at every stage of life because it interferes with the developing child's burgeoning need for self-determination. Parents who rely more on Control than on Guidance intrude on the child's self-awareness and self-expression in all of its possible forms, maintaining their own status at her expense, and create an environment in which love and acceptance are contingent on her sacrificing her identity and being the person that *others* want her to be rather than the person that *she* wants to be. Once children feel that they cannot be true to their inner selves, motivation will always be deflected and self-reliance will always be detained—they will live the life of a puppet or a slave.

While no parent resides entirely on one side of this spectrum or the other, most of us like to envision ourselves as more guiding than controlling. Often, though, families reveal to me that there's been a good deal more controlling than guiding going on, and a reorganization of the family system is what's necessary to promote growth.

The patently obvious form of Parental Control is maltreatment—abuse, abandonment, and neglect are the most extreme, and the most extremely *damaging*, ways of preventing a child's growth. Overall, few parents regularly resort to such strategies. However, just because there's an absence of maltreatment does not mean that there is an absence of Parental Control—it's just that the controlling efforts are not only more nuanced, but seem sensible and justifiable, even as they are directed at a wide range of their child's thoughts, feelings, and actions. Here are some typical examples of what I refer to as "hurtful helping":

- *withdrawal of love and affection:* spurning, rejecting, or ignoring her when she does not do or see things your way;
- *attacking:* yelling, threatening, shaming, imposing corporal punishment;

- *overemphasizing competition:* pressuring her to "win at all costs" rather than "do your best" or "try to excel";
- *inducing guilt:* manipulating and coercing her to be different by exploiting her loyalty *to* you and reliance *on* you;
- *overprotecting:* keeping her from making her own decisions and dealing with the consequences of learning how to handle winning or losing on her own;
- *blaming and scapegoating:* convincing her that she's always at fault while you are always in the right;
- *overevaluating:* constantly praising or criticizing her performance and conduct;
- *inducing anxiety and fear:* inhibiting initiative and ambition through creating a disquieting or alarming depiction of the world outside of the family;
- *inappropriate reinforcing:* providing an overabundance of *external* rewards, such as verbal and nonverbal incentives, reinforcements, and enticements, for behaviors that should be personally and *internally* rewarding for the child.

While all of us have surely engaged in some of these Parental Controls at times, it is when they are regularly used that a child's growth is hindered and developmental inertia is soldered into place. Of course, simply because parents are not exclusively applying control does not automatically mean that that they are creating the context out of which the young adult's motivation will arise; in addition to *limiting* Parental Control behaviors we have to *augment* Parental Guidance. But I have found that the balance between Parental Guidance and Control that is established over the years is generally a robust predictor of a young adult's level of motivation and her related capacity to maneuver her way toward self-sufficiency.

The heart of motivation, which is the engine that drives us toward self-sufficiency, can be found in our sense of our autonomy. When we feel autonomous, more or less able to stand on our own two feet and think and do for ourselves, we do things with creativity, enthusiasm, and dedication because we *believe* in what we are doing. Further, we believe in what we are doing because it feels like a natural expression of who we truly are, rather than of who others want us to be. It is only when we feel autonomous that we ultimately are motivated to succeed, and to *feel* like a success when we do succeed. Without autonomy, we are either doomed to fail, doomed to *feel* like a failure, or doomed to feel like we are someone *else's* success (which is simply failure of another kind).

People who feel autonomous not only have a better relationship with themselves, but they also have a better relationship with others: they tend to be more engaging and open, less insecure, irritable, and standoffish. Autonomy allows us to be more *responsive* to our most essential drives and ambitions, which guarantees that we will be more *responsible*, both to ourselves and to everyone else who is important to us.

Autonomy is not rooted in ignoring the expectations of others, disregarding beliefs, or living above or outside the law without adherence to relational or societal rules. What is different when we feel autonomous is that it does not feel like we have "ingested" these rules without making them our own, and, as a result, that we have to either submit to them or rebel against them. Instead, when we feel autonomous it is as if we have "digested" rules, processed them, metabolized and internalized them so that they become a part of us, so that there is a workable harmony between our interior rules and expectations and the rules and expectations of others.

In other words, autonomy is revealed when we behave in the way that we do because we choose to and want to rather than because we have to and feel compelled to. And when we do what we do out of choice, out of genuine willingness and desire, we will always be more invested in what we do, and more motivated to achieve competence, mastery, and perhaps even virtuosity. People who feel autonomous will naturally and spontaneously establish their own goals, develop their own standards, monitor their own progress, achieve their own objectives, put up with tasks and duties that are boring or unpleasant in the service of some larger objective, and regard themselves in an overall positive light.

As noted above, we undermine a child's developing sense of autonomy whenever we emphasize Parental Control over Guidance. And when we feel controlled by others, there are really only two options, *compliance* or *defiance*.

- *Compliance* can be understood as doing something because you are *told* to, not because you believe that it is *best* for you.
- *Defiance* can be understood as doing the *opposite* of what you are told to, not because you think it is best, but simply because it's your automatic reaction to being controlled, "bossed around."

The two are flip sides of the same coin, and individuals who feel more externally controlled than internally motivated may, in fact, flip back and forth between compliance and defiance, or display elements of both at the same time. Your son may have been highly obedient through elementary, middle, and high school, for example—well-behaved, studious, and polite—and then erupt into a surprising phase of mischief and misconduct when he leaves for college, drinking heavily with his fraternity brothers and sleeping through half of his classes. Your daughter might appear dutiful and demure when ensconced in her church youth group on Friday night, and then behave seductively, bordering on promiscuously, at parties on Saturday night.

Just as commonly, compliance and defiance may cancel each other out, resulting in a "foot on the gas, foot on the brake" scenario in which there is much noise, but no actual progress. This accounts for the half-hearted, uneven path that many young adults find themselves on, in which there is an absence of any net growth because they are complying and defying at the same time, neutralizing the possibility of progress. I see this when young adults obediently follow the career path laid out by their parents, but ensure that they don't actually succeed at it because it doesn't really feel like their own. For example, a young woman plods through law school but never passes the bar exam, or a young man becomes an accountant but, because of his perfunctory, listless work habits, he is the first to get laid off when the firm needs to make staffing cuts.

What we also need to keep in mind is that when young adults feel more controlled than autonomous, they will tend to behave in ways that actually elicit and engender those very controls that they complain about.

In the case of extreme *compliance,* a young adult will be unable to muster even the most basic drive toward self-sufficiency, and will become aimless and lethargic as the last threads of initiative and ambition gradually dissolve completely. His directionless anomie and passivity will prompt his parents, and possibly others, to become more and more involved with trying to rock him out of his rut. Meanwhile, he steadfastly rejects or cleverly repels their efforts, leaving him feeling more controlled and less motivated even while he protests everyone's well-intentioned interventions on his behalf.

In a case of extreme *defiance,* a young adult may not only flagrantly break school or family rules, but also societal rules, perhaps even leading to run-ins with the justice system and the subsequent imposition of *legal* controls—supervision, probation, enforced treatment, court-ordered rehabilitation, or even incarceration. He will howl that he is being deprived of his freedom without fully understanding that he never felt free to start with, that it was his *lack* of freedom and resultant lack of responsibility—in other words, the absence of autonomy—that led to his insistent (though unspoken) request for more rigid restrictions.

It is the dearth of autonomy that leads to the motivational impasse—an impasse that has its roots in excessive compliance, defiance, or a mixture of both—and when that blockage is in place it becomes impossible for young adults to spread their wings and leave the safety of home behind.

So if we know that motivation is the key to self-reliance, and that autonomy is the basis for motivation, how do we promote autonomy in our young adults? The best way is assess your ratio of Parental Guidance to Parental Control, and to adjust this ratio to the balance that's right for your family. Let's take a look at how this can be done.

Every family is characterized by competing tendencies toward continuity and adaptation, between family connectedness and individual separateness. The former is crucial to each family member in developing a sense of tradition, relatedness, and stability, while the latter is crucial to each family member in developing a sense of creativity, initiative, and self-reliance. The energy for a healthy departure results from this ongoing tension (or competition) between the two.

For independence to develop, a family needs to renegotiate its equilibrium. In response to the pressures exerted by young teens and their desire for freedom during early adolescence (these pressures intensify through middle and late adolescence into early adulthood), the family's status quo is disrupted, gently or rudely, and all are challenged to evolve.

Some families respond to these pressures by constructively reacclimating: by modifying their expectations of each other and transforming the rules under which they all operate, they allow and invite new and more suitable attitudes and behaviors on every member's part to take root and blossom. Under most circumstances, families are very resilient organisms with a tremendous capacity for self-correction and realignment.

Sometimes, however, the forces that have kept the family in its steady state for the last several years, or for the last couple of decades, remain so firmly in place that the family system becomes stiff and calcified. Unable to shift gears easily from "the way we've always done things" despite circumstances that dictate revision (such as children maturing), parents remain attached to their outdated approaches to childrearing, even in the face of irrefutable evidence that these are no longer doing the trick.

Instead of taking the risk of negotiating a new balance, one or both generations desperately try to re-create and reinforce their familiar ways, often with more insistence than before. This leaves the family confined to its old patterns of interaction, no matter how unproductive and irrelevant these patterns have become. As a result, progress is nipped in the bud and family members stagnate. Or, if there is growth, it is toward rebellion on the part of the frustrated young adults.

For example, a father and his five-day-old son who are inseparable could be described as appropriately—even lovingly—connected with each other. A father and a five-*year*-old son who are inseparable are *inappropriately* connected with each other. A father and a *fifteen*-year-old son who are inseparable would be considered to be *problematically* connected with each other. And a father and a *twenty-five*-year-old son who are inseparable would be considered to be *pathologically* connected with each other. A connection that is functional and growth-promoting at one stage of development can quite clearly be described as *dys*functional and growth-*inhibiting* at subsequent stages.

When families inflexibly resist growth, a young adult's development is squelched and we see evidence of the Regrouping, Meandering, Floundering, and Recovering behavior that I described in the Introduction. Things will worsen when the parents—as almost all mothers and fathers will do—begin to focus on their young adult's obstinacy, rather than on their own or the obstinate stasis that the family unit has come to restlessly reside in.

At this point, a family is essentially sinking in psychological quicksand—the more everyone thrashes about trying to address the young adult's disinclination to leave the nest, the more that unwillingness sucks everyone down, prompting further efforts to eliminate the problem (assumed to be only in the young adult), which further sidesteps the need to make necessary changes, leading to further disinclination.

This process explains why our tendency to rapidly label children with a variety of dire disorders and clinical verdicts is misguided. Their problems rarely reside within *them*, but are the outcome of an imbalanced *family system*, so only through changing that system will these problems get resolved. When it comes to young adults, instead of spending so much time and energy applying the fashionable diagnosis du jour, we should resist this easy temptation and take on the more complicated task of diagnosing and reconfiguring the obstructing family (or social) circumstances that checkmate their growth.

Two axes along which we typically see a handicapping imbalance are in the areas of Power and Responsibility. Let's take a look at each of them to see how we can learn to rebalance the family and create the conditions in which the young adult's motivation can blossom.

POWER IMBALANCES

During the launching phase, parents must learn to share power with their young adult, who is perhaps still somewhat dependent. There is no tidy algorithm that tells us exactly how to continue to display family leadership yet to do so in ways that unmistakably recognize and promote his development, for example by trusting him or her to have good common sense. More art than science, it is truly impossible to avoid erring in one direction or another—in other words, either giving up too *much*, or too *little*, power.

Some parents make the mistake of ceding too much authority too soon, while others never establish sufficient authority in the first place, before their children even make it to adolescence or young adulthood. It is as if the family was inverted, built heels over head, with the younger generation calling the shots.

During the postadolescent years, young adults in these families may continue to behave in ways to which parents have become unhappily accustomed—demanding, provoking, and demeaning. The parents appear helpless and defensive in the face of such confrontations, eager to do anything that will appease their offspring's demands in an effort to calm them down, even momentarily. Of course, the only thing that would truly calm them down is a restoration of appropriate order. But power, being as addictive as it is, can be very difficult to pry away from someone who's used to possessing it.

Parents of young adults may have had many reasons for disavowing their parental duties and abdicating power, but usually it has had something to do with their long-standing fear of what does or will happen if they pull rank and lay down the law. ("My child won't like me anymore.") Frightful imaginary scenarios sometimes prevent parents from taking decisive action, and thus render them as disenfranchised leaders, figureheads without any meaningful influence.

Doyle, for example, a 17-year-old living at home with his parents, had gotten his learner's permit and was working toward completing the 60 hours of supervised instruction required to take the driving test. However, even with one of his parents sitting next to him in the front seat, he drove recklessly, ignoring such basic rules as complete stops at stop signs, and often accelerated well past the speed limit on residential roads. His mother became nervous and upset after several harrowing trips and refused to supervise his driving any longer.

Doyle pleaded with his father to continue driving with him, desperate to accumulate the necessary hours required for his license, and his father relented. However, the son continued driving unsafely, refusing to obey speed limits and encountering several near accidents as a result of his carelessness. He also took the car out late one night without his parents' permission and smashed one of the taillights during his surreptitious excursion.

After all this, one might expect that Doyle's father would simply have followed his wife's lead and shut down Doyle's driving privileges entirely until he agreed to drive safely, rather than condoning such hazardous behavior. After all, driving is a privilege, not a right, and in this particular instance Doyle needed his parents more than they needed him. He had shown ample and repeated evidence that he was not yet mature enough to handle a car responsibly.

But, as I came to find out, Doyle had basically intimidated his parents for many years into surrendering to his incessant demands, and this situation was no different. His enraged tantrums in the face of attempts to set limits had become so insufferable since early adolescence that one or both parents would eventually submit to his outrageous demands just to shut him up and get him off their backs. The parents' capitulations reinforced the cycle and encouraged Doyle to become more and more outrageous, and less responsive not only to the family's rules, but to society's as well. So his father continued to drive with Doyle, and, ultimately, another impulsive driver was allowed on the road.

When I work with defiant young adults like Doyle, the key is helping the parents to reclaim their authority. That can be daunting after many years without parental authority having been exerted, as there is a "runaway train" quality to the young adult's brazen belligerence. But restoring order is absolutely essential because unless the young adult learns to blend his commitment to serving his own needs with some deference to the needs of others, he will be unlikely to make it in a world that will be far less lenient and tolerant than his own parents have been.

Other families display the opposite power imbalance: the parents have had no difficulty wielding power, but can't figure out how to distribute it in a form that respects their young adult's competence and desire for independence. In these cases, differences of opinion between parent and young adult are viewed as epic battles to be won or lost, and the concepts of concession, negotiation, or even just "going with the flow" are seen as abject defeats, losses of respect, or renunciations of parental authority.

Hinda, 18, a senior in high school, was doing little of the work necessary to select a college and complete her applications. The harder her parents pushed her to write her essays and submit the necessary forms, the less she seemed to produce. Now that it was November, with many applications already due or about to be, the family was in a tense crisis.

During our initial family meeting, Hinda's mother, Phyllis, brusquely laid out what she felt to be the best college options. While all five of these schools seemed to me to be reasonably good matches, there appeared to have been little consideration of the preferences of Hinda herself.

Hinda said she had visited all five schools with her mother, but none of them had stood out as a favorite. When I inquired, she admitted that there were, in fact, two other colleges that did interest her, based on what her friends and a couple of favorite teachers had told her, but both possibilities had been quickly ruled out by her mother and no visits had been arranged just to check them out. Phyllis, a successful and high-ranking government official, appeared to be running the college search process as tightly and formidably as she ran her streamlined federal agency.

Not surprisingly, the daughter displayed little interest in this clamped-down approach. Not being given any clout when it came to determining her future, she responded by folding her cards, running the risk of foreclosing her educational future entirely.

When I work with determinedly passive individuals like Hinda, my job is to help the parents to release their grasp in order to allow room for the development of their young adult's autonomy, which will invariably motivate her to start her engine and get herself in gear. The apathy and indifference that they display are hallmarks of having been ruled with too much Parental Control and gasping for the invigorating air of autonomy.

RESPONSIBILITY IMBALANCES

As is the case with imbalances in power, parents can find themselves bestowing too much or too little responsibility on their young adults. Sometimes families burden young adults with responsibilities that far exceed their capacity, resulting in feelings of stress, futility, sadness, and anxiety. In other families, young adults are granted a reprieve from responsibility to such a large extent that they feel no obligation to perform duties that benefit anyone other than themselves, and thus they don't build the self-respect that comes with taking appropriate responsibility.

Twenty-four-year-old Sascha had returned home to live with her father for her final semester of college in an attempt to save money and eventually get her own apartment with a girlfriend. More than two years after graduating, however, she was still at home with him, and, more problematically, she was not moving ahead with her life in any kind of meaningful way. She had majored in criminology and had a long-standing interest in becoming a police officer or an FBI or Secret Service agent, yet she was working twenty hours a week at the same

local crafts store where she had gotten her first job during her sophomore year of high school. She occasionally went out with fellow employees, but had not been seriously involved with anyone since her
freshman year of college.

I learned that her mother had died of breast cancer when Sascha
was a senior in high school and that her father, Ilya, had not remarried since then, and did not date. Ilya struck me as a very bright but
lonely and depressed man who had not recovered from the loss of his
wife. Sascha appeared to be the sole light in his life, and he took great
delight in relating her many attributes and talents (almost none of
which she was capitalizing on) and describing how the two of them
still enjoyed playing cards and watching reality TV shows together in
the evening.

Sascha, however, was not quite so content with this arrangement as
her father was.

"Does your father have much of a social life?" I asked at one point.

"I wish he would, I can tell you that," she replied, wearily. "Sometimes I think that *I'm* his social life."

"What's it like being his social life?"

"What do you *think* it's like? I mean, I love my father, and I know
he's terribly lonely, but I wish he didn't depend on me so much."

"What motivates you to continue to promote his dependence on
you?"

"What am I supposed to do? Not come home? Stay out all night
just to avoid him? That doesn't seem right."

"Nor does sacrificing your own life in the hopes that it takes the
edge off of his loneliness."

She frowned. "Look, if someone offers me a great job, believe me,
I'll take it. If I great guy throws himself at my feet, believe me, I'll go
out with him. But there's nothing out there on either front right now.
What else do you want me to do?"

"There might not be anything out there on either front because
you're committed to being such a dutiful daughter. You may be isolat-
ing yourself enough to ensure that a great job offer is not going to come

about and a great guy is never going to be able to find you. You're not making it very easy to be sought out."

"But he's my father, I can't just abandon him. My mom has already done that..."

Sascha had been recruited to take on so much *inappropriate* responsibility—the responsibility of keeping her father from descending into loneliness and despair—that she didn't feel able to take on the more *appropriate* responsibilities of expanding her social life and pursuing a profession so that she could eventually become more productive and self-reliant. Without anyone encouraging her to understand that it really wasn't her job to stay home and be her father's companion, and with her father understandably eager for her to carry on this role nonetheless, she simply didn't have the requisite motivation to propel her own life forward.

In Sascha's case, her apparent *lack* of responsibility was the result of her being covertly asked to shoulder too *much* responsibility. In other families, a young adult's insufficient level of responsibility is the result of too little being expected of him. In the latter situation, parents are so hyper-responsible that there is no need for children to learn to take on any real responsibility. There are many reasons why we may fall into this pattern. Sometimes it's a reaction to how much responsibility we had when *we* were growing up. One father told me that he was so busy watching over his four younger siblings when he was a child that there was no time left over for him to go out with friends or participate in sports. As a result, as a way of belatedly compensating for his tough early years, he vowed that he would never ask his children to have to do anywhere *near* this amount of caregiving.

Sometimes our decision to rescue our children from responsibility is rooted in our guilt. For instance, because we went through a divorce, because we worked too hard, because we were impatient or volatile or self-absorbed, we try to compensate by easing, and sometimes taking on, their burdens. Similarly, our expecting too little of them may be an expression of our feeling sorry for them: because they're dyslexic, or overweight, or have diabetes, we try to help them out by not *asking* them to help out.

And in many families, a child is deprived of responsibility in a (usually subconscious) effort on the parents' part to maintain their importance to the child. In other words, as long as the young adult is not self-reliant, the parents are still indispensable to them, which may help to stave off the feelings of irrelevance and mortality that begin to grow as the child gravitates toward young adulthood (a topic we will explore in more detail in Chapter Eight).

Along these lines, one high school senior complained to me that whenever she started to make dinner for herself in the kitchen, her father would appear out of nowhere and take over. His insistence on being perpetually necessary to her might have been masking his anxiety that, sometime soon, he would be less necessary to her, and, as a result, he would have to find some other source of meaning in his life.

For any one or more of these reasons, parents of young adults find it difficult to establish a new status quo, and their high level of responsibility virtually guarantees the young adult's low level of responsibility. This is when we find parents contacting the dean of housing at their son's college to help him to get a single room because he can't get along well with his roommate, or emailing the human resources director at their daughter's first job on her behalf to see if her health insurance coverage will be adequate.

In examining imbalances in power and responsibility in the families I treat, I have often noticed that the parents vary between giving too much or too little power or responsibility, and, in their unpredictable oscillations, they confuse and infuriate their young adult children. Having difficulty locating a reasonable middle ground, they toggle back and forth between extremes, displaying unyielding toughness or crystalline clarity one moment and squishy leniency or erratic waffling the next.

Young adults generally react with bewilderment to this kind of instability because they don't know which parent is going to "show up," or which one to respond to—the brutish enforcer or the benevolent pamperer—and the twisting back and forth makes it difficult for them to acquire and get comfortable with a right-sized sum of power or responsibility.

Sometimes this discrepancy resides between the two parents—one playing "Good Cop" while the other plays "Bad Cop"—and sometimes both parents are, in a strangely symmetrical way, lurching unpredictably between sharing too much or too little power or responsibility. It is not a surprise, then, that young adults rarely display meaningful forward motion for very long in these families, for the parents are so busy changing back and forth that there isn't much of a chance for the young adult to forge ahead and sustain regular progress.

Nineteen-year-old Asher was proceeding at a glacial pace through community college, taking a couple of courses per semester, sometimes withdrawing from one or both before the semester was over. His parents believed that this casual approach to his education left him with plenty of time to get a part-time job as well, either in his field of interest, computers, or anywhere he would be paid.

I learned during our first session that not only was Asher not being asked to help pay for his education, for room and board at home, or his health and car insurance, but that he was given a credit card for essentially unlimited and unexamined spending on clothing, gas, and random food purchases, a monthly bill that was covered by his parents without any questions asked. Even more surprisingly, he was also provided with a cash allowance of $25 a week for entertainment and miscellaneous expenses (movies, concert tickets, etc.), apparently a holdover from when he was in high school, before he had a credit card.

I half-jokingly told his parents that I was tempted to move in to their home and sign up for such an appealing arrangement myself, so little was being asked of Asher in return for his being offered so much. Surely there was not much motivation for Asher to find a job when he had so little fiscal responsibility and all his needs were so munificently handled for him. With this in mind, I advised them to take a step in the direction of promoting his self-reliance by cutting off his allowance, and asking that he pay for all other incidental expenses except gas, and health and car insurance, suggesting that this might bump up his incentive to secure a job.

His parents agreed to this arrangement without hesitation. At their next session, however, I learned that Asher was still not employed, and that he had hit up his father for some cash so that he could go to a movie with friends a few nights before, and his father had agreed, without consulting with his wife. She was understandably annoyed, and so we clarified the terms of the agreement.

Upon their return two weeks later, Asher again had not found a job, but this time his father angrily reported that Asher had used the credit card to purchase a pair of athletic shoes without asking either of them for permission, a purchase that the mother had heard about and agreed to cover.

"I thought we decided that he has to handle these kinds of expenses by himself," the father reminded her.

"I know we did, but he needed shoes. Have you seen his shoes? They've got holes in them. He can't wear them."

"Yes, I've seen his shoes, but we've got to teach him to be more responsible. We agreed that he would handle all of his own clothing purchases."

"Do you want to amend the contract and provide him with a clothing allowance?" I asked.

They batted it around for a while and eventually concluded that, for now, Asher would be expected to manage clothing purchases on his own.

When they returned two weeks later, Asher remained out of work, and had once again slithered through a loophole in his parents' supposedly ironclad agreement. He had blown out a tire in the community college parking lot, and asked his father to help him pay for a replacement. Once more, Asher was able to get what he wanted without having to pay for it. "How am I supposed to find a job or get back and forth to school without being able to drive my car?" he had pleaded to his father, who told me that he just didn't want either he or his wife to have to transport Asher back and forth each day, so he had agreed to buy a replacement.

"Are you crazy?" Sarah shrieked at him in my office. "We're paying Dr. Sachs for his advice and we don't even follow it!"

Back and forth these two parents went, alternately rescuing Asher from becoming more responsible while complaining about the lack of self-reliance that they were diligently authorizing.

                                                          ⸎ ⸎

We have been exploring the ways in which you can help to foster and induce your young adult's motivation by emphasizing Parental Guidance over Parental Control, and shifting the family's balance of power and responsibility in growth-promoting ways. It's never a simple matter of "getting tough" or "giving in," but of finding a middle ground that allows for authority without rigidity, leadership without tyranny, and involvement without intrusiveness. When parents comfortably find such a middle ground during the launching phase, the odds are greatly heightened that your young adult will discover his own motivation, meaning that a healthy leave-taking is on the horizon. At this point, there are additional strategies that you can put into action to support and promote it, and it is these strategies that we will now investigate.

CHAPTER FOUR

THE RITES AND WRONGS OF PASSAGE

DEVELOPMENTAL TASKS FOR PARENTS

As we have seen in the previous chapters, young adults are often in a developmentally amphibious state, belonging neither entirely in or out of their family of origin. This obviously makes it hard on parents, who have to stay constantly vigilant and flexible when it comes to knowing how or whether to respond when concerns present themselves or worries arise.

There is a word from the Hebrew Bible, *ezer,* which has two seemingly unrelated meanings: "to rescue" and "to be strong." But embedded in this word is the understanding that effectively helping someone requires that you be strong, as well as the understanding that help, at its best, should increase the strength of the person you are helping.

In this chapter I will recommend some basic strategies for managing matters effectively while the nest is being emptied so that you have the strength to appropriately support your young adult, and so that your support promotes his strength as he is launched toward success and self-reliance.

PATIENCE AND EMPATHY

One of my favorite Far Side cartoons depicts two women peering out the window at a monstrous entity perched on their doorstep. One says to the other, "Calm down, Edna. Yes, it is a giant, hideous insect, but it may be a giant hideous insect in need of help."

Many times parents respond to the ongoing presence, or the prospective return home, of their young adult as if he is a giant hideous insect, a monster destined to at least disrupt, if not destroy, their lives. The reality is that as "hideous" as the young adult may appear, he may still be in need of help, and your job at these times is to determine the kind of assistance that will be the foundation for his forays toward independence.

You may be unsure about the new dynamic with your young adult child who is still living with you or who has returned for a period of time. You might ask yourself such questions as, Does he want me involved or not? Should I offer aid or stay out of it? Do I enfold him in a welcoming, protective embrace, or do I steel myself and send him back out into the cruel, pitiless world? Frequently, there will be no right answer to these questions, just a lave-like series of wrong or vague responses that seem to scald both generations as each has expectations of the other that are impossible to meet.

It is also challenging both for the young adult, as well as her parents, to understand what she is in the midst of. (Remember the five categories from the Introduction: Progressing, Regrouping, Meandering, Recovering, and Floundering.) Is she regressing, or stepping backward in preparation for moving forward? Is she simply "zoned out," or preparing to move into a new zone? Is she stable, in stasis, or just stagnating? Growth during young adulthood may often appear less like a freight train's straightforward progress and more like a sailboat's tacking back and forth in an effort to catch the right wind at the right time. As parents, we aren't always privileged to witness solid, steady progress. You might at times need to apply firm but gentle pressure to enable your child to figure out her next step to keep some "tension on the line." At the same time, the more patience and empathy you can call forth, the better. (Remember what we discussed in Chapter Three: Parental Guidance is generally more helpful than Parental Control.)

Kirk's 19-year-old son, Evan, was a part-time community college student and had been working as a server at a restaurant, but never more than a few nights a week. Kirk had been insisting that Evan try to get more hours, and Evan had insisted that business was slow and extra shifts just weren't available. One day, Evan showed up for work and found the doors locked and the windows whitewashed: the restaurant had shut down the night before, unable to make their rent.

Evan knew that he needed to get a new job, and in discussing this with his father during a session, said that he'd start submitting some new applications but wanted to "take a break" before getting back to work.

Kirk, not surprisingly, hit the ceiling: "A break?! You want to take a break?! You've only been working two nights a week. What do you need to take a break *from?* I work sixty hours a week. I'd *love* a break, but if I took one, we wouldn't have any food."

Evan tried to convince his father that this was only a temporary pause and that he was still committed to finishing up his school and working. But Kirk thought he had been patient enough already.

"As far as I'm concerned, you've been bumming around for the last six months! Ten hours of work a week and a couple of community college classes? And you expect to get ahead with that kind of schedule? You probably don't even have a hundred dollars in the bank, you're still living at home, and I'm still paying your car insurance. You won't have your college degree for another twenty years at this point . . . and you're convinced you need a vacation?!"

"Alright, fine, Dad, forget it. I'll go out right now and start trying to find a job. Look at me, here I go . . ." and Evan stormed out of my office, slamming the door behind him.

"Now what do I do?" Kirk pleaded.

"The first thing you need to do is to remember that Evan's probably struggling with this issue more than he's acknowledging. Young adults are ingenious at getting their parents to be more upset about things than they are, because it's always easier if someone else carries the emotional load for them."

"But that's the problem," said Kirk. "He doesn't seem to be upset at all. *You* heard him! Instead of figuring out what he's going to do next, he's going to put his feet up for a few weeks. And, by the way, he should have seen this coming. I know the economy is tight right now, but if you've got your ear to the ground, you probably know when your workplace is going belly-up. He probably wasn't even paying attention, just assumed that everything was going to be fine."

I said, "It's possible that he's as relaxed and devil-may-care as he appears. It's also possible that he's terrified. You are probably correct that, if he had been paying closer attention, he might have seen that the restaurant was about to fold. On the other hand, that might be exactly what he's upset by: here he thought he had a decent job, and then the rug got pulled out from under him. So, rather than being angry with himself for not seeing this coming and not creating some alternatives, he sets it up so that you're the one who's angry, and then he can be angry with you, rather than with himself."

"Great," muttered Kirk. "So I'm angry with him instead of his being angry with himself. That's another responsibility of his that I've now got to shoulder. When will he grow up already?"

"He'll be more likely to grow up when you resist stepping in to shoulder that anger for him, and allow him to simmer in it himself."

"How do I do that?"

"By sitting back and waiting to see what happens. By letting him solve this problem. And also, going back to what you said a moment ago, by not subsidizing him so unquestionably."

"What do you mean?"

"Well, for starters, I don't think you have to pay for his car insurance. If that was placed back on his shoulders, he might take making a living a little more seriously."

"Oh, sure, but if I don't pay that, and he doesn't have the money for it, then he can't drive a car and then he won't be able to get to school or keep a job, and then I'll get blamed for that."

"You don't have to pull it cold turkey, though. You can tell him that you'd like him to begin contributing a certain amount, and that unless he's good for it, he'll eventually lose his insurance and be unable to drive."

"But isn't that just doing the same thing you described a moment ago—my being angry at him instead of his being angry at himself?"

"I don't think setting limits and promoting responsible behavior is the same thing as being angry or punitive. You can set limits without being angry about it. In fact, that's the best way to set those limits. Parents tend to get the most angry when they're *not* setting limits, because it's at those times that they tend to feel taken advantage of by their children. And I believe that's what's happening here."

Kirk decided to take this approach, and it initially got Evan's dander up, but eventually he took some steps forward.

"He was all pissed at first," Kirk reported later, "asking me why I waited until he was unemployed to start asking for car insurance payments. But I told him first of all that I was sorry that I had gotten so angry with him for wanting to take a break from work. Then I told him that I had faith in him and that I thought it was time that he started to feel more self-sufficient. I said that maybe I wasn't doing my job as a father if I was preventing him from being more responsible."

"What did he say?"

"Well, of course he asked how much money I wanted from him and when he needed to start paying. But then he started to talk about the restaurant, and how he had the sense that something was going on, but he looked the other way. He told me it's always been like that, this feeling that he's not really in the flow, that he's missing out on something important.

"So we had a really good conversation about this. One thing about Evan that I haven't told you is that his mom had a very serious bout with cancer when he was very little, around three years old. For the next few years after the diagnosis, we really couldn't focus on him at all because we were so busy with medical matters. And even though she eventually recovered, there's always been this sort of spaced-out quality to Evan, and I wonder sometimes if it's a result of those 'missing years' when his mom was so sick and we just basically ignored him."

I commented, "I think you're pointing to something very important, Kirk. He may have learned during that time to 'tune out,' which was, in a way, what you and his mom *wanted* him to do, and what he *needed* to do, to avoid becoming overwhelmed by fear and dread. So he may not ever have learned to 'tune back in,' and now he needs to learn this if he's going to succeed. That may be exactly why he didn't pick up on the vibe at the restaurant: he had the sense that something distressing was happening, but the modus operandi, the 'way of dealing' that he has cultivated over the years is to shut down in the face of distress."

Evan and I scheduled a couple of sessions to revisit this period in his life and to work on his learning to be more attentive to his environment. Within a month, he had latched on to another serving job. This time, however, he started applying some of the techniques to stay tuned in that we had talked about, such as making sure he touched base with his manager on a weekly basis to see how he was doing, and keeping a journal of his work experience. His newly cultivated attentiveness paid off: within three months he was promoted to assistant manager and given a higher level of responsibility than he had ever had at a job.

He started using some of these same strategies at college—checking in with his instructors, keeping a log of his class work and homework—which led to positive results there, too. Opening his eyes even led him to take note of the work habits of his fellow students. He told me during one session, "There's a guy I'm friends with in one of my classes and we always walk out together, but then head out in different directions. So the other day I asked him where he went after class, and he said he always goes to the computer lab to get started on our assignment before he forgets what he's supposed to do.

"Well, believe it or not, all these months I've been there and I didn't even know that our school *had* a computer lab! So I went and it was amazing. There are computers and printers and people to help you, and I realized I could go in between classes just like he did, rather than wandering around looking for coffee like I've been doing."

Kirk's anger and frustration with Evan were understandable, but once he found a way to be both firm and empathetic with his son, Evan responded positively and took some steps toward maturity. When you find the right balance between clearly stated expectations and patient understanding—seeing your young adult as capable, but still in some ways vulnerable—you will see him fly with more speed in the direction of his most meaningful personal horizons.

REFLECTING BACK SO THAT YOU MOVE FORWARD

We see our children at various points in their development through the lens of how we remember ourselves when we were their age. And we nurture them according to how we were raised when we were at that stage. This is particularly true when it comes to young adulthood, because our memory of our own departure from the nest is going to be sharper than that of our adolescence or childhood.

If you recall marching effortlessly from high school into young adulthood—college, graduate school, career, marriage, and child-rearing, for example—you might expect the same of your child, and become overly disappointed and critical if her path is not quite as straightforward as you remember yours as having been.

On the contrary, if your transition into young adulthood was not so straight, or was tumultuous, you might anticipate the same kind of transition for your child and overreact counterproductively to some of her initial mistakes and missteps in an effort to turn things around for her.

If you felt as if your parents pulled the plug on parenthood too quickly as you were finishing adolescence, and they weren't there for you when you were making your first attempts to liberate yourself, you might be prone to holding on too tightly when it comes to your own child's departure. Or, if you remember your parents as overbearing even after you had moved away from home, you might swing in the other direction and provide too wide a berth for your child, neglecting to instill some of the structure and contact that still might be necessary to cultivate additional growth.

As a psychologist I strongly advise parents to think back on their early adulthood with as much accuracy and objectivity as they can so that they operate with as much flexibility as possible, rather than unconsciously repeating old patterns, or reflexively opposing them. Much of that reflection entails rediscovering, with the perspective and wisdom of adulthood, exactly how your own leave-taking went. What aspects would you want your child to repeat, and what would you rather she did differently? What are you proudest of yourself for, and what do you most regret? Which friends were you jealous of, and why?

This is also a good time to revisit the role that your parents played in your own movement into independence. How did they encourage and help you, and how did they hinder your progress? What did they say that you found supportive and inspiring, and what did they say that felt demoralizing or hurtful? What qualities in your friends' parents did you find yourself envying?

In addition, it is worthwhile to consider being more honest with your young adult regarding what your life was like when you were his age. Maintaining secrecy about your youth may have had some protective value during the adolescent years, when children are still quite impressionable and, as a result, vulnerable to "doing as you *did,* not as you say." It may not be wise, for example, for a mother to share with her teenage daughter the promiscuous phase she went through in high school, or for a father to share with his teenage son detailed accounts of his acid trips when he was in college.

But the same restraint is not necessary, or even advisable, when raising young adults. In fact, trying to maintain secrecy at this stage of parenthood often backfires. Not only does it deprive your child of learning from your experience, but it compromises some of the closeness and candor that can benefit both generations. It takes a lot of pressure off the young adult when the parent admits to having made mistakes, especially if you can poke a little fun at yourself.

You don't have to go into all the "gory details" of every choice that you still regret, but there is value in having frank and informative conversations about important decisions you made when you were younger and how you now understand and evaluate them in retrospect.

CONNECTING TO YOUR ADULT CHILD

Raising a child requires an enormous, lifelong emotional investment, and we're much more likely to make that investment if we find a way to connect with the child whom we're investing in, such as by seeing ourselves or others in her. That is one of the reasons why new parents begin this process early on—"Oh, look, he sleeps in the same position as I do!" or "She definitely has her grandfather's eyes!"—because it helps them feel that their baby is literally more *familiar,* not a stranger.

Complications arise, however, when we assign characteristics to our child that may not be relevant to who she actually is. Say, for example, your toddler's ill-tempered outbursts are to be expected as part of her normal growth process, but when she's in tantrum mode she reminds you of your mother, who too often became nasty and acerbic. So you instinctively react to your daughter as you reacted to your mother decades before—fearful, cringing, and cowed. This response actually contributes to a self-fulfilling prophecy, because since you don't have the resolve to take your daughter on and help her learn to manage her temper more effectively at a young age, she tends, without any firm limits in place, to become more and more unglued, which of course reminds you even more of your mother. "Why am I being tormented by both generations?" you complain, not realizing the ways in which your victimization by your mother has helped you to actually produce a similar victimization by your daughter and engender similar behaviors.

Sometimes this process of making inaccurate and pejorative associations begins very early on and continues through adolescence and early adulthood, and sometimes it may start later on—but, either way, if not seen for what it really is, it can interfere with an adult child's efforts to grow up and out of the nest.

For example, Ginger's older brother Sal is a 54-year-old alcoholic who lives a marginal existence, is sporadically employed, has been divorced twice, has no money to his name, and is still moving in and out of their parents' home, despite their very limited means. Ginger has been disgusted with Sal for years and wishes he would finally grow up, or at least stop sapping their mother and father, who are in their eighties, of what little savings they have. She knows, however, that this is unlikely to happen, and that her parents will probably be exploited by their indigent son for as long as they live.

Meanwhile, Ginger's 20-year-old son, Everson, has been struggling to make headway in life but hasn't yet met with any consistent success. His heavy drinking during high school ran him aground and placed a very low ceiling on his level of achievement. College was out of the question, and his first year after finishing high school was essentially spent in a drunken haze, earning a DWI and a suspended driver's license rather than any income or undergraduate credits.

It was not surprising that Everson was uncomfortably and unnervingly reminding his mother of her "loser of a brother," and she was understandably responding to him as if he were the reincarnation of his derelict uncle. However, this was making it difficult for her to see the progress that Everson was in fact making, which in turn made it difficult for her to support that progress.

For example, Everson had recently begun attending Alcoholics Anonymous meetings and was beginning for the first time to string together some significant periods of sobriety. But when I asked her, initially, to consider going to some Al-Anon meetings (for spouses, partners, parents, and children of alcoholics) as a way of possibly augmenting his recovery, I was met with a blunt refusal.

"I don't need to learn anything about alcoholics," she announced irritably. "I've got a brother who's taught me everything I need to know."

"But there might be some guidance or perspective that could be useful to you as you try to support Everson's sobriety."

"If he stops drinking, he stops drinking. It won't be because *I* go to any meetings."

"Well, you're right about that, his recovery is definitely in his hands, not yours. But you might benefit from some support as he struggles through this, and that can be valuable. Plus, you don't want to inadvertently enable him, and there might be some parents there who help you to stay out of his way as he's figuring things out."

"Nope, not for me. My parents actually have been to some Al-Anon meetings, and look at all the good it's done for them. My brother still drinks like a fish and meanwhile they put up with his nonsense, year after year."

"Do you know when they first went to an Al-Anon meeting?"

She thought for a moment. "It probably wasn't until my brother's first rehab, after his second marriage ended. He was probably thirty or so."

"So Sal was ten years farther along than your son is before your parents tried to take a different tack."

"What are you saying?"

"Maybe if they had gotten some support and direction earlier on, things might not be as bad as they are now. No guarantee, but who knows?"

"I don't know, I just don't see the point. It's going to run its course, I'm afraid. I can see myself thirty years from now with Everson living in my basement, still telling me he's going to get his act together, just like my brother does with my parents. Pretty sad, I tell you, pretty sad."

In this family, Ginger's son and brother were so inextricably fused in her mind that she was unable to distinguish them as two separate individuals. She couldn't see that Everson was actually beginning to make some progress and that there were ways in which she might be able to give some additional impetus to that progress.

It is for these reasons that when I am working with families with struggling young adults I will generally ask the parents if their son or daughter reminds them of anyone in their family. I inquire because it is not unusual to find someone else in their lives who has struggled in similar ways (sometimes, of course, it is one of the parents himself or herself whom the child reminds them of). If these intergenerational echoes are reverberating, then some effort has to be devoted to distinguishing the two individuals in question so that the parents see their child as who he actually *is,* not as a disquieting clone of someone he is *not.* As I often remind parents, "Tendency is not Destiny."

GETTING ALIGNED

As parents, we are prone to getting upended whenever our offspring enter new life stages. We may have been in agreement about how to potty train the two-year-old, but now we have different outlooks on how to convince Junior to find a job. One of the key themes I'd like to emphasize in guiding your adult child toward independence is the work that you and your coparent need to do. Now, I don't presume to know what lies behind any long-term relationship—perhaps you and your child's father have long since divorced; maybe you are a widow or widower, or it could be that your current wife is your child's stepmother. Perhaps you are still married to the coparent of your child but have a fractious relationship, or maybe you have an otherwise wonderful marriage that your difficult young adult seems to be jeopardizing. Any of this is possible. But in all these cases, if you are not solo parenting and your child is subject to the influence of his other parent, the two of you need to communicate and align yourself on a course of action you can both follow.

It is of course impossible to spend a couple of decades, plus or minus a few years, raising children without experiencing many moments of not seeing eye to eye. When it comes to finishing things off the right way, however, it's essential that you achieve as much congruence as possible with your partner in parenting.

Many couples who are not seeing positive results fall into a pattern of denouncing each other for the lack of progress that they are seeing. Not only is this unpleasant, but it is a significant distraction, and ultimately absolves the young adult from being more responsible for his actions. You want to parent as a team, as coequal partners.

Edward and Carmen were very frustrated by 20-year-old Kyle's grouchy behavior. Although he had a couple of very part-time jobs, he still was not earning enough money to move out, and he was making their lives miserable at home. Surly and selfish, he did almost nothing that they asked him to do, basically using the house as a "crash pad" when he wasn't at work, and often insulting his parents when they tried to get him to change his churlish ways.

Edward blamed Carmen for this state of affairs, noting in great detail for me the long history of what he saw as his wife's coercive and demanding behavior. "She's always in his face, she's never satisfied. It's been building like this for years. It's no wonder that he's so unpleasant. Who do you think he learned it from?"

Carmen, in turn, blamed Edward, omitting no detail in describing the long history of what she saw as his inept and feeble fatherhood. "He's basically been a wimp. Kyle's been bossing him around ever since he started middle school. My husband has never stood up to him, never been willing to set a limit. You know how some people bend but never break? Well, Edward bends *and* breaks, and that's why Kyle's so impossible."

At this point in the family life cycle, Edward and Carmen are squandering their time and energy pointing fingers at each other. Their current focus shouldn't be to fault each other for how Kyle turned out, but rather to form a united front concerning what is and what is not acceptable behavior. Only then will Kyle begin to consider renouncing his indignant, ungrateful stance and change his attitude.

One of the specific challenges that such a realignment may necessitate has to do with the need to acknowledge sometimes that your parenting partner may have been more correct about certain matters than you were. This kind of "pride swallowing" isn't easy, but it beats the alternative, where you're divided, frustrated, and getting nowhere.

Difficult as it may be, your young adult (and your marriage, too, as we'll see in Chapter Seven) will always reap the benefits of greater parental congruence.

GETTING ALIGNED AFTER A DIVORCE

You are probably familiar with the fable of the turtle and the scorpion, but just to review: a scorpion, unable to swim, asked a turtle to carry him on his back across a river. "Are you crazy?" the turtle exclaimed. "Surely you'll sting me while I'm swimming and I'll die."

"My dear turtle," chuckled the scorpion, "why would I do that? If I were to sting you while I was on your back, you would certainly die, but so, too, would I—we'd *both* drown!"

"Good point, I can't argue with your logic," admitted the turtle with relief. "Hop on my back, and off we go."

Of course, they weren't halfway across the river before the scorpion gave the turtle a powerful sting. As the poison quickly coursed its way through his body and he found himself unable to swim, the turtle dejectedly asked, "You knew that if you stung and killed me, we'd both die—so why did you do it?"

"It's in my nature," explained the scorpion with a shrug, as the two of them sank down to their watery graves.

I have worked with many couples who have divorced in civil and dignified ways, and who have clearly kept the needs of their children foremost, despite the emotional complexities entailed with dismantling a marriage and possibly moving on to create a blended family. These parents deserve enormous credit for protecting their children from unnecessary distress, despite whatever emotional compromises needed to be made to keep the coparenting relationship respectfully intact.

While nobody marries and starts a family intending to divorce, and while psychological research has demonstrated that there are formidable lifelong ramifications for the children of divorce, the fact remains that the breakup does not have to be traumatic. And, in addition, the outcome does not have to be irredeemably negative, either.

Many parents become more diligent and involved once they are put in the position of encountering single parenthood for a short or long period of time, and a more fairly distributed coparenting relationship can emerge. If the marriage has been a particularly embittered one, it is often a great relief to the children to be released from the hostile atmosphere. And if one or both parents remarry, the extended family stretches a little farther, and there can be a wider range of peers (half-sibling, step-sibling) and adults (stepparent, step-grandparent, step-aunts and -uncles) to draw from. A child's sense of security does not have to evaporate in the face of a divorce—in fact, it can be expanded and reinvented if the newly orchestrated ensemble of caregivers have worked to create two safe, loving homes that aren't at war with each other.

On the other hand, the story of the turtle and the scorpion reminds me of many divorced parents I have treated who repeatedly sting each other in ways that put the entire family at risk, leaving them all floundering, if not drowning, in rancor. While they justify their stinging as an unavoidable response to their partner's provocation, just as the scorpion attributes his stinging to his nature, the reality is that everybody suffers.

Whether a divorce has occurred years before or very recently, you still need to be aware of its potential impact on your young adult's development, and negotiate an accommodating and cooperative arrangement with your ex-spouse so that everyone, especially your child, can stay afloat and keep on swimming. At this stage of life, though, your new, long-standing, or rekindled resentment may make achieving this state of affairs troublesome.

The fact of your divorce can make your young adult's impending leave-taking feel like an abandonment rather than an advance, akin to ripping a scab off of a healing wound. Perhaps your spouse has soared ahead with his professional life while you sacrificed yours to attend to the children—so now that you are divorced you must struggle to make ends meet while he is close to retirement or buying a boat or taking long, expensive vacations with his new partner. Maybe your ex-spouse seems much more involved with her new family than the family that she started with you, and you feel both angry and sad as you realize that you may not be able to celebrate your children's rites of passage together in the coming years.

And the fact that you have developed a particularly close relationship with your young adult as the result of being a single parent for some time may make her leave-taking particularly painful to bear. Obviously, you won't have your coparent as physically or emotionally available to be a source of comfort and strength as this leave-taking evolves. In fact, if your child's presence has provided some form of glue between you and your former spouse—a legitimate reason for the two of you to be in some form of regular contact—her leave-taking will dissolve that bond and leave you contemplating a much larger chasm between your "together past" and your "asunder present."

On the other hand, divorced parents do have certain advantages when it comes to launching young adults. Due to child-sharing arrangements, they may have already learned how to make significant adjustments when it comes to seeing their children less frequently and having less direct influence over them. They may have already learned how to grieve, forgive, and move on—all of which are necessary parental tasks at this stage, as well, as we shall see in Chapter Eight. And they may have already been forced to become more honestly acquainted with themselves, and with their sometimes negative effect on others, as a result of having undergone the difficult process of separation and divorce, insight that can be put to good use while emptying the nest.

It is these strengths that need to be harnessed so that you, your co-parent, and your young adult can all successfully cross the sometimes rough terrain of life after divorce. You will need to continue to reassure your child that even though you are no longer husband and wife, you will always function as mother and father. This can be conveyed in many different ways, including:

- clarifying cooperatively how you'll handle the various parental duties that you are both still responsible for, such as paying for college;
- developing fairly consistent expectations across your different households while your young adult is still visiting or living at home;
- providing emotional support while still respecting your child's need to maintain a loving relationship with his other parent, your ex-spouse;
- tolerating those phases when your child seems more connected with your ex-spouse than with you;
- finding ways to come together around important discussions (such as which college to attend) or milestones (such as graduations);
- avoiding the creation of loyalty binds; that is, situations in which your child feels that positive experiences with one parent are likely to betray or injure the other parent (in other words,

not being rigid about how your child divides her time between two homes during visits or vacations, or about which house she chooses to live in during a return home).

When parents find ways to remain aligned even when they are no longer married to each other, it can help to take the "sting" out of the divorce, and catalyze a timely and healthy departure for the young adult.

OPEN MIND, OPEN HEART

The great anthropologist Margaret Mead wrote, "You must be free to take a path / whose end I feel no need to know." In a similar vein, although in a different way, Mae West suggested, "Those who are shocked easily should be shocked more often." Parents must give their young adult children permission to explore what is of interest to them . . . but sometimes what is of interest to them is somewhat foreign to us.

In the Introduction, we examined the many ways in which post-adolescent life is very different for your child than it was for you. Much has changed, and what has changed is likely to continue to change with equal if not greater rapidity. You might be optimistic or pessimistic about the ways in which things are different these days, but, like it or not, there's no turning back the clock.

So the more open you are to the vast array of possibilities that await your young adult, the more likely she will be to pursue some of those opportunities in satisfying and productive ways, to take risks and find her own way. Such a pursuit is less likely, however, if you're living in the past and insisting that she stay there with you.

One of the best ways to maintain your broad-mindedness is to shift from trying to get your child to learn from you, and instead to see what you can learn from her. Rather than assuming that the "rules of engagement" that you have been playing by have remained immutable, take some time to ask her what the world of higher education and work is really like these days. Not only will your young adult feel valued, but she may also provide you with perspective that will enable you to be more effective in your efforts to support her.

Remember that it can be pleasantly reassuring when the road your child travels is similar to the one that you traveled, particularly if it worked out well for you. But most careers, and career paths, are not what they were when you were making your own career decisions. In fact, many jobs in our modern economy did not even exist back in the Dark Ages of your own (and my) young adulthood.

Of course, there may be other choices that your young adult makes that trouble you besides his career path and choice. His decisions at this stage of his life are going to have more powerful and enduring consequences than the choices he made, for example, when he was in high school—whom he dated in his freshman year, what level French he took as a sophomore, or whether he ran cross-country in his junior year. You may worry that he appears to be repudiating everything that you taught and espoused, or you may misinterpret his emerging individuality as rebellious immaturity, or possibly as servile conformity.

The young man your daughter is dating, for example, may ultimately turn out to be her husband, and the father of your grandchild, and from your perspective this may or may not be a good thing. The college she attends will surely affect her subsequent flight path and influence some of the destinations that she will arrive at in her twenties, and possibly beyond. The somewhat extremist political group he joins may have cultish overtones, and you may wonder if you're going to lose him to some Svengali-like mentor whose tenets he seems to adhere to too credulously.

So it will inevitably be rough going when your child strikes out in a completely different direction from what you did or what you would prefer, and it's best to be as curious and welcoming as possible as he forges ahead toward terra incognita.

Remember also that life rarely follows the blueprint that we so carefully draw out. Mythologist Joseph Campbell wisely observed, "We must give up the life we planned so that we can discover the life that awaits." While planning certainly has its place, the reality is that many other unpredictable, uncontrollable factors did and will influence our own life's trajectory, and those same factors—which we call fate, coincidence, serendipity, tragedy, destiny, fortune, and misfortune—are going to play a role in your young adult's trajectory as well.

SHINING NEW LIGHT, FINDING NEW SOLUTIONS

Making frequent adjustments is one of the prerequisites of effective parenting at every stage of development, up to and including young adulthood. One of the most important adjustments during the launching phase is finding innovative ways to cultivate and promote an attachment to your child without either ejecting or engulfing her. This means finding a middle ground between the "centrifugal launching" (prematurely shoving your young adult out of the nest before she has confidence in her capacity to fly) and the "centripetal launching" (tethering your young adult so tightly that she isn't free to leave the nest and discover the capacity to fly) that we explored in Chapter Two.

Tolerating the inevitable conflicts and disappointments that are likely to crop up without losing sight of the undercurrent of caring and love that can still exist is one of your chief objectives when young adults are launching and liberating themselves.

Recently a rabbi told me a touching story about his 18-year-old son, who, unlike his three siblings, seemed to be actively rejecting his religion, despite the family's having actively and enthusiastically honored Jewish traditions over the years. Not surprisingly, this was a source of great distress for the rabbi, who had obviously hoped and trusted that his children would continue to live in religiously observant ways as they made their way into adulthood. He went to a senior rabbi for advice on what to do, and the advice arrived in three simple words: "Love him more." Not to sermonize, not to preach, not to convince, not to persuade, but to *love*.

You can keep this flow of love alive in many different ways. For example, as the parent of a young adult, you need to make the family structure more malleable in an effort to accommodate growth. This might mean updating or putting to rest family activities that have been satisfyingly in place for some time, and instead creating new ones and including your young adult's friends and significant others. It may also mean loosening your hold on your child, even when your instinct is to clutch tighter. Loving can sometimes mean relaxing your grip. No matter how you do it, there has to be a recognition that the family organism is evolving, and a willingness to establish room for more supple and adaptive arrangements.

One of the many ways to keep shining new light and finding new solutions harks back to Chapter One, when we discussed how it is important for the young adult to create a broader, more expansive narrative of her life. Just as she has to elongate her neat and tidy version of her history and destiny for her to grow, so must you as well. That means contemplating explanations and understandings that are different from and more subtle or sophisticated than those that you have hitherto been relying upon.

For example, 22-year-old Karl got a DUI while still on probation for a previous DUI. This meant that he was now facing the possibility of incarceration, not just probation. In our initial session, after his parents quickly attempted to explain away his behavior as being the result of the "low-rent company that he keeps," he complained vigorously to them about their ongoing tendency to blame his problems on his friends.

"You've always assumed that I get into trouble because I'm hanging around with the wrong crowd, the bad kids. You've been saying this ever since Victor gave me my first joint back in seventh grade. Don't you guys see that it's *me*, not them? Don't you see that *I'm* one of the bad kids? Don't you see that there are parents who don't want their kids hanging around *me*, that it's not just the other way around? Don't you guys get it that I can f**k up perfectly well on my own, I don't need the help of anyone else, thank you very much?"

Karl was making an important point: his parents' unceasing tendency to absolve him of responsibility, a habit that they had been perpetuating for almost ten years now, had clearly outlived its purpose. In fact, as he was astutely noting, it was inhibiting his parents' capacity to see him more clearly and help him to reverse his course.

Updating your parental philosophy can be a tall order when you have worked so hard for so many years to craft it, but thoughtful revision is required in order to help ease your young adult forward.

KEEPING THE FAITH

One of the most difficult but essential aspects of childrearing is having more faith in your child than she has in herself. When you convey to your young adult that you believe in her, she absorbs and assimilates that belief, and it will ultimately become her own, to be embodied and acted on. Of course, having more faith in your child than she has in herself can sometimes feel like quite a large *leap* of faith, but it's a leap worth taking.

Sometimes you can convey this faith by reminding her of the times when she has successfully adapted to difficulties in the recent or distant past, or has risen to challenging occasions and beaten the odds. Sometimes you can convey this faith by sharing inspirational stories from your own life, from the lives of family members, or from the lives of role models who might be meaningful to her. Sometimes the most powerful way you can convey this faith is by ratcheting up your expectations and, through so doing, making it unmistakably clear that you trust in her competence.

For example, 20-year-old Allison was living at home after having withdrawn from college, and had been dipping in and out of community college classes, often without completing them. She wasn't working, either, and spent most of her time with her boyfriend, a nice young man who had a reasonably solid job with a flooring company. Allison had a 24-year-old brother, Gordon, who was now a graduate student in the history of science and had already precociously published two well-received scholarly articles.

There wasn't a significant amount of tension at home between Allison and her parents, but that, to me, appeared to be one of the problems. They didn't ask much of her, and because they didn't ask much of her, there was little movement.

Allison's father, Leonard, explained, "We learned early on that you just don't push Allison. If you push Allison, she just pushes back, and you get nowhere. Now with Gordon, you could push, and he would respond. The harder we pushed him, the faster he went. That's probably why he's gotten as far as he's gotten. But with Allison, that clearly doesn't work."

"What *does* work?" I asked.

"That's why we're here: we don't know," Leonard responded. "*Nothing* seems to work."

In talking with Allison, I wondered what it was like for her to take note of this discrepancy between how she and her brother had been treated.

"Of course I've seen the difference. It's like they're saying, 'Oh, Gordon, you're so smart, you can do anything, but, poor, dumb Allison, you're never going to amount to anything.'"

"Why do you think they treated the two of you so differently?" I inquired.

"Look, I guess he got the brains in the family."

"And what did you get?"

"I don't know, that's a good question. I can tell you I've got a better social life than my brother, that's for sure. I've always had tons of friends. I've got a great boyfriend, but Gordon, he's kind of on the lonely side. I don't even think he's ever dated, let alone had a girlfriend. He really keeps to himself."

"You talk like it's all or nothing, though, like it's not possible for both of you to have gotten some of the family's brains."

"Well, they certainly don't act like I'm very smart. They were just happy to have me get *into* a college. I wasn't much of a student in high school, so they didn't spend a whole lot of time figuring out which college I should go to. With Gordon, it seemed like every day was spent figuring out where he should go and what essay he should write and how much scholarship money he would get. I remember just sitting around watching TV in the family room while they sat around the kitchen table night after night, discussing his future."

It was clear that Allison did not believe that her intellect was taken very seriously by her parents, certainly not in comparison with her scholarly older brother. It was also clear that she had internalized this lack of faith in her intelligence, which may have been one of the reasons why she had not succeeded when she went away to college and why her subsequent educational efforts had been tepid. It struck me that, ironically, she had been using much of her intellect to find ways to *doubt* her own intelligence.

In this case, the goal was not to "push" Allison—as we have already noted, pushing young adults tends not to produce lasting positive results. Instead, it was to hammer away at the image she had of herself as scholastically inert, and attempt to *lure* her into believing that she had more brainpower than she had previously concluded.

Allison had had a psychoeducational evaluation performed on her back in fourth grade that showed that she was dyslexic. While she had received specialized tutoring for several years to help her compensate for this, and her reading scores had gradually improved to grade level by the end of middle school as a result of these services, she was still left with the belief, partly because of her disability and partly because of the constant comparisons with her talented brother, that she just did not have "the brains."

She and I spent some time going over that evaluation with her parents present, an evaluation that concluded that, despite her dyslexia, her global cognitive potential was well above normal. I reminded her that a learning disability says nothing about one's overall smarts.

"Then how come I never did very well at school?" she wondered.

"I'm not exactly sure—perhaps somehow you mistakenly decided that if you were dyslexic, you simply couldn't achieve at a high level. Perhaps you thought that it would be unfair to your brother if you succeeded academically as well as socially, when he was only shining in the academic world, so you 'blunted your sword,' so to speak, and made sure you didn't surpass him.

"Perhaps," and here I looked at her parents, "your mom and dad felt that they had to go easy on you because they didn't want to set up expectations that you couldn't meet."

"That's true, that's true," Allison's mother, Joan, quickly chimed in. "We were told by the experts not to push you, not to expect too much. We got you the tutoring, we knew that was helping, but we didn't want you to think that we expected you to be like Gordon."

"But don't you see that I *wanted* to be like Gordon?" Allison replied, tears in her eyes. "I wanted so much to be smart like him, but I knew I just didn't have it, and I knew that *you* guys knew I just didn't have it."

"But we were just taking our cues from the evaluation, honey. You had been having a hard time reading, you were always frustrated. That's why we got the assessment in the first place, because we knew that you were smart, but that something was holding you back."

"But it's like you just threw in your cards after that. 'Oh, my daughter's dyslexic. Oh, she'll never be a good student, not like her brilliant brother, not like Gordon the Genius.'"

"Allison, that's not what we meant," Leonard insisted.

"But that's how it *felt*," Allison noted, sadly, then added after a moment, "and that's how it still feels. You didn't spend *half* the time helping me find a college that you spent with Gordon."

"You also weren't that interested in colleges, Allison," Leonard reminded her. "You didn't want to go on any tours, you didn't look at the stuff that came in the mail. We were trying to read you, trying to figure out where you were at. We didn't want to go on some intense search for the perfect college if you weren't interested."

"But maybe if you had been more intense, I would've gotten more involved."

The family was bravely uncovering some old hurts that needed to be addressed for Allison to get unstuck and make progress. The truth of the matter and the solution to the dilemma, as we have generally seen, did not lie entirely in either the parents' or Allison's behaviors, but in the *interaction* between their respective behaviors.

Leonard and Joan were trying to be good parents and not get too pushy about school achievement or college applications. Allison interpreted this as most adolescents would, as a signal that her wise parents must know, at some level, that she was not that intellectually capable. So she continued acting like the person she saw reflected by their behavior, which in turn convinced her parents that their approach was the correct one. The painful result, after many years, was that all three of them had lost faith in Allison's intellect.

Our objective was to help Allison harness the intellectual horsepower that she had been ignoring for years instead of just browbeating her into a firmer academic commitment. We spent the remainder of this session, and our next couple of sessions, illuminating Allison's cognitive strengths and showing her that they were there all along. Her parents pulled examples from her childhood when she shone at school, before she became convinced that her brother was the brains of the family.

I encouraged her to go to the career center at her community college to take some vocational inventories, and it turned out that science was one of the categories that seemed best suited to her. What was painful to Allison and her parents was that she had given up on one of the subjects that she was actually most qualified for, simply because no one had helped her to believe in herself, and she had concluded that such belief was not warranted.

I suggested that they consider four-year colleges, particularly those that had good programs for dyslexic students (which her previous college did not have), so that she would have some goals in mind as she recommended accumulating community college credits. It was heartening for me to see how delighted Allison was by the time and energy that the three of them devoted to this process: it was a reparative experience, a way to compensate for the attention that they had dedicated to Gordon's college search years earlier.

With this shift in tone, Allison began taking her courses more seriously, and, as a result, achieving at a higher level. She decided to stay at her community college to earn her associate's degree, and then was admitted to a four-year college, where she eventually earned a bachelor's degree with honors in biology. Then she went to graduate school, just as her brother had done, choosing marine biology.

When her parents took the risk of encouraging her and instilling in her some of the faith in herself that had been lost, she was able to begin drawing on her vast but hitherto sealed-off reserves of intellectual capital and more confidently invest in her future.

NETS VERSUS NESTS

The difficulty involved with finding respectful ways to stay connected with your young adult often creates a breeding ground for worry: he may attempt to stay connected with you by giving you something to worry about, while you may attempt to stay connected by finding reasons to worry. Of course, the two processes simultaneously reinforce each other, an interaction that keeps both generations stuck.

That is one of the reasons why I focus on the image of building a "net" rather than a "nest" at this stage of parenthood. As we have seen, the young adult needs an opportunity to spread her wings and fly, but she'll be more likely to leave the nest if she knows that there's a safety net below that will cushion her if necessary. The building of a net provides you with something useful to focus on instead of free-floating parental anxiety, and the reassuring presence of a secure net provides your young adult with less reason to feel her *own* anxiety, which in turn, of course, will make her less likely to make *you* anxious.

Parents who shift their energies from the nest to the net display some of the following behaviors:

- They provide plenty of space for their young adult to make mistakes, along with the subsequent emotional support that might help him *learn* from these mistakes and not repeat them.
- They adopt the "long view" and remember that their child has many years to sort things out and define a trajectory, despite whatever periods of waywardness, backsliding, and uncertainty may occur.

- They share with their young adult their own uncertainty regarding what role they should be playing, and they invite their young adult's feedback regarding the optimal balance of netlike versus nestlike behaviors.
- They continue to perform a more sophisticated, finely tuned version of "picking him up and dusting him off," much as they have done when their child tripped and fell, literally or figuratively, since his earliest years.

FINALLY . . .

Remind yourself constantly that your young adult is not you, nor is she supposed to be. You may be absolutely convinced that she is making decisions that she will pay dearly for, based on your own experiences. And, at times, sadly, you may be correct. But you will surely not be correct all of the time, for she is not the same person as you are, her circumstances are different, and she will only learn from her mistakes if allowed to make them, just like you did.

I wish that there were some method of learning important lessons other than by making some bad decisions, but, as much as I've searched, I have yet to find such a method. However, most errors do not result in lifelong consequences, and, even if they do, the consequences are rarely entirely negative.

So keep in mind that neither Father nor Mother knows best. Don't be so arrogant as to believe that you know with absolute certainty what choices will turn out to be the optimal ones for your child. Life, we must acknowledge, will always provide us with plenty of unanticipated plot lines, and no matter how vast your experience and wisdom may be, there is still no crystal ball that will accurately predict your child's future.

In the last several chapters, we have been exploring the many different ways in which parents can promote young adults' development. As you have probably already noted, however, almost all of these strategies and techniques depend on clear and effective communication. Our next chapter will sketch an outline for parent–young adult dialogue that will carry you through the emptying of your nest and continue to have relevance in the years beyond.

CHAPTER FIVE

GETTING BEYOND "WHATEVER"

GROWTH PROMOTING COMMUNICATION DURING THE YOUNG ADULT YEARS

Successful family communication is not so much a matter of getting your point across or making sure that everyone is in agreement, but of parent and child *making the effort* to understand each other, and of each of them feeling that they are understood, or at least listened to.

True, you communicate with your adult children in ways not dissimilar to how you've communicated with your younger children all along. But some of the techniques that worked at earlier stages of development will actually be counterproductive during the launching phase, and you will also have to be prepared to implement some innovative methods.

Because young adults are preparing to move into a new constellation of relationships in the coming years—with roommates, colleagues, employers, intimate partners, perhaps children of their own—creating a more supple and sophisticated mode of exploring, debating, and resolving matters will serve them well as they enter this next phase of their life. New ways of communicating will also carry you through the subsequent decades of your relationship with your adult child, so they are definitely worth becoming acquainted with.

Of course, there are numerous impediments to establishing effective communication during the launching phase. First of all, despite the fact that technology now offers us many more ways to communicate, the myriad modern options also present a barrier to genuine communication that results from our accelerated lives and demanding schedules. Good communication takes time, and we have far too little of it no matter what gadgets are at our disposal.

Also, if unproductive communication patterns have been established over the years, your young adult will understandably be reluctant to engage in discussions that tend to have unpleasant or heated outcomes, particularly if she's no longer living at home and these can now be conveniently sidestepped.

Further, as part of her evolution as a young adult, she naturally has to keep some boundaries in place and give more seasoned thought to the sometimes subtle distinctions between privacy and secrecy, between openness and overexposure. This will likely require a period of time distinguished by more selective verbal disclosure and interaction as she seeks to square up her relationship with you and other important individuals.

But even with these challenges in place, it is possible for you to become fluent in a new tongue, and what follows is a compendium of age- and stage-relevant approaches that will not only help you make the effort to understand your young adult child, but also will result in your being better understood by her as well.

STEPPING ASIDE

Perhaps the most significant shift in approach is that your job is no longer to put forth your own viewpoints and values in an effort to mold your child, but to set up conversations that enable her to develop *her own* viewpoints and values. It becomes less and less important that she understand your perspective, and more important that she clarify and broaden her own. It is no longer required that she think the same way you do, but it is essential that she think differently about herself and become more interested in her own cognitive process.

There is a Hebrew word with a lovely sound, *tzimtzum,* loosely translated as "contraction," which captures this concept. Some Jewish mystics teach that God began the process of creation by shrinking heavenly omnipotence and infinite presence in order to allow for the existence of an independent world. Only through the withdrawal of divine energy and essence could a space for imperfect humanity, and for human growth, became possible. Likewise, parents of young adults must "contract" themselves, condense their presence so that their child has space and room in which to grow and think more independently.

Young adults tend to battle parents as a stand-in for the combatants who lurk inside of them. You may believe that your 20-year-old daughter's pot smoking is keeping her stuck, but until *she* is able to contemplate this possibility, not only will her self-destructive behavior continue, but you will become increasingly estranged from each other and she'll be less receptive to whatever influence you try to exert.

She may blindly flail about, swinging her sword at demons that you can't even see, but it is no longer your function to leap into the room, boldly declare yourself her adversary, and engage in a dedicated thrust and parry with her. Instead, you must stand to the side and simply illuminate the room so that she can enter the skirmish within herself with more vision, skill, and clarity.

So your dialogue with her needs to be designed not as an evangelical sermon designed to convert her to your way of thinking, but as a series of conversations structured to *attract her curiosity* about why she does what she does, so that changes take root and germinate from the inside out.

INSTEAD OF SAYING:

"You *must* be able to see that smoking pot every day is keeping you stuck, making you irritable, and destroying some brain cells. And please don't try to explain to me that you think better and are more creative when you're high. I don't buy that for one minute."

TRY SOMETHING LIKE:

"We may never see eye to eye on pot use—you're convinced it's good for you, I'm convinced it's bad for you; you have your evidence, I have mine. We've established our positions quite clearly, so for now, we're going to have to agree to disagree. But I do hope that you observe yourself carefully, and perhaps even take a break from pot for a week or two at some point just to see how it feels, so that you have as much factual evidence as possible to determine its risks and benefits for you in the coming years."

DEFINING WHO'S RESPONSIBLE

I pay very careful attention to the words that parents select, because they are always quite revealing. I find many parents of younger children, for example, speaking in the first-person plural, as in "We haven't gotten very good grades this quarter," or "We've thrown a lot of tantrums this week." The "we" is usually indicative of a blurring of the lines of responsibility, subtly suggesting a tacit agreement that the parent is just as accountable as the child, if not more so, for problems that have cropped up.

I hear similarly revealing word choices when working with parents of young adults as well. In one family session, for instance, I learned that the mother's birthday was coming up, and I asked her what she would like to receive from her unemployed 22-year-old son as a present. Her reply—"The best present for *me* would be for *him* to get a job"—was understandable, and, if delivered, would probably indeed be met with great enthusiasm, as her son had been without a job since graduating from college four months earlier. Nevertheless, it suggested that her son's employment was as much a gift to her as to himself (if not more so), as though he had no investment in gainful work.

I've heard other parents plead, "Just do it for me," where the "it" could be anything from getting sober to finding a mate. When a parent beseeches a young adult to achieve a goal "for me," it almost guarantees that either the goal is not going to be achieved, or is going to be achieved for the wrong reasons and in such a way that it won't *feel* like an achievement, or is not going to be achieved without some form of sabotage that undercuts its value.

One of the most important foundations for effective communication during the launching phase is clarifying *who is responsible for what*. Parents need to be able to live by, and convey to their young adult, the following dicta:

- I am responsible for what *I* do, not for what *you* do.
- I am not here to solve your problems for you, and you are not here to solve mine for me.
- If something upsets me about what you are doing and I want you to know, I need to say something to you directly, and not expect you to read my mind.
- If what worries me does not worry you, then I'll need to decide how to handle that, rather than insist that you be as worried as I am, or that you feel obligated to make me feel less worried.
- If you have a problem or concern and want my help, you need to let me know that—otherwise, I will assume that you can manage on your own.
- If I decide, for whatever reasons, not to offer the help that you have requested, you are entitled to be disappointed, but you will still have to work it out on your own.
- If I ask you to work it out on your own, I have to accept your method of doing so, even if I might have done it differently myself, and allow you to live, happily or unhappily, with whatever consequences ensue.

HOW DO YOUR WORDS AFFECT HIS SENSE OF EFFICACY AND JUDGMENT?

There will always be times when it appears to you that your young adult has run aground, and would benefit from your guidance or perspective.

But imposing yourself on her ("Look, here's what you need to do") without first soliciting her input, or inflicting yourself on her in judgmental, critical ways that bruise her self-regard ("*Your* way clearly doesn't seem to be working, so it's time for you to try things *my* way") will invariably hobble your good intentions. The occasions when you might most desire a good talk with her are often the times when she is most reluctant to talk. She may be feeling embarrassment, disappointment, or shame—but one or more will close her off to your efforts.

You can be more certain that you are approaching her in a way that is respectful of her autonomy if you are thoughtful about how you introduce your concerns. This involves being attentive to how you receive her response, how you validate her concerns, how you reassure her that you believe in her, and how you remind her of how she has survived adversity in the past.

Here are some ways to draw near that won't reflexively provoke a freeze-out:

- "You've been looking like you've got some things on your mind—did you want to run any of them by me? I can't tell if my being a sounding board would be helpful to you or not..."
- "Do you think, at your age, that you can turn to me for support or direction without feeling like you're still a child, or too dependent on me?"
- "I have some thoughts about what your options are, but am not sure that you want to hear them. Would this be a good time? If not, there's no hurry, I can be patient..."
- "I have the sense that you're holding back from letting me in on your struggles, maybe because you believe I might be critical or disappointed, as I acknowledge I've been in the past. Am I near the mark? Are you willing to give me a second chance?"
- "You're in a complicated situation here, and there's no simple solution. Do you have a sense of how you want to handle it yet? Did you want to lay out some of the possibilities so that we can evaluate them together?"

- "How are you managing things these days? If you're starting to feel overwhelmed by your predicament, I'm available. But I can also respect your desire to try to manage things on your own."

Needless nags and admonitions should be avoided at all costs. When you leave the house for work and remind your son, "Don't forget to finish those job applications this afternoon," it suggests to him that you don't believe that he has the maturity and sense to follow through on matters independently. Now, of course, refraining from saying those words certainly doesn't guarantee that he *will* complete the job applications. But citing them places him squarely in the Compliance/Defiance bind that we discussed earlier, and whether it's complying or defying, neither will make him feel more motivated.

DON'T USE WORDS AS A SUBSTITUTE FOR ACTIONS, AND DON'T MINCE THE WORDS YOU USE

Talk is cheap, and actions always speak louder than words when it comes to family life. No matter how logical you think you are being, you can never reason another person out of a position that he didn't use reason to get himself into.

So, as we have seen in many of our case examples, simply telling your young adult "We want you to get off of the Xbox and get a job" is unlikely to have much impact unless he is made uncomfortable enough that he has to get a job to ease his own discomfort. It shouldn't really matter to your child whether or not you "want" him to get a job—what should matter is that, for example, you are no longer going to pay for his car insurance or his cell phone plan, meaning that if he wants to drive or text, he's going to have to get a job.

And when you do choose to rely on words to make your point, make sure that you "say what you mean, and mean what you say": don't beat around the bush, hoping that he eventually gets your point. Many of the parents I work with, in their efforts to be patient and gentle, end up padding their words with so many pillows that he never gets the point.

INSTEAD OF SAYING:

"Are you sure that graduate school is a good idea for you to pursue right now, especially since you don't have much money in the bank? It's quite expensive, you know . . ."

TRY SOMETHING LIKE:

"You can certainly apply to graduate school if you want, and education is never a waste of money, but I want to make it clear up front that unless we win the lottery, we won't be able to subsidize this endeavor. We still have your younger brother's college to pay for and your grandmother's health is declining; she's going to need our support in the coming years. So it's your call, but we want you to be able to make that call with the right data in hand."

PREVENT THE PREVENTABLE

Because of the long and complex history between parent and offspring, parents are not always the best sources of counsel for their young adult children. Many conflicts can be prevented or subverted simply by subtracting yourself from a discussion and putting your young adult in contact with another "authority figure," one who may say the same thing that you have been saying, but in a way that will enable it to be better heard.

INSTEAD OF SAYING:

"How do you think you're going to be able to get a truck loan when you've only been working for the past month? Don't you understand that the dealer's going to need to see pay stubs, three bank statements, and your year-to-date earnings?"

TRY SOMETHING LIKE:

"I'm not sure how easy it is to get truck loans these days, but why don't you head over to our bank and talk to someone over there to get the latest information and rates? If you'd like, I'll go with you."

PREFACE YOUR CONCERNS
WITH YOUR INTENTIONS

Children of any age will always be prone to feeling judged or criticized by their parents. This leads them to automatically interpret your words as attacks or assaults, so young adults will react with an offensive or defensive posture. When you are bringing up something that is worrying or upsetting you, it's helpful to let them know right up front that you are not looking to demean them.

INSTEAD OF SAYING:

"I think you're making a big mistake by relying on Craigslist to find a job. You can say all you want about the wonders of the Internet, but there's really no substitute for getting out there and pounding the pavement."

TRY SOMETHING LIKE:

"I know that you want to find work, and I have seen that you are making efforts to do so online. I am not interested in telling you how to conduct a job search. I know that things are very different now than they were when I was your age. But I'm curious: how much longer do you think you're going to give it before you may consider some other strategies besides relying on the Internet?"

BE CAUTIOUS WITH PRAISE

As I constantly remind parents, praise is like penicillin: the right dosage can promote healing, but overdoing it can be poisonous. As we saw when we discussed the basis for motivation, once you confer your own celebratory assessment of an accomplishment, it might take away from her own celebration, making it feel more like a feather in your cap than hers, and prompting her to take fewer steps, or even some steps backward. It's better to give her an opportunity to reflect upon her achievement and assign it the proper weight, than to douse it with your own appraisal, however exultant you may be.

Taking this approach means that you have to be careful not to carry forth your own evaluation of her progress, or lack thereof, but to lay back enough so that she engages in a frank and forthright *self*-evaluation.

INSTEAD OF SAYING:

"That's so wonderful that you finally got your college applications done, you must be very proud of yourself—I know that we're very proud of you, that's for sure."

TRY SOMETHING LIKE:

"I've seen you working hard to get these applications completed by deadline. How's it feel now that you've taken care of them?"

RENOUNCE REPETITIVE AND INTRUSIVE INQUIRIES

The more questions that young adults are asked by others, the less questions they ask of themselves, partially because they wind up spending a good portion of their energy fending off these incoming inquiries rather than putting forth their own. Posing questions that have to do with matters that *they* should be responsible for actually diminishes their level of responsibility, because they learn to count on you to bring up subjects that they need to learn to bring up for themselves.

INSTEAD OF SAYING:

"Are you staying on top of math this semester? I know that was your downfall *last* semester, and that you probably don't want to have to take it for a third time *next* semester..."

TRY SOMETHING LIKE:

(intentionally blank)

SOLICIT YOUR YOUNG ADULT'S PERSPECTIVE ON YOUR ROLE

Another difference in communicating with a young adult as opposed to a child is that now your son or daughter has the capacity to think and speak with greater maturity and versatility—and this is something that can work to the advantage of both of you.

Many parents struggle unnecessarily because they refrain from simply asking their young adult what role he believes they should be playing in his life. This is not something that you should have to figure out on your own. Inviting his perspective not only will help you to more sensitively fine-tune your relationship with him, but it will also be another statement of your belief in his capacity to ask for what he needs and decline what he doesn't.

INSTEAD OF SAYING:

"I see from your bank statement that you've bounced checks again, and now owe 300 dollars in overdraft fees. I think it's time that I held on to your bank card, and that we went over to the bank together to see if we can get some of those fees reduced."

"I see from your bank statement that you've overdrawn again, and now have to deal with returned check fees, as well. Are there ways in which you believe that I can be of some help as you learn to manage your finances, or is this the sort of thing that you want to work out on your own?"

FOREGO COURTROOM INTERROGATIONS

One of the more maddening aspects of communicating with young adults occurs when they engage in what we might politely call "revisionist history," such as when their description of certain events sounds radically different from what you recall. Displaying a (sometimes cheerful) disregard for truth or authenticity, they may prefer to gild and polish, or falsify and misrepresent, in a way that meshes better with how they think in the present.

While it is tempting at these times to flatly correct her revision, this generally accomplishes nothing. You should certainly feel free to articulate your own account, but not to the point where you engage in a hopelessly subjective dispute that is unlikely to resolve itself, but *very* likely to engender anger and polarization. It is far more important to talk to her in a way that will help her to come to terms with the feelings or wishes that lie at the root of her revisionist tendencies.

For example, in response to your daughter's comment that, "I really wanted to go to College A, but decided on College B because that was where *you* wanted me to go, and now I'm unhappy at College B and wish that I had gone to College A like I originally wanted to . . ."

INSTEAD OF SAYING:

"No, no, that's not true at all, you fell in love with College B, don't you remember? That's all you could talk about! In fact, you didn't even *like* College A. You came back from the tour telling us you couldn't see yourself fitting in. We didn't push you at all, it was entirely your decision."

TRY SOMETHING LIKE:

"I'm not certain I remember it the same way you do, but I do hear that you're having some regrets about the choice you made. It's impossible to make a decision this big with any kind of satisfaction guaranteed, and all of us know the pain of wishing we'd chosen differently. At this point, did you want to tell me more about what's not going right for you? Would you like to talk about how to make things better where you are, or discuss maybe transferring to College A, or somewhere else?"

DON'T BE AFRAID TO APOLOGIZE

All of us lug behind us a sack of regrets regarding the decisions we have made as parents, and it's not exactly a day at the beach to have to revisit all of them. Yet such a review is often insisted upon by your child as he ventures forward and tries to make sense of his own personal history.

When your young adult brings up a hurt from the past, it's best to allow him to talk about it so that healing becomes possible. Expecting him to "bury it alive" because it's in the past will only create larger problems down the road. Of course, incessant complaints about the past can get tiresome, indeed—"Okay, okay," you want to say, "I know I wasn't perfect, but it's enough already. Maybe you should be using your mind to focus on finishing college rather than prosecuting me as an incompetent parent." Sometimes you might feel like Joseph K. in Kafka's *The Trial*, apprehended and punished for obscure, unspecified crimes that you don't even recall having committed.

But usually when I hear a young adult pummeling away at his parent with the same complaint, it's because he hasn't yet felt that his grievance has truly been heard. Or, the formulaic "I'm sorry" that has been repetitively offered sounds to him more like, "I'm sorry that you took it the wrong way," a thinly veiled way of saying, "I'm sorry that you're still so immature, fragile and thin-skinned." But when there is an acknowledgment of contrition and remorse, of a sincere effort by the parent to understand, I find that most young adults are much more easily able to let go and move on, difficult as it may be for the parent to summon an authentic apology.

Eppie had begun an affair with her current husband, Grady, while still married to her first husband, Peter, ten years earlier. Her love affair with Grady quickly led to her divorce from Peter and marriage to Grady, all of which occurred when their son, Jonathan, was 12 years old. Shortly thereafter, Peter reconnected and moved in with a former girlfriend who now lived in another state, leaving Jonathan and his two younger sisters to be raised by his mother and stepfather, seeing their father only a couple of times a year for brief vacations.

Ten years later, at 22, Jonathan was floundering, living at home and continually stalling out in his effort to get moving, and angrily blaming much of this on his mother's affair and the succeeding upheavals in his life. Her general tactic had been to avoid acknowledging that her decisions had had any deleterious impact on Jonathan's life. Here's a verbal snapshot from one of our initial sessions:

"I was very unhappy with your father, but you weren't that happy with him either. You used to complain all the time about how grouchy he was, how he was always in a bad mood. That was one of the reasons that I was so miserable. But Grady always took an interest in you, and he treated you like you were his own son. That was one of the things I liked about him. I wouldn't have married him if I hadn't thought he would be a good stepfather to you guys."

"He basically kissed my ass, Mom, and the reason he kissed my ass is because he wanted to impress you. If he's so terrific, why did he have an affair with a married woman? And if you were so unhappy with Dad, why didn't you get divorced and *then* start a relationship with someone? Do you know how awkward it was for me, having to move into Grady's house right after you and Dad split?"

"It wasn't exactly 'right after,' Jonathan, it was—"

"Oh, come on, Mom, maybe not the day after, but it was pretty soon after . . . and then Dad winds up leaving because you left him, and now I never see Dad, and it's like nothing ever worked out for me after that."

"But you weren't very close to your father, Jonathan. You used to—"

"*Stop* telling me what I used to say, Mom, he's my father. He's my only father. All sons fight with their fathers, and, let's remember, Grady is *not* my father, no matter how you try to paint it. He's not my father, and he's never going to *be* my father."

"But you won't let him in, Jonathan, you make it so hard for him. Your sisters adore him, he's been great to them."

"I don't care what my sisters think. They—"

"He's a good man, Jonathan. He wants nothing more than to be close to you."

"Sure, a good man, that's what he is, a good man who screwed up my whole life because he wanted to get into bed and *screw* you and you couldn't resist. Doesn't sound like a good man to me."

"Well, no one told your father that he had to fall in love with someone halfway across the country and move out there with her, you know."

"Blaming Dad for moving doesn't do anything, Mom. Let's face it, he wouldn't have done that if you hadn't gotten involved with Grady. He'd still be here with us. What was he supposed to do, sit around here and twiddle his thumbs while you had your love affair?"

Clearly, Eppie's defensiveness isn't doing much to take the edge off of Jonathan's lingering hurt and resentment. While she feels justified in having ended her first marriage and believes she selected a better man the second time around, she also needs to come to terms with the role she played in disrupting her son's life and the wreckage that ensued.

After Eppie and I met a couple of times individually to devise a different approach, here is the direction that their conversation took as she became more willing to take fuller ownership for the consequences of her decision:

"One thing I realize is that I never apologized to you for having gotten involved with Grady and ending my marriage to your dad. I had my reasons for doing so, and I believe it's worked out much better for me, and for your sisters, but I can hear that you don't feel that it's worked out better for *you*."

"You're darn right that it hasn't. And a lot of good your apology does for me now."

"I know that an apology doesn't turn back the hands of time, and doesn't make the pain go away. But I'm starting to understand more about how hard it must have been for you when all of these changes came about so quickly."

"It's about time..."

"I obviously wish that I had been able to stay in love with your father, but we just weren't happy together—he knew it, and I knew it. But you are right, it's one thing to be unhappy in a marriage, it's another thing to have an affair and end a marriage and ask a 12-year-old boy to suddenly live with another man and treat him like a father."

"Why did you do it?"

"I can't answer that easily, Jonathan. A dying marriage is a terrible thing to live through. We can talk more about that at some point. It's very complicated. But for now I just want you to know that I really do apologize for all that I put you through, even though I tried to make it as easy for you as possible."

"It was never easy, Mom."

"I know, I know."

"What you did changed everything."

"It did, you are right. I am truly sorry for the pain that I caused."

Jonathan was silent for a few moments, and then softly said, "But I guess that change is something that we all have to deal with."

Here you can see how the conversation begins to move in a different direction. Eppie's ability to walk through her own pain, and to hear out her son's, moved their discussion out of the world of disputation toward reconciliation. Jonathan began to contemplate the possibility that he was not just a hapless victim of his mom's selfishness, and that for him to move forward, he had to focus less on what had changed in the past, and more on how to make changes in the present. This included the need for him to heal his relationship not only with his mother, but also with his distant father, which turned out to be the next phase of our work together.

DON'T ALWAYS TAKE THEIR WORDS AT FACE VALUE

What young adults are saying to us may often be an echo of what they are saying to, and feeling about, themselves. When your son exclaims, "I just can't stand living here with you guys!" it is often better to translate it as, "I just can't stand living in here with *myself*." When your daughter squawks, "Why won't you stop *nagging* me and leave me alone already?" she may also mean, "I am so tired of nagging myself and not seeing any results." "I want to be treated like an adult!" may be best decoded as, "I am terrified of being treated like an adult and no longer having the right to be taken care of." When she grumbles that you're always "yelling" at her, it may be because she's so busy yelling at herself in rich, interior, stereophonic sound.

It is natural to want to respond to the hostile "lyrics" that are coming across, but there is a music behind the lyrics that has to be attended to, as well. If you counterattack in the face of these dismal assessments, you will lose the chance to help your young adult understand more about his dismal *self*-assessment, a crucial precursor to springing himself free.

INSTEAD OF SAYING:

"You can't stand living with *me*? What do you think it's like for me to have to live with *you*?"

TRY SOMETHING LIKE:

"I'm sure it's not very easy for you, and it's not very easy for me, either. What is it that you need to do to move on so that we're not so entangled with each other?"

INSTEAD OF SAYING:

"I wouldn't have to nag you if you'd simply clean up after yourself and take care of what I've asked you to..."

TRY SOMETHING LIKE:

"I'm truly puzzled by your wondering why I still nag you, since it's clear that I nag you when you haven't done what you said you were going to do. But I will acknowledge that my nagging doesn't seem to be getting me what I want, which is more responsible behavior on your part. So I guess I'll have to figure out another way to deal with this. In the meantime, you might want to think about why you behave in a way that invites the nagging that you have understandably grown so tired of."

TACKLING HEAD-ON

I am often struck by how parents and young adults seem to "circle around" their changing relationship without actually addressing it directly. There may or may not have been a long history of circumventing discussions of this sort, but delving into them in straightforward ways always pays off.

Here are some questions that you could start with that might lead to a useful, revealing conversation:

- What would you change about our relationship with each other at this point? What would you like to see more or less of between us?
- How would you like our relationship with each other to evolve in the coming years?
- What about our connection with each other would you like to have in place when *you're* the parent of a young adult, and what would you like to be different or better?
- What aspects of our relationship with each other at this point are surprising, or somehow different than you thought it would be? What parts are about what you expected?
- Are we doing enough together, or too little, or too much?
- Are there ways in which some of your friends or colleagues connect with their parents that you envy?

- What is it about me, about you, about our relationship with each other that you think makes it difficult to have a conversation like this one?
- As you move on and move out, what are the ways in which we can remain close while still giving each other space?

The timing of these conversation starters is important, of course—it's always better to introduce these questions during a moment of connectedness, rather than abruptly, from out of the blue, or just after a bruising clash—but most young adults are looking for some guidance as they move forward, and helping to initiate or frame a discussion of this sort always helps.

EMBRACE CONTROVERSY

No matter how healthy your relationship is with your young adult, there are still going to be arguments—and there *should* be. As long as these respectful, "loving fights" are relatively infrequent and don't incur wounds too deep to heal, they can serve a useful purpose: helping two people to see each other's perspectives with more clarity and empathy, and clearing the air by discharging built-up tension.

Also, children can learn to fight fairly and constructively through their scuffles with their parents (as well as through their observations of their *parents'* loving fights), so the more that you help them learn to argue productively, the better they'll be able to work things out in their own adult relationships.

But for arguments to be productive, they have to follow mutually established ground rules. In a moment of calm, when an argument is neither brewing nor just being recovered from, it's advisable to sit down together and come up with a set of guidelines that can be followed so that both parties learn something from their disputes.

Typically, the articles of your family's Geneva Convention may turn out to be fairly obvious and self-evident, such as avoiding interruptions, name-calling, obscenities, blaming, raised voices, storming out, or threats, while emphasizing reflective listening, empathy, I-statements, and mutual problem-solving. But the act of requesting his thoughts about how to promote civility in your discourse will automatically lead to more civil discourse. It's just another way of growing him up and inviting him to be a more responsible relational correspondent.

Remember, also, that the best way to resolve an argument and prevent needless repetitions is often just to follow up at a later point—with additional thoughts, with new ideas, with respect or contrition, with care and an expressed desire to stay connected despite the fallout. Many of the families that I work with never quite "close the loop" after a fractious dispute, which is akin to leaving an open abscess, one that is then extremely vulnerable to becoming reinfected.

UNDERSTAND YOUR ANGER

Anger is a complicated emotion, because it is often a cover for other emotions. Many times when we're feeling troubled or overwhelmed by sadness, grief, worry, or fear—our emotional circuit board sizzles out and we short-circuit into dependable, reliable anger. The anger that we experience *feels* real, and to some extent *is* real, but because it may be disguising other emotions that presaged our rage, it is not going to be an effective vehicle for conveying these emotions. Instead, we find that our words simply gush forth in a blistering torrent, rendering us unable to make sense of the many important feelings that we are actually feeling while antagonizing or injuring the individual whom we want and need to share them with.

The key is to peel away the layers of the emotional onion so that you are better able to see what lies at the core. Sometimes anger is simply anger, and completely legitimate, but often in the parent–young adult relationship a parent's anger is actually composed of other emotions. When we feel like we're making too many sacrifices for our child, we tend to get angry (with resentment). We also get angry when we worry about our child, or when we feel too depended upon (resentment again). And when young adults feel dependent, they get angry at the person on whom they're depending, which is often you.

Dissecting your anger into its numerous parts and identifying its sources will endow you with the capacity to distinguish between justified and unjustified anger, and prevent you from alienating your young adult with unwarranted attacks or scorching invective.

INSTEAD OF SAYING:

"I am *so* sick of your lazy, ungrateful attitude, the way you lay around the house not doing a thing while I'm at work all day and then you go out at night without even offering to help clean up."

TRY SOMETHING LIKE:

"Recently, I've been feeling taken advantage of. You seem to see our home as a free hotel where you can come and go as you please without helping out at all. I'm definitely angry about this, but I'm feeling worried, too—worried that you're not understanding how things really work, worried about how you'll do on your own once you're no longer living with us. And I guess there's some sadness and regret in there, too, as I think about how I might have contributed to your belief that you're entitled to live here—or anywhere—without contributing."

Even when your anger is, in fact, legitimate and not just masquerading for another emotion, it doesn't necessarily mean that your young adult has done something wrong, only that you did not get what you wanted. When you understand that your anger arises in the context of your unmet expectations, you'll be better able to express it with clarity, respect, and consideration, rather than through an aggressive rant or a fault-finding screed.

TAKE YOUR TIME

I've written in some of my other books about the Dark Side of the Moon phenomenon, one that often begins during adolescence but that can continue well into young adulthood. When an individual is heading around the Dark Side of the Moon, effective communication is blocked, but it doesn't mean that he's not going to eventually come around. It *does* mean, however, that you have to learn to abide these troubling periods of silence or emotional remoteness without overreacting or making things worse.

Technology can obviously make communication easier, but it can also make us that much more frustrated when it doesn't yield contact. You call and get voice mail but no return call, you email without response, you try texting but don't receive a reply, you try to "friend" your daughter on Facebook, but she ignores your request (as perhaps she should).

There are many reasons why the protection of the moon's Dark Side is sought. Some young adults are hesitant to share much with their parents because they don't want to worry them. Others, particularly those who are still living at home, or who are not yet that confident about their independent functioning, feel compelled to erect sturdy walls in an effort to reassure and convince themselves, and their parents, that they are now truly separate, autonomous beings. And those who have fought hard to establish their own territory may not want to risk making contact and being reeled back in by their family's gravitational pull (especially in a strongly centripetal family as discussed in Chapter Two).

It's important to maintain patience and not overreact, even when you are not getting the kind of response you would like. You may think "It's really not such a big deal for him to simply reply to a text or an email, or make a quick phone call; I'm not asking for a 30-minute conversation," but remember that part of his establishing independence entails his being able to set the terms of his relationship with you, and there often have to be periods of relative distance for your young adult to know how to establish the right level of closeness. Again, sometimes loving means releasing.

REMEMBER, YOU'RE (BOTH) ONLY HUMAN, AND FALLIBLE

Despite his bravado, his apparent certainty regarding all matters, and his lack of hesitancy to criticize you, many a young adult still idealizes his parents, which may leave him feeling ineffectual and diminished. With this in mind, it's often wise to share stories of your own struggles, even if these stories are painful ones to have to relive through the telling.

You are probably not proud of how you handled every single one of the crossroads and phases that you encountered during your own early adult years, but you deserve to share some of your more notable slips, trips, and bungles, both as a way of softening your own self-criticalness and as a way of buffeting your child against some of his own self-criticalness.

INSTEAD OF SAYING:

"You're not really handling things with a lot of maturity, I can tell you that. By the time I was your age, I was not only working full-time, but I was already engaged to your mom and saving money for our first house. I certainly wasn't busy trying to 'find myself' or figure out what I wanted to do with my life like you still are."

TRY SOMETHING LIKE:

"I may have been a little farther along than you professionally when I was your age, but I can tell you that I was pretty immature, too, and didn't have much of a grasp of relationships and how to make them work. I didn't always treat your mom with as much respect as I should have, and I didn't get along very well with my boss at my first job. It actually took me quite a while to figure some of those things out, and I wasn't always sure I was going to. But I hung in there and things eventually started to click, and I'm sure the same thing will happen for you if you hang in there, too."

MAINTAIN EQUANIMITY AND
DON'T PANIC (TOO OFTEN)

The numerous case examples that we have studied thus far make it clear that it is often difficult to predict ultimate outcomes based on several steps forward, sideways, or backward. Because of this, it is best to remain emotionally balanced because young adults are always "moving targets," and their lives will most likely continue to oscillate over time.

INSTEAD OF SAYING:

"It's just great that you're finishing your community college degree, so now it's time to decide where to complete your undergraduate studies, right?"

TRY SOMETHING LIKE:

"Now that you're finishing community college, what are some of your thoughts regarding your next move? Are you feeling any hesitancy about moving on from here?"

INSTEAD OF SAYING:

"Losing that job is certainly a bitter pill to swallow, you're stuck in a pretty deep hole right now, what with no income and no prospects for another job."

TRY SOMETHING LIKE:

"Losing a job, even one you weren't crazy about, is hard. On the other hand, it's an opportunity to move forward in some different ways. What are you thinking this will free you up to do?"

Also, keep in mind that while some young adults play their cards close to the vest and disclose very little of their angst to their parents, many tend to share generously only when they are in crisis mode, giving their parents a distorted view of their lives—distressingly detailed portraits of her at her worst, but only infrequent glimpses of her at her best.

One mother complained to me, "It seems like I only hear from my daughter when she's crying. She calls me and cries about how awful her boss is, she calls me and cries about how awful her boyfriend is. So I wind up figuring that she's a complete mess, that she's basically suicidal. But then I go on her Facebook page and I see all of these friendly, happy interactions with everyone else. And later on, when I ask her about whatever she was upset about, it, she acts like it was no big deal and wonders why I'm so worried. So I don't know which one is the real Elise and which one is the fake Elise."

Other young adults are prone to floating their half-baked ideas past their parents, not because they are necessarily convinced that these ideas are worth pursuing, but simply to elicit feedback, to see how they sound when they're given airtime. But don't panic: just because he's talking about moving in with his girlfriend doesn't mean that the two of them have already picked out an apartment and signed a lease. Just because she's considering withdrawing from college and working on an organic orchid farm in El Salvador doesn't mean that she's already bought her plane ticket and applied for her passport. Just because he wants to move to a state that legalized medical marijuana so that he can become a pot distributor doesn't mean that he's got his bags packed.

It's generally unwise to presume that what you actually hear about is the sum total of your young adult's thinking and to react anxiously to this misguided presumption. Maintain as calm a demeanor as possible, even in the face of prospects that might have you temporarily gasping for air, because the more you panic, the more likely that your young adult will panic and lose her powers of judgment (and maybe even lean toward doing the thing that freaks you out).

If you do lose your temper, as we are all liable to do, this can be neutralized by some good-natured words once you've reclaimed your perspective.

AFTER YOU'VE VENTED SOMETHING LIKE THIS:

"I can't believe you've wrecked the car! Now *I'll* have to drive you to work and if I'm late, my boss will kill me, and who knows when we'll get it back, and, meanwhile, if you lose *your* job, you lose your health insurance, and we can't get you back on my plan anymore! Plus, who knows if you'll even be able to *afford* car insurance now, your rates are going to skyrocket! This is a complete disaster!"

YOU CAN ALWAYS TRY:

"Look, neither of us wanted this to happen, but I'm glad you're okay, even though the car isn't. I guess we're going to have to muddle through unhappily for the next few weeks until things get sorted out, so we'd both better be on our best behavior for a while or we'll make each other miserable. Just remember, though—if I'm driving you to work in *my* car, it's *my* radio station we're listening to, not yours."

SIGNAL YOUR TURNS

Because family communication patterns have been in place for a long time, deviations from the norm may not always be noticed. So if you're going to implement some of the changes that we have been discussing, it's a good idea to let your child *know* that you're implementing them— to heighten his awareness of what is different—so that he doesn't miss out on them, and so that he's likely to display some positive deviations as well.

INSTEAD OF SAYING:

"So did you register for your LSAT's yet? You know the deadline is just a week away, and you missed the last deadline by a hair. Do you need any help filling out the registration form? Just let me know when you need my credit card . . ."

TRY SOMETHING LIKE:

"I'm aware that the LSAT deadline is just about here, and this is the point at which I usually tend to step in and start reminding you what to do. But I'm realizing that these decisions have to be your decisions, handled by you alone. So this is the last mention of this matter that I will be making . . . it's up to you how to proceed from here."

LISTEN

I generally conclude all of my lectures to parents—no matter what the topic—with this one-word piece of advice: *Listen*. We tend to associate communication with talking, but, in reality, listening is by far the most important component of communication—indeed, of any relationship—and it cannot be faked or forged. We instantly know when we are being listened to wholeheartedly, devotedly, respectfully—and when we are being listened to in a distracted, incomplete way.

Full-bodied listening is the greatest gift that we can offer to someone, and far surpasses any other relational attribute, any tactic or strategy. Our deepest wish as human beings is to be listened to attentively by those who matter to us. So if you come away from reading this book with nothing more than an unswerving commitment to being "all ears" for your young adult as you prepare for her departure from the nest, and if you commit yourself to allow the words "I'm not entirely sure—what do *you* think?" to guide your conversations, then I can promise you that it will definitely have been worth it.

"I am *here* for you"—the words that all parents want their children to understand and believe—will only mean something to the child if you also make it clear that "I *hear* you."

We have been looking at a wide spectrum of important tasks that need to be completed on both generations' part to successfully empty the nest. In our next chapter, we will examine several complicated family situations in greater detail to see how parent and young adult can combine their efforts to set the stage for liberation and transformation.

CHAPTER SIX

PREPARATION FOR
SEPARATION

PUTTING IT ALL INTO ACTION

No matter how intelligently and persistently we try to empty the nest, there will still be challenging and discouraging times.

Sometimes these are short-term crises or rough patches that test our patience as well as our love and require a reexamination of our family's history and structure so that we can break old, outmoded ways. At other times, a family finds it is facing a siege or blockade more than a crisis—a long-standing and seemingly intractable situation that resists all efforts to resolve the issue. In fact, these efforts at mediation, well-intentioned as they may be, sometimes cause the problem to harden or intensify, making every family member feel more and more hopeless. In the end, whether it's a crisis or blockade, the young adult starts to seem to everyone involved like a failure—a professional ne'er-do-well, a permanent black sheep—and while the family remains involved with him, it's often only in the most malfunctioning ways.

I see my efforts to usher families through their crises and blockades as akin to the initiation ceremonies developed by native cultures to ritualize an individual's movement across an important threshold. While my suggestions may appear counterintuitive and sometimes hard to put into practice, the ultimate goal is to spring the young adult free from childhood and his dependence on his family, as well as his family's dependence on him, and help them all to institute more freely functional lives.

In this chapter we will weave together what we have been discussing in the previous chapters by looking in greater depth at an assortment of vexing situations and viewing them through the lens of the family's spoken and unspoken rules.

In my experience as a clinician, I have never come across an individual who has created a significant family problem entirely by him- or herself. It always takes the contributions of at least two (and usually more) family members to create the knottiest difficulties.

Every organization operates by a certain set of rules, and a family, which is the most intimate and powerful organization that we will ever be a part of, is no exception. While most families generally create rules that lead to good feelings and growth-promoting experiences for all of their members, sometimes family rules inadvertently cause unhappiness and inhibit growth while making their members practically unable to connect amicably with other family members.

The interesting thing that I have noticed in my consultation room is that it is generally impossible for people to not follow rules, even though, as we have observed, sometimes these rules are confusing or upsetting. In fact, children tend to be the most profoundly affected when the family's rule structure is severely problematic because nobody can figure out how to change the rules for the better.

When it comes to the launching stage of parenthood, typical rule-based problems tend to fall into one or more of the following categories:

- The rules are no longer appropriate for the developmental stage of the young adult ("Even though you're in college, you're still living with us, so you need to be home by 6:30 every evening for family dinner").

- The rules are not clearly stated and are left vague and open-ended ("You need to show some respect around here" without defining what "respect" is).
- The rules are not enforced, or there is no clear consequence established for when a rule is broken ("I'll be very upset with you if I find out that you're still smoking pot").
- A stated rule conflicts with an unstated rule, one usually being more explicit than the other, making it impossible for the young adult to follow rules without simultaneously breaking rules (Overt rule: "You must learn to get yourself up in the morning, using your own alarm clock rather than relying on me." Covert rule: "You must allow me to continue to feel relevant as a parent, so please ignore your alarm clock so that I am forced to wake you up each morning").

Young adults who are having the hardest time embarking on a successful departure may appear to be breaking the most explicit family rules—such as the rule that one must study hard or avoid drugs or finish college or find a job—but in most cases they are simply trying to protest or renegotiate rules that do not effectively address who they are or the predicament they find themselves in. They may be trying desperately to navigate between incompatible rules, a process that leaves them mired in motivational quandries, feeling stuck and hopelessly frustrated.

While it might seem odd in these situations to imagine that exasperating young adult children are actually "following the rules," that their negative behavior actually has a cooperative quality to it, that, indeed, is almost always the case.

So the trick lies not simply in asking him to not follow rules, but in changing the rules and making them more adaptive to the young person's needs. When we adjust the rules, we will notice a behavioral change, too.

Here is my blueprint for helping idling young adults get into gear:

1. Define the problem as one that results from counterproductive rules.
2. Examine the counterproductive rule and try to revise it so that it is more aligned with the young adult's needs at this point in his development.
3. Develop a plan to make it clear to the young adult that the rules are changing.
4. Observe the ways in which the young adult's behavior does or doesn't change in response to the change in family rules.
5. Assess progress: if positive changes result, carry on; if not, revise the plan and make a different modification of the counterproductive rule (or rules).

Let's now look at five different families and examine how changing the rules, and rule-based behavior, can get young adults unstuck and on their way.

COUNTERPRODUCTIVE RULE: WOMEN MUST PUT THE NEEDS OF OTHERS BEFORE THEMSELVES

Susan had been upset for quite some time with her 20-year-old daughter, Cecelia, for constantly making sacrifices that benefited Cecelia's 22-year-old, boyfriend, Alex. Most recently, Cecelia had put her job at a child care center in jeopardy by frequently arriving late after dropping Alex off at work while his car was in the repair shop following an accident. Transporting Alex wouldn't necessarily have to make Cecilia late for work, except that he was so slow to get moving in the morning that when she swung by to get him, he was rarely ready to go.

When Susan heard that Cecelia might lose her job—one that was hard to find and truly enjoyable—she became incensed and told her daughter that she simply had to leave for work when it was time to leave, whether Alex was ready or not.

"But then Alex might lose his job if he doesn't get to work," Cecelia countered.

"I don't care whether Alex loses his job or not—*you're* going to lose *your* job. You're the one I'm worried about here, not Alex," Susan replied with exasperation.

"You don't worry about Alex because you don't care about Alex. If you want me to break up with him, say so. Just stop making believe that this has to do with your being worried about my keeping my job."

Clearly, Susan was worried about Cecelia's tendency to make inappropriate sacrifices for her irresponsible boyfriend. But questioning Cecelia's judgment and the basis for her relationship with Alex was doing nothing but putting her daughter on guard and getting them off track.

In speaking with Susan, I learned that she, too, had a long history of making sacrifices for others. As the eldest of four with a depressed mother and a workaholic father, she had functioned as the de facto caregiver for her three younger siblings. Her first marriage, to Cecelia's father, Ralph, ended in a divorce due to his drinking. But she eventually found the internal strength and external support required to extricate herself from her marriage. She acknowledged the numerous self-sacrificing behaviors she had designed to rescue Ralph from the consequences of his drinking, such as calling in sick for him when he was too drunk to get to work.

Susan had remarried three years before the present occasion to a much healthier husband, Antonio, who was caring and supportive. Antonio also played a paternal role with Cecelia, and she was growing to trust him.

As Susan and I discussed her family of origin, I learned that Susan's own mother, Ruth, had been raised by an alcoholic mother, and that Ruth, too, had been a "parental child," becoming hyper-responsible for keeping an eye on younger siblings as well as her mother's drinking. So there was clearly a long and enduring legacy of female self-sacrifice in this family, one that Susan was not happy about acknowledging but that was filtering down through the generational strata nonetheless.

With this history in mind, I suggested that Susan approach Cecelia through what they had in common, rather than through judgment and criticism.

"I don't want her to repeat the pattern that I fell into, and that her grandmother fell into, too," Susan worried.

"But talking to her about this history might help her to see things differently, which might then enable her to begin to behave differently."

"But, honestly, I'm ashamed of so much of what I did. I'm embarrassed to tell her how I covered for her father, I'm embarrassed by how much I put up with, how much I tolerated. . . . I've always tried to protect her from this."

"I'm not saying it was unwise for you to have protected her when she was younger. But she's at a more advanced point in her development now, and, with this in mind, she needs more advanced information and perspective. She deserves to know how you used to cope with your childhood and with her father's drinking, even if it wasn't always in the most adaptive way. That will help her to appreciate how you ultimately came to cope in a healthier way, which in turn will make it more likely that she'll do the same. You might begin by letting her know more about what her grandmother was up against and what you were up against, and how powerful those lessons of female self-sacrifice grew to be. You could then suggest to her that perhaps she's in the midst of deciding the extent to which she's going to fulfill that legacy herself. You might simply leave her with a question, like 'Does the long history of females sacrificing their growth and ambition for the sake of men in our family make you more or less likely to do the same?'"

"And then she'll stop rescuing Alex and being late for work?"

"It might not be that simple and it might not be that immediate. But at least you'll have the opportunity to open up the conversation in a way that enables her to look at herself and her decisions in a new light, and maybe turn over a new leaf. And that will ultimately work to her advantage better than either sacrificing herself on the altar of her boyfriend's immaturity, or getting annoyed with you, which are the two options to which she is limiting herself."

Susan agreed to give this a try, and reported back to me that they had had a very touching and revealing conversation. Cecelia knew little of what Susan had to tell her about her family history, and made it clear that she had a fresh appreciation for her mother's courage.

"She told me that she had no idea how hard it must have been for me, and that she wished I had told her more about this when she was younger. Here I was feeling ashamed and embarrassed about how I lived, but my daughter found it inspiring that I was able to get out of that hellhole and make a better life for myself. In fact, she said that she found herself wanting to do the same thing for herself, wanting to be with someone like Antonio, and wondering if Alex was ever going to fit that bill.

"It was a relief for me to hear how frustrated she gets with him, although it was also upsetting to hear about some of the other details about their relationship, which reminded me way too much of my marriage to her father. But you were right, the conversation was completely different than me telling her to stop picking Alex up and her telling me that I didn't understand."

"She's probably more ambivalent about Alex than she lets on," I proposed. "That's one of the reasons she fights with you: it's easier for her to assign to you the role of not liking Alex because she's too uncomfortable to handle it herself. That way she's free to play the liking-Alex role and ignore some of her fears and misgivings about the relationship."

When Susan returned two weeks later for a follow-up, she told me that Cecelia had, on her own, laid down the law with Alex and made it clear that she was not going to imperil her job anymore, and that if he wasn't ready on time, she'd be heading off to work without him. Alex hit the ceiling and told Cecelia that he didn't need her in his life if she couldn't be "supportive," prompting Cecelia to suggest that maybe it was time to take a break from their relationship.

In this family, the counterproductive (and unstated) rule was, "Women must always put others before themselves." When Susan helped Cecelia change that rule, and create a larger context within which to understand her behavior, Cecelia was ultimately able to change her behavior for the better.

COUNTERPRODUCTIVE RULE: WE MUST PROTECT OUR SON FROM DEPRESSION

Ken, the father of Duane, a high school senior, couldn't step back from his son's college application process. Since August, he had been hectoring Duane constantly about the need to download applications, get teacher recommendations, finish his essays, and register for a final SAT II exam, but all to no avail. In fact, as is often the case in situations like this, the more he pushed, the less Duane did. Meanwhile, the tension level at home was escalating rapidly, with arguments breaking out almost every night. The entire process had ground to a quarrelsome halt.

"Here it is November, almost Thanksgiving," Ken complained, "and he still hasn't gotten anything moving. Many applications are due December 1, and he doesn't have a single one completed. He was supposed to have worked with a tutor all summer on his essays, but he found one way or another to avoid it, so now we're in a big hole."

It was interesting to hear his use of the word "we" when he talked about being in a hole. Ken was apparently struggling with this as much, if not more than, Duane.

"I know that he'll probably eventually go to college, and it's not like I'm pressuring him to go to any particular school. But the biggest problem is that if he doesn't get in anywhere, he's going to have an awful time next August when all of his friends go away to *their* colleges and leave him behind.

"Duane's always had a tendency toward depression, and for all of his buddies to ship out and leave him behind would be the absolute worst thing for him. I don't care if he works instead of going away to college. I don't care if he goes to community college instead of going away to college. But I don't want him to fall into a major depression, and if he gets these applications in, then at least he has the option of going somewhere and not feeling deserted."

Ken's fears were legitimate ones: I learned that Duane had gotten seriously depressed on two different occasions, once in ninth grade and once in eleventh, and had spoken about taking his life and suggested the world being better off without him. Each time, he received psychological treatment, and his bleakness gradually lifted, but Ken had certainly not forgotten those harrowing periods, and his fears for his son were understandably great. At the same time, it was hard not to imagine what Duane was thinking: after going through such dark tunnels on two separate occasions, how could he not be afraid of a relapse, especially the possibility of that relapse occurring while he was living away from home for the first time?

So while Ken was thinking that the best way to prevent a depressive episode would be to get Duane to leave home at the same time his peers did, Duane was probably thinking that the best way to prevent a third depressive episode would be to avoid making any potentially destabilizing changes or departures in the coming months.

This hypothesis was borne out when I met with Duane. While he didn't come out and say, "I'm too scared to go away to college, and too ashamed of myself to admit this, so I'll just sidestep the whole process," his overall perspective seemed to support this. He spoke vividly about how painful and embarrassing his depressive episodes had been. He also talked about how important it was for him to make his parents proud of him, which probably diminished the likelihood that he could share his ambivalence with them, ambivalence that was creating his internal stalemate. I mentioned this outlook to Ken and his wife, Marjorie, who both understood, yet were still perplexed.

"We know that it's got to be scary for him, but all we're asking him to do is to apply to these colleges. We're not asking him to commit to going, we just want him to have that option, because, who knows, nine months from now, when it's August, he may be feeling fine and wondering why he didn't create a doorway for himself," Marjorie emphasized.

"But it seems clear that your current strategy—to lean on him more and more heavily—is not working. You are right, one of the risks of backing off is nothing happening. But you are running some bigger risks right now, because if you keep pushing, there are several likely outcomes. He's either going to continue defying you, in which case he's less, rather than more, likely to get his applications in on time. Or he's going to comply and complete some applications, but he'll do so in a way that doesn't present him in the best possible light, diminishing the likelihood that he'll get admitted anywhere. Or, he's going to complete some applications and get admitted somewhere, but feel unprepared to go since it was never fully self-endorsed. In that case, he may not make a positive adjustment to college, and, as a result, he will feel like a failure and once again be highly vulnerable to becoming depressed."

"So what do we do?" Marjorie asked.

"I believe the best thing for you to do is to leave it entirely in his hands. You need to make it clear that applying to college is entirely up to him. And you should all remember it's not a permanent or irreversible decision. Should he regret it when many of his friends are leaving home, that will probably prompt him to get moving with his applications for the following year. And there are certainly many productive things that he can be doing if he doesn't go away to college that will keep him engaged with the world and in contact with like-minded peers. So it's not like it has to be a wasted, depression-filled year.

"And one other thing: while there's no question that it's getting late, it's not too late. He still has several weeks to do what needs to be done, and he wouldn't be the first high school senior I've worked with who waited until the last minute, or even beyond, and still managed to create some college possibilities. There's a collective momentum among his classmates right now that may sweep him up at the eleventh hour and push him to take care of business."

"Interesting," Ken noted, "because that's sort of what happened with driving. Duane had no interest in getting his license, but we thought that once his friends starting driving, that would get him motivated. It didn't, though, and then we found ourselves wondering if he'd ever get his license. But then—and I remember the day distinctly—we were sitting at dinner, just talking about random stuff, and all of a sudden his sister, Rhonda, blurted out, 'Oh my God, I can get my learner's permit in less than six months!'

"And I swear to you, the very next day Duane came to me and asked if we could head over to the Motor Vehicle Administration to get his learner's permit. It was one thing for his friends to be driving before him, but the thought of his younger sister driving before him was apparently too much for him to bear. And he got his permit, got his driving hours, and got his license without our having to do anything."

With this framework in mind, Ken and Marjorie spoke to Duane about their decision to back off. They saw no change in his behavior for several weeks, which made it even harder for them to stay on the periphery, but then, in the middle of December, he presented to them some parent forms that needed to be completed for a couple of four-year, in-state colleges, and asked for their credit card number so that he could register for an SAT II exam. They also learned that not only had he quietly gotten to work filling out two applications, but that he had asked his English teacher for help editing the essays that he had written.

In this family, the counterproductive rule was "Everything must be done to protect Duane from the possibility of depression." Once Ken and Marjorie were able to change this rule, placing the responsibility for the college application process in their son's hands, Duane was able to follow through on his own, knowing that it was his decision, rather than theirs. Their faith in him, which he quickly began to incorporate as his own, would turn out to be a much more effective antidepressant than trying in vain to push and pull him through the college application gauntlet.

COUNTERPRODUCTIVE RULE: NOT KNOWING YOUR MOTHER IS BETTER THAN KNOWING AN ABSENT MOTHER

Twenty-year-old Melissa had spent the last two years of her life moving in and out of her parents' home. She would meet a guy, usually at least several years older than her, quickly fall in love and shack up with him, and then return in several months once the relationship imploded, as would inevitably happen. Not surprisingly, Melissa had not made much progress cultivating her own future, so invested did she become in this sequence of marginal men. Aside from a part-time job in retail and a few community college credits, she had little on her resume.

Melissa's early years had been difficult and unstable. Her mother, Jeanne, had left her and her younger brother with her father, Mark, when she was three and her brother was just a baby, and Jeanne had remained an inconsistent part of Melissa's life, going through phases of contacting her and visiting her regularly, and then disappearing for months at a time, usually because she had become involved with someone. It was striking how closely Melissa was replicating her mother's destructive pattern of overly intense and then quickly dissolving relationships.

Mark had struggled to provide a solid foundation for his daughter— he raised her by himself for nine years after Jeanne left him, until Melissa was 12, and then he met and married Dina, who had two younger children of her own from a previous marriage. Dina became a caring and involved stepmother to Melissa and her brother, but there had still been many years during which Melissa was effectively on her own, without a reliable mother, and with a father who had to work full-time to make ends meet.

Mark initially contacted me because he was concerned about Melissa and his inability to help her get some momentum.

"I hate to say this, but she's turning out to be just like her mother, and that's the last thing that I want, and probably the last thing that Melissa wants as well. But I can't seem to talk her out of it. Worse, she doesn't even seem to acknowledge how similar they are. I don't understand why she doesn't take a different path. Doesn't she see how much better her stepmother's life is than her mother's?"

"I'm sure she does, but let's remember, she's still her mother's daughter and still has some loyalty to her. "

"Loyalty?! To her mother?!" Mark exclaimed. "Her mother's never been loyal to her, so why should Melissa bother being loyal to her mother?"

"I know that it doesn't make sense, but some part of us is always loyal to the person who gives birth to us. After all, we wouldn't exist unless that person did give birth to us."

"But she must see that this sort of loyalty to her mother is going to make for a very miserable life."

"I suspect she does, but her vision is probably blurred by her grief. It is impossible to overestimate how painful it is to have your own mother abandon you, and the only way left for Melissa to connect to her mother is to display loyalty to her by being like her in some way. And the most obvious way for Melissa to be like her mother is to copy her unhealthy, unstable relationships with men. That is how she keeps her mother close and is able to see herself as a good daughter. What we have to do is help her find a different way of connecting with her mother, one that doesn't handicap her to such a large extent."

"So how do we do this?"

I explained that the most effective way would be to provide Melissa with some other aspect of her mother that she could connect with and identify with, something that would be healthier and more positive.

"Well, that's going to be a problem," said Mark. "This is a woman who abandoned her own children for months and years at a time, who, as far as I can tell, has never held a steady job, who doesn't even talk to *her* mother."

"But you were married to her, which means that you must have courted her, and if you courted her, you must have been attracted to her in some ways—otherwise you wouldn't have married her."

"I don't think I can even remember why I was drawn to her."

"But that's what I want you to think about. As upset and embarrassed about your relationship with Jeanne as you may be, even after all these years, I want you to go back in time and think about what it was that drew you to her. It's extremely important that you do this because what you come up with will be what enables Melissa to begin moving herself forward. While Melissa has had you, she hasn't had her mother, her fellow female role model. So that's why you have to help her to create, even retroactively, a healthier image of her mother."

A few weeks later, Mark returned with some thoughts and memories.

"You are right, while Jeanne and I met when we were too young, she did have some positive qualities that I liked. For one thing, she was very pretty, as is Melissa. For another thing, she was quite creative: her artwork was always on display at our high school, and she went to a trade school for graphic arts after high school, before we were married. And she was pretty involved with the youth group at our church. She was one of the leaders there, and people really looked up to her."

"How much of this does Melissa know?" I inquired.

He chuckled. "Probably none of it. Although I do remember that Melissa used to like sitting and drawing with her mother. That was probably the only time that Jeanne was a true mother to her. They used to spread out on the floor and Jeanne loved watching Melissa scribble."

Mark paused, and his eyes reddened. "How did things turn out so terribly? How do we make such a mess out of our lives?"

"I don't have a simple answer for that, Mark, but we can do what we can to give Melissa some opportunities that her mother was never able to take advantage of. I'd like you to share this information with Melissa, fill in the details of her empty portrait of her mother, and let's see how she responds."

Mark showed up for his next appointment and told me how it went.

"It was the strangest thing. I started by saying that I thought that it might be important for her to know more about who her mother was, and began by describing her mother's artistic abilities. At that moment she dashed up to her room and came right back with a notebook that I had never seen before. She opened it up and it was a series of pictures, page after page, of a woman. And the woman, she told me, was her mother. 'Whenever I would get lonely for Mom, I would draw a picture of her.'

"Here she had been keeping this artistic journal of her mother who was, in fact, very artistic, and it just blew me away. And some of the pictures were sad-looking and some were happy-looking, some were quite beautiful and some were quite ugly. It's like she was trying to capture all of the different facets of her mother . . . "

"And all of her different feelings about her mother, too," I added.

"I guess you're right, the happy feelings, the sad feelings, the nice feelings, the ugly feelings. It was all right there in the notebook. But what was amazing was that she didn't really know that her mother was artistic, and when I was telling her about her and her mother sitting on the floor drawing together she started crying."

"Just like you did when you recalled that scene," I reminded him.

"Just like I did," he agreed, his eyes brimming with tears. He paused to regroup.

"And then we started talking about her life and where she had been and where she was going. She told me that she really wanted to get into fashion and design, that one of the only things she liked about her job was the one time she had been asked to decorate the store window, and how pleased everyone was with her work. So we thought about how to pursue that, and she brought her laptop down and we started looking at some fashion institutes for her to study at. It's like she suddenly awoke!"

"She awoke because you gave her a reason to wake up. How difficult it must have been for her to feel like the only way to be a good daughter was to follow her mother's troubled roads. And what a tremendous relief it must have been for her to know that she could be a good daughter in a way that worked to her advantage, by being creative rather than self-destructive. You gave her a great gift by helping her to compose a broader, more detailed portrayal of her mother."

In this family, the counterproductive rule was, "Melissa must be protected from any identification with her birth mother." Once Mark broke this rule and helped his daughter find a way to identify more positively with her missing parent, she got out of her rut and started moving forward.

COUNTERPRODUCTIVE RULE: DON'T TELL YOUR CHILD WHAT YOU REALLY FEEL

Sometimes what holds a young adult back is not just a lack of self-confidence, but a certain amount of shame, a stubborn belief that he doesn't deserve to thrust himself forward into the world.

Wayne had entered community college four years earlier, planning on obtaining his associate's degree in two years, and then transferring to a four-year college to pursue his interest in musical composition. While he had done decently in his first two semesters, his academic progress had become much more erratic over the past three years: he would register for four or five classes, drop one or two by midsemester, and often fail at least one of the classes that he had intended to complete. Though he had finished eight courses during his first year, he had finished a grand total of six in the following three years.

Puzzled by his persistent lack of progress, he met with me at the behest of his parents. During our second session, Wayne reluctantly disclosed to me that he was gay. His experience coming out had not been traumatic, at least not thus far. He first told his older sister, with whom he had always shared a warm and supportive relationship, and then his parents, who responded without obvious shock or displeasure. His mother even began to get involved in the local gay community, attending PFLAG (Parents, Families, and Friends of Lesbians and Gays) meetings and making herself available to fellow parents of gay and lesbian adolescents.

Toward the end of his high school years, Wayne began coming out to a few of his close friends as well, and had even started dating a young man whom he had gotten to know online. While the relationship did not endure for very long and ended in heartbreak, he still appeared to be further along in defining a healthy sexual identity than many gay young adults. Nevertheless, he also appeared to be burdened by a good amount of shame and embarrassment. For example, the year before, on a Mother's Day card, he had written a short poem for his mother, Shayla:

You've always loved me, you've always been great,
Even though I'll never be straight

And that same year, for Father's Day, he composed the following and gave it to Donell, his father:

You've understood what it means to be gay
Though I won't be the son you wanted to raise

Evidently, despite having made a very positive adjustment to being gay, Wayne was still carrying a significant amount of self-loathing. With this in mind, we began speculating about his lack of academic progress, considering some possibilities while ruling out others.

"I suppose we can rule out the possibility of your being over-matched academically, since you had a solid first year of college," I opined.

"That's what I can't figure out. I start each semester off like gang-busters, and feel like I've got everything under control, and then all of a sudden I'm falling behind, dropping classes, and completely lost."

"So there must be something holding you back. Do you have any idea what it is?"

"Not really. I mean, I really want to move on to a four-year college. I've just gotta get my act together and nail these last few classes."

"What thought have you given to what your life will be like once you're no longer living at home?

"I don't know ... I guess I'm looking forward to it. I mean, my parents are great, but it's not a whole lot of fun living at home. They're pretty cool about my coming and going, but I still have to let them know when I'm leaving and when I'm back. Feels a little odd, being that I'm almost 21 already."

"What have you thought about how you'll handle being gay when you're living more independently?"

Here Wayne stopped, twisting a strand of his hair while mulling this over.

"I don't know, really. I've visited the website of the college I'd like to transfer to if I ever finish this degree, and they have a fairly active gay community, with a lot of resources ..." His voice trailed off.

"That sounds good, but you sound sort of hesitant."

"I guess I am. Here's what it is—as long as I'm living at home, I don't really have to live like I'm gay. My parents know, a few friends know, I've dated a bit, but that's about it. It's like I'm practicing being gay, but not really gay. When I think about going to college, though, I realize that I can actually live like I'm gay—spend my time with other gays, date, hopefully fall in love. It will be the real thing, and I'm just not sure I'm ready for that."

Wayne was gradually revealing to himself why he might have been disrupting his own progress: if he were to work up to his intellectual potential and finish community college, then he'd be forced to confront his sexual identity more vividly than he had ever had to before. The prospect of this confrontation wasn't one that he was confident he wanted to take on.

With this hypothesis in mind, we spent a few sessions discussing what it would be like to take some further strides toward a fuller acknowledgment of being gay. At one point he confessed that as long as he was living at home, he believed (irrationally, he knew) that he might be able to "turn things around" and somehow magically wind up straight. But once he left home, in his mind, the die was cast, and there was no longer any going back. No wonder he had gone to such great pains to academically disable himself.

With his ambivalence in mind, I suggested that Wayne visit the college he had in mind and make an appointment with one of the deans who was in charge of gay campus life, and contact a few of the students who were willing to be resources for prospective gay students.

Wayne followed through on these assignments, and came back with a much more lucid frame of mind. The dean, who was also gay, had been very helpful, and they'd had an in-depth conversation not only about gay life on campus, but about gay life in general. He also hit it off with one of the student counselors whom he had gotten in touch with, and their friendship blossomed in the ensuing months. The revolutionary thought that began to occur to him was that moving ahead with his life might, in actuality, help him to feel more positive about being gay.

I also scheduled a couple of family sessions and brought Wayne's parents, Donell and Shayla, into the discussion. I couldn't get Wayne's self-deprecating Mother's Day and Father's Day poems out of my mind, and wondered if they reflected some hidden parental disenchantment with his sexual orientation.

Shayla maintained that the fact that Wayne was gay created little distress for her. "Honestly, I think it's harder being African American than being gay. You don't automatically see that someone's gay, certainly not someone like Wayne... but you do automatically see someone's skin color, and when your skin color is black, then you have to deal with all of the prejudicial nonsense associated with that."

Donell, however, unlike his upbeat wife, revealed some aggravation. "Look, I love Wayne, and it's not that I'm homophobic or anything, but the fact that he's black and gay is going to make his life hell. One or the other is hard enough, but both? So it's not that I want to talk him out of it, but I sure wish he would have an easier lot in life, and it's not going to be easy to be on the receiving end of so much 'prejudicial nonsense,' as my wife puts it. I have not wanted to say any of this, because I know how hard it is for Wayne, but I really can't keep it to myself any longer."

It was not surprising that Donell had concerns about Wayne's life as a gay black man, but the honesty with which he spoke had a tremendous impact on his son. Rather than making him feel worse, as Donell had feared it might, it actually made Wayne feel better:

"Dad, you and Mom have been great. You didn't even bat an eye when I came out, and you've been unbelievably supportive. But I've always known that this wasn't your wish, so it's a relief to hear you say what you've said. It's like you see me as an adult, as someone who's man enough to take it, man enough to be gay without having to be ashamed of it. That means a lot to me."

Rather than hurting Wayne, Donell's candor actually freed his son to continue to come to terms with being gay, and he was then able to remove some of the self-imposed roadblocks to his progress. He entered what turned out to be his final semester of community college, passed all four of his classes, applied to the university and was admitted. When his father allowed himself to break the rule of "I mustn't tell my son what I really feel," Wayne was able to understand more about why he was holding himself back, which allowed him to move forward.

COUNTERPRODUCTIVE RULE: THE MOTHER MUST PROVIDE FOR ALL OF HER CHILD'S NEEDS

Olga called me because of the increasingly high tension level in her house once her son, Dmitri, returned home after college. Dmitri appeared to be trying to find a full-time job and insisted that he wanted to earn enough money to move out on his own. During this interim period, however, which had now been going on for almost a year, he was driving his mother crazy with his many demands, while sporadically working on weekends for a caterer.

"He became a vegan while he was away at college, plus he's a real 'green freak,' so he's constantly going around pointing out what we can do differently to be more ecologically sound. And it's not that I'm averse to being ecologically sound, but I don't need my 21-year-old son marching around the house issuing orders for how I'm supposed to be doing things."

"What are some of his orders?"

"Some I'm really okay with, like replacing our light bulbs with the new energy-efficient ones—that's simple enough. A new water filter for the kitchen sink? That's alright, too. But it doesn't end there. He wants *me* to become vegan, which I'm not going to do, and some of the things he's talking about are expensive, like replacing all of our windows with better-insulated ones. Listen, if he was paying for all of these things, that'd be fine by me, but all he does is tell me what I should be doing while quoting dire statistics about greenhouse gases and global warming."

"What are you asking of him, now that he's back to living at home?"

"Not much, really. I ask him to help with the dishes, and to keep his bedroom and bathroom clean. He does the dishes, but, honestly, for all of his interest in being ecologically sound, his bedroom and bathroom are disgusting. He doesn't clean up at all; there's got to be all kinds of things growing in those rooms. He appears to be using books as plates and his clothes as napkins."

"Does he pay rent?"

"How can I ask him to pay rent? He doesn't even have a regular job, and his catering gig is very intermittent. He majored in political science, and, let's be honest here, that's not going to get him very far, not in this economy. I believe that things are pretty slim out there when it comes to young experts in kremlinology."

"But he could try to find a better or more substantial part-time job or two while he's looking for full-time work in his field, right? You said that he's been home for almost a year, now. That's a long time to only be working a few days a month."

"I guess you're right. But, basically I just want him to get off my back while he's living here, and get a job and move out. I'm sure he wants to move on, as well."

"What other expenses of his do you cover?"

"His cell phone—I've always kept him on my plan. And his car insurance. And of course health insurance. And, of course, I buy all the food, too."

"So is there anything that he's contributing to the upkeep or functioning of the house?"

Olga was silent for a moment. "I suppose not," she said, almost surprised by her answer.

As I listened, everything seemed topsy-turvy in this family. Fifty-four-year-old Olga, who worked full-time as a bank teller and had faithfully paid the mortgage by herself for over twenty years, was being brazenly criticized and ordered about by her underemployed 21-year-old son, whose every need she fulfilled. Not only was this unpleasant for her, but it didn't seem to be spurring any progress on Dmitri's part, who sounded to me a little too comfortably ensconced in this inverted situation.

To make things easier for Olga, and to spring Dmitri forward, this cushy arrangement would have to be disrupted. I began by suggesting to her that she establish a base rent that Dmitri would have to come up with, and proposed that if he didn't have the money, he would have to earn his keep through some kind of labor on her behalf—yard work, painting the basement, any chore that was not part of her baseline expectations for him. Also, he was to be put in charge of setting up his own cell phone account.

"And what if he doesn't pay the rent or perform the chores?" she asked apprehensively.

"You have to establish this as more of a landlord-tenant relationship than a mother-son relationship. Otherwise, he'll continue to exploit you, and there will be little motivation for him to get moving with his life."

"So what should I do if he doesn't pay the rent or perform the chores?"

"What would a landlord do?"

"A landlord would kick him out! Are you saying I should kick my own son out of his house?"

"Remember that it's *your* house, not his. Who pays the mortgage? Remember also that you're giving him plenty of room to maneuver here. You're telling him he can either pay you in cash or in labor, while many landlords would insist on the former only. But you're not preparing him for real life unless you establish a more realistic arrangement here at home. He's going to have to learn how to pay rent or handle a mortgage at some point, so he might as well learn while he's living with you."

"I just can't see him agreeing to this."

"But he doesn't have to agree to it. You're the landlord, he's the tenant. He's not in a position to dictate the terms of the lease. You're the one who owns the property, not him."

Olga puzzled over this, mulling over the possibility that she had more power here than she had originally thought.

"I can do that?"

"Of course you can do that. And not only can you do that, but it'll be better for both of you if you do. You'll feel less resentful and annoyed, and he'll start to acquire some self-respect, which he desperately needs right now. He certainly can't be very proud of himself, a college graduate hanging around the house all day and cleaning up after other people's parties on the weekend. That's probably one of the reasons he keeps nagging you about being more green. Perhaps if he was earning more money and had more 'green' in his pocket, he wouldn't be bugging you so much about your ecological correctness."

Olga returned after laying things out for Dmitri, but informed me that, from her vantage point, their discussion had gone terribly.

"He was outraged. How dare I ask my own son for rent? he exclaimed. What kind of mother would charge her own son to live in her own house? he shouted. He was stomping around the kitchen, and I wound up going to my room just to get away from him."

"I understand that this wasn't a very serene encounter," I said, "but I'm not sure why you think it went so badly. You laid out the terms of the agreement, and he wasn't happy with them. But what's more important than his getting over his anger is his getting on with his life. If he is temporarily upset with your insistence that he uphold his end of the bargain, that's a small price to pay if the result is his ultimate independence. And, just so you know, in my experience, young adults are a lot less angry with their parents when they are less dependent on them. What you're doing here is not increasing the likelihood that he'll be angry with you over time, but actually diminishing it."

Olga agreed to hold her ground with Dmitri, which wasn't easy, especially because he cleverly implemented the "silent treatment," knowing this would be difficult for her to handle. As hard as it was for her to have to listen to his disapproval of her home's ecosystem, it was even harder for her to not have anything to listen to. But she didn't yield, and changes slowly came about. He went out and got his own cell phone after she canceled his service, and grumpily handed over his $50 monthly rent after one of his Saturday night catering gigs. She missed their conversations—there had been some times, if he wasn't disparaging her, when they had enjoyed chatting about politics—but she did take note of the fact that he was following through and making progress.

His enforcement of the silent treatment gradually softened, and in less than a month's time, Dmitri came home and proudly announced that he had gotten a full-time job, one that didn't pay very well but that blended his interests, working for a lobbying group in Washington, D.C., that promoted environmental causes. He told Olga that he would like to continue living at home for the time being and commuting, which she agreed to. However, clearly having gotten the hang of things, she made it clear to him that now that he was making more money, she'd be doubling his rent and asking him to cover at least half of his car insurance. This time Dmitri respectfully agreed, and slowly began to engage on more friendly terms with his mother.

In this family, the counterproductive rule was that "Once a son returns home, he is to be welcomed without any expectations or limits." Olga's willingness to raise her expectations, set limits, and risk the attendant (and temporary) loss of affection was apparently all it took to rock Dmitri out of his rut and get him back on the road to self-reliance.

❧ ☙

Changing the family rules that you have thoughtfully established and abided by for many years is a difficult enterprise, but one that is an essential component of successfully launching your young adult. It requires you to assess, with as much objectivity and clarity as possible, whether the rules are supporting or thwarting your child's progress at this stage in his development. But when parents don't fall asleep at the wheel and instead stay awake and make the necessary revisions to family rules—and if they are patient and persistent enough to enforce the changed rules—the invariable result is the enhanced growth and freedom that both generations deserve to take delight in.

CHAPTER SEVEN

ENDURING INTIMACY

YOUR MARRIAGE AT THE LAUNCHING PHASE

"[Love] no longer unfolds spontaneously according to its unknown laws in a heart wondrously awed and captivated. Now we tinker with it, we push and distort it with the help of memory and suggestion. When we recognize one of its symptoms, we remember others and thus give love a new lease."

—*Marcel Proust*

A Roz Chast cartoon depicts a husband and wife, each antagonistically seated on opposite ends of a couch, staring angrily into space. The caption: "Not Quite Empty-Enough-Nest Syndrome." You may be preparing to empty the nest of your children, but if you're still married, the nest will not be completely emptied: what remains behind, for better or for worse, is the spousal relationship that was cemented together by the very children who are now in the process of figuring out how to depart. While we tend, as mothers and fathers, to pay very careful attention to how our child-rearing behaviors affect our children's development, we tend to minimize or even ignore how our marital behaviors affect our children's development and the interaction between our lives as couples and as parents.

As you have surely observed in some of the case examples that we have explored thus far, the relationship between a husband and wife can have an enormously positive or negative impact on a young adult's efforts to separate and become self-sufficient. What we also want to pay attention to is the ways in which the young adult's liberation can in return promote the parents' liberation. We will tackle the issue of individual growth at midlife in our next chapter, but for now let's turn our attention to how marital growth occurs in this time period.

The introduction of a child always illuminates the underlying weaknesses of a couple's relationship—anything from conflicts with in-laws to sexual tension, from asymmetrical divisions of labor to radically opposed child-rearing approaches. Sometimes couples respond positively to the challenge and use parenthood to shore up their vulnerabilities and significantly upgrade their relationship. Sometimes, though, the presence of a child distracts couples from addressing their marriage's structural flaws, or provides them with a young lightning rod to draw off their unresolved tensions, thus exacerbating a couple's relational limitations, putting the marriage at significant risk or contributing to its demise.

No matter how a couple has learned to manage and adapt in the early years of family life, however, when the child as a young adult begins his leave-taking, whatever frailties and fault lines have developed in the previous decades will be nakedly exposed. And older parents have the same options that younger ones do: they can rise to the occasion and fortify the foundation of their bond, or they can allow themselves to be sidetracked, deflect their problems onto their offspring, or collapse under the weight of change.

So, just as couples at the beginning of parenthood had to learn to shift the focus from a preoccupation with themselves as a dyad to being engrossed with child-rearing responsibilities, so do couples farther along the parenting time line have to learn to shift the focus from a preoccupation with child-rearing responsibilities back to focusing on their relationship as a twosome. The marriage, which may have been gradually shoved to the sidelines by family life, now needs to charge back onto the playing field once again and get back into the game.

In Chapter Two I described three different types of family dynamics, and the ways in which they sometimes produced stiff headwinds that prevent a young adult's successful leave-taking. To review, centripetal families (seeking the center, or pointing inward) make it difficult for the young adult to leave the nest because departure is made to feel like a betrayal. Centrifugal families (fleeing the center, or pointing outward), on the other hand, eject him prematurely and thus fail to provide him with enough of the psychological nutrients that he needs to become self-reliant. Mission impossible families, while supportive of the young adult's departure, burden him with responsibilities that are either so incongruent or overwhelming that the attempted departure eventually caves in under the strain.

When I work with couples who are trying to empty their nest and wind down their parenting machinery, I usually see echoes of these dynamics in their marital life. In centripetal marriages, there is often ongoing relational deadlock, a chafing under overly restrictive rules that makes it difficult for one or both partners to develop fully as individuals and establish the kind of sturdy intimacy that can only come about when there is a healthy amount of independence in place. As I often explain to couples, you can only be as married as you are separate: it is the balance between the two that keeps an enduring relationship vigorous and resilient.

In centrifugal marriages, a growing distance between the two partners that began either before or after they started their family can become a seemingly unbridgeable chasm, making intimacy of any sort—emotional or physical—a challenge.

In mission impossible marriages, ongoing clashes result from a couple's opposing expectations of each other, such as how much intimacy there should be, or what roles they should play in each other's lives.

Finding ways to realign your marriage during the launching phase helps, in both direct and indirect ways, to resolve a young adult's hesitancy and ambivalence about moving on. And just as importantly, the

ult's ability to move on invariably gives couples the opportu-
___ ___ake important marital adjustments, producing a positive feedback loop wherein growth displayed in one part of the family augments
and supports growth in another. So let's take a closer look at the three
kinds of stalemates that typically afflict marriages and see what can be
done to resolve them.

A CENTRIPETAL MARRIAGE

Hank and Carla began dating during their junior year in college, became engaged during their senior year, and married two years after they
graduated. They had two children: Tanya, 25, who had just finished her
training as an occupational therapist but was continuing to live at home
rent-free, and Stephan, 22, who was also living at home rent-free, and
without any observable direction.

Neither Hank nor Carla had been seriously involved with any
other partners prior to their marriage. Both were rather shy, and they
found in each other a kindred spirit. They took the responsibilities of
work and home life very seriously, but it seemed clear that their relationship had, in significant ways, protected them from having to develop as people. Although they were friendly with some other couples
in their neighborhood and through their church, neither had any close
individual friendships. Although they were active weekly participants
in a local square-dancing group, neither engaged in any meaningful
individual hobbies or pursuits. And while both worked separate jobs,
neither took much pleasure in their mostly tedious bureaucratic employment. When Hank and Carla did go out as a couple, it was the
"same old, same old," a monthly Saturday night dinner at a local
restaurant, followed by a return home to watch a DVD, and then to
bed. Just about everything they did seemed to revolve on the axis of
their relationship with each other.

Perhaps because of this limited variety there was a stunted quality to
their interactions: they had grown so symbiotically entwined with each

other over the years that it was difficult to see the separate spouses that comprised their marriage. With this in mind, I was not surprised to learn that their sexual interactions were infrequent and perfunctory—after all, for sexual arousal to take place, there has to be a certain excitement that can only exist if there are interesting spaces and differences between the two partners. Without any separateness between these two, sexuality had gradually been snuffed out, like a flame that had lost its supply of oxygen.

Both children seemed to be struggling to find a way out of this suffocating emotional confinement. While Tanya had at least begun the process of becoming more independent by obtaining an education and the skills to get a job, Stephan was making few moves toward autonomy.

He had gotten into a four-year college and initially talked about becoming a lawyer, but accumulated only a year's worth of college credits in his first two years, and was then asked to withdraw. Since then, he had stopped taking courses altogether, and now was essentially a layabout, working 15 hours a week in the shoe department at a sporting goods store and hanging out with a group of fellow ne'er-do-wells every evening to play video games. It appeared as if the energy that it would take to escape from this benign prison was too much for him to conjure, and he had basically tossed in the towel and agreed to live the life of a passionless inmate.

With this family I focused initially on Hank and Carla, rather than on Stephan. I began by asking each of them to cultivate an independent interest, and to devote at least two hours per week to it. Both seemed bemused by my suggestion, but agreed to follow through. Upon their return, Hank announced that he had dug up his old camera and was going to start taking photographs again, while Carla told me that she was going recommence playing the clarinet; both were diversions that neither had explored much at all since college, almost three decades earlier.

It was striking for me to note the change in their relationship as Hank and Carla discussed their pursuits with me. Carla listened intently as Hank talked about the darkroom that he had set up in his bedroom as a teenager, and his long-held wish to be a photojournalist, a possible vocation he had abandoned early in college. Hank joked good-naturedly about how squeaky Carla's clarinet sounded during her first few practice sessions during the past week, but also told me how much he had enjoyed attending her college symphony concerts when they were dating, and how she was the first person to teach him about classical music.

For their next assignment, I asked each of them to find a way to use their interest to connect with other people. A couple of weeks later, when they returned, Hank told me that he had set up an account on Flickr, an online photography site, and had also signed up to take a six-week course on digital photography. Carla told me that she had found a clarinet teacher and was going to take lessons again, aiming to join a local wind ensemble.

Again, I was struck by how their interaction with each other appeared to have been reinvigorated, as if a dehydrated plant was slowly and carefully being watered. Hank spoke excitedly about once again having the opportunity to watch his wife perform, and Carla was looking forward to seeing Hank's photographs of plants and wildlife, which had always made up his best work. All it took was someone on the outside to help them break their deadlock for Hank and Carla to resume the individual growth that had been checked early on in their relationship.

Seeing progress in their marriage, I was then able to focus more on Stephan. Trying to help him separate from his family without his seeing any compelling evidence that a safe and healthy separation was a viable option would have been impossible. But once his parents made it clear that creating some personal space was sanctioned and doable, there was suddenly some room for him to maneuver.

When I asked Stephan to tell me honestly which class he had gotten the most out of while he was in college, he self-consciously chuckled and admitted, "Beer Appreciation." In discussing this, however, it quickly became apparent that he was not just looking for inventive ways to become intoxicated, but that he was truly interested in the art and business of brewing. He spoke enthusiastically about the many different microbrews that he had learned about in the seminar, and the ways in which Americans, from his perspective, were now beginning to take beer-tasting as seriously as wine-tasting.

When I asked him if he had given much thought to how he might expand his interest and translate it into more of a hobby, or even a career, he initially drew a blank. But when I offered some fairly simple suggestions, such as getting a job in a liquor store, becoming a beer salesperson, writing about beers for a newspaper, website, or blog, he told me that the other night he had stopped in at a liquor store advertising weekly beer tastings, and that he was also regularly surfing the Web in search of the newest craft and artisanal beers.

I asked Stephan to follow up on some of these possibilities, and he happily returned to report that he had joined a local home-brewing association that held monthly discussions and tastings, and that the liquor store he had visited was willing to train him to host their beer-tastings, initially on an unpaid intern basis, but perhaps eventually for pay.

These endeavors became the basis for his gradually developing some separateness and autonomy over the course of the next year. He made several new friends through the home-brewing group and the beer-tasting internship, and he was invited to contribute his thoughts to a food-and-wine column in a local magazine. This motivated him to become a certified bartender, which in turn led to his getting a job at a nearby hotel lounge. While he wasn't yet financially stable enough to move out of the house, he was developing some solid skills, becoming more involved with other people, and gaining self-confidence.

Also, in a very touching example of what-goes-around-comes-around, Stephan arranged for his father's photographs to be displayed at the hotel where he worked, resulting in several sales, the first time that Hank had ever been paid for his photography.

It is certainly possible that Stephan might have responded to some of my suggestions without his parents having already begun making changes on their own, but I doubt that this would have happened. After all, he had already made many false starts, and my sense was that he never gained any traction because of the suffocating centripetality of the family, embodied most vividly in his parents' squelching marriage. Before his parents began reviving their own individual interests, it was as though there simply weren't any doors out of the house.

At the same time, a close girlfriend of Tanya's from their college days moved back into town and contacted her about the possibility of sharing an apartment. Tanya had staunchly rejected offers of this sort before, but this time she seemed open to the idea, and the two of them quickly found a place and signed a lease. Again, while it was certainly possible that Tanya might have agreed to move out if her friend had contacted her a year or two before, most likely she would've stayed put.

It was only when Hank and Carla got to work creating a different relational climate and developing their individual lives that their marriage improved. This in turn spurred their children to feel more comfortable pursuing their own interests and developing *their* individual lives, leading to a sunnier future for all four of them.

A CENTRIFUGAL MARRIAGE

Landry and Mara had both been incessantly involved with their children's athletic endeavors since the three boys were toddlers. One or both had played just about every role imaginable over the years—coach, team manager, league commissioner, and host or hostess for innumerable team banquets and parties.

They loved what they did, but between these tireless efforts, and their jobs, their relationship had clearly taken a backseat. Over the years, they had devised a work schedule that usually allowed for one of them to be home and available to the children, which meant many alternating overnight and weekend shifts at the hospital where both worked as emergency room nurses. Because of this, several days would go by during which they might not see each other at all, or share only the briefest of conversations. They were highly organized, extremely efficient, and quite caring, but when it came to their marriage, they led almost entirely parallel lives,

All three of the boys had graduated from high school, but only the middle one had sustained any ongoing independence in his adult life. Martin was currently a junior in college, planning on going into sports medicine (not surprisingly). Their eldest, Denny, had gone away to college, returned home after one year, departed for college again, and then returned home once again, each time because of his inability to stay on top of his academic work. He was now languishing, without any clear plans or motivation. Their youngest, Trevor, lost athletic eligibility during his senior year of high school due to low grades and absenteeism, didn't apply to any colleges, and was now living at home and working as an aide at the same hospital where his parents worked, a job his father had arranged for him.

In obtaining their marital history, it quickly became clear how far apart Landry and Mara had grown over the past two decades. Their children's athletic undertakings had been the glue that had kept the two of them together. Never having developed any other relational adhesive, it was not surprising that, without this glue in place, there was nothing holding these two parents close. In fact, even with all three of their children eighteen years and older, they still hadn't made any adjustments in their work schedule to allow them to spend more time together; they continued to alternate weekend and overnight shifts as if nothing had changed.

In situations like these, children sometimes step in to fill the void in their parents' relationship, sacrificing their own development to keep their parents linked up. Somehow it had been silently determined that Martin was free of this responsibility, meaning that by remaining at home, Denny and Trevor were left holding the bag, keeping an eye on their mother and father and ensuring that they didn't drift so far apart that there was no way to bring them back. And each was doing a fine job: between Denny's ongoing shuttle back and forth between college and home and Trevor's refusal to even make a plan to leave home, Landry and Mara never really had to confront the emptiness that characterized their relationship. They could continue to imagine that time stood still and that there were children around who needed them, and who were also needed to distract them from the possibility of addressing their remoteness from each other.

With this couple I needed to find a way to gently move them into closer orbits so that they could find a way to re-create their attachment to one another. In that way, all three of their sons, rather than just one, would be able to contemplate *their* future without feeling as though doing so would imperil their *parents'* future.

I began by asking Landry and Mara to restructure their work shifts so that they were more aligned, rather than alternating, allowing them more time to be with each other. While both protested that this was easier said than done due to scheduling complexities at the hospital, I nevertheless asked them to stay on it, even if it meant putting in shift requests that wouldn't kick in until months down the road.

I also asked them to talk more about what had initially drawn them together. The main attraction, not surprisingly, turned out to be sports. They had met shortly after both had finished nursing school while playing in a coed lacrosse league, and had continued in various other coed leagues, as well: softball, flag football, and soccer. They were expecting Denny within a year after getting married, and Martin and Trevor had each followed 18 months apart. Of course, between work, and the responsibilities entailed with raising three small boys very close in age, there was little time for their own athletic activities, so the one original shared interest that had yoked them so nicely together was abruptly disabled, and with their staggered work schedules they were left with no overlap at all.

I reminded them that they now had the opportunity to revisit the activity that had first brought them together. They quickly reminded me in return that they had both grown so out of shape over the intervening years that the idea of joining lacrosse or soccer leagues was, in Landry's words, "a shortcut to a heart attack."

Keeping this in mind, I suggested that they begin going to the gym together three times a week in an effort to lose weight and get back into reasonable shape. I also asked them to come up with one other hobby or activity besides athletics that they might want to cultivate, something that they might or might not have explored before. Some combination of old/familiar and new/challenging might be required to bring a couple's relationship back from its distant fringes.

Landry and Mara gave it some thought and returned to tell me that, back when they were first dating, they had dreamed of setting up some kind of business together. After bouncing around some ideas over the past couple of weeks, they had come up with the concept of establishing an agency that provided on-site first aid specialists for high school athletic contests and tournaments.

Both were very excited about this project, and their interest in making this dream a reality motivated them to begin spending significantly more time in contact and conversation with each other—networking with colleagues, meeting with attorneys, bankers, and insurance companies, and marketing to coaches and athletic directors. Interestingly, their endeavor seemed to not only reenergize their marriage, but also energize their two lagging sons.

Trevor decided that he wanted to be a part of things, and enrolled in an emergency medical technician (EMT) class taught at the fire department so that he'd qualify to be one of the first on-site staff people. Denny, meanwhile, wanted to handle the financial end of this incipient family business, so he signed up for some evening classes in bookkeeping while contemplating a return to college to become an accountant. Of course, Martin, already planning on going into sports medicine, was looking forward to becoming medical director once he had completed his residency.

Bringing this far-flung couple back into more engagement with each other not only helped them move into the next stage of marital development, but also helped their children proceed down more prosperous pathways.

A MISSION IMPOSSIBLE MARRIAGE

Ray and Darlene had been stuck in a contentious marriage for many years, punctuated by precarious truces or sulky silences during which they tried, usually in vain, to remain undisturbed by each other. Invariably, however, some event would trigger a renewal of hostilities, and they would make each other and their children miserable. In my work with couples who are trapped in this kind of vicious cycle, I generally find that things did not start off that way.

Ray was initially attracted to Darlene's quiet demeanor, which was in stark contrast to his moody and volatile mother, who often exploded into fits of rage. Darlene was initially attracted to Ray's clever sense of humor and clarity of thought, which was in stark contrast to her mopey father, a man who had recently died broke and friendless.

Over the years, however, what looked appealing to each of them at first take began to transform itself in a negative way. Darlene's quiet eventually slid into a wintry aloofness: Ray found it increasingly difficult to make emotional or physical contact with her as she retreated further and further away from him, unavailable to give or receive affection or support. Ray's intellect and clarity eventually began expressing itself as bullying condescension and cruel sarcasm; as he became more sharp-tongued, Darlene found him increasingly difficult to bear.

They gradually became less and less able to control, or distract themselves from, the growing backlog of frustration and barely subdued irritation each had with their marriage. The more impassive and detached Darlene became, the more harsh Ray turned, prompting her to distance herself even further, which in turn prompted him to become even more callous and inconsiderate. Not surprisingly, their sex life completely evaporated, and each commenced a relationship with someone outside of the marriage.

Ray, an attorney, engaged in a series of brief sexual affairs, including one with a client that almost ended his legal career. Darlene, a city planner, was involved with an unmarried colleague of hers who seemed to be subtly wooing her with his constant attentiveness and availability. While the two of them weren't physically intimate, they texted and emailed throughout the day and went out for coffee several times a week. In other words, she spent far more emotional energy on him than she did on her husband.

Each of them, of course, felt hurt by the other partner's betrayal of intimacy, but neither seemed able to discuss it in a constructive way or understand how these affairs had been operating as both cause and effect of their separateness. While divorce was frequently brought up, usually in the context of a blistering fight, it was never seriously pursued—the idea of fracturing the family, as well as the financial challenges it would entail, steered them away from this cliff, as did the slim flame of their initial attraction to each other, which still flickered from time to time.

So they remained, year after year, in a desultory deadlock. And, not atypically for couples in this kind of situation, they could not help but enlist their children as personal allies in their ongoing relational siege.

Nineteen-year-old Ray Jr. was belligerent at home, casually referring to his younger sister as "slutty" and frequently telling his mother to "f**k off" when she asked him to do something. Ray Sr. did little to curb his son's behavior and make it clear this was not to be tolerated. By not correcting his son, Ray Sr. was tacitly sanctioning such verbal abuse: Junior was simply the mouthpiece, giving voice to his father's not-so-secret attitude. Naturally, it was devastating for Darlene that her husband wouldn't defend her in the face of her son's unbridled verbal aggression.

Meanwhile, 17-year-old Christa seemed to be acting out her mother's unmet desires for love and physical affection. Christa dressed provocatively, flirted with boys incessantly, and had become sexually active with Corey, her boyfriend of three months. Darlene, rather than attempting to persuade her daughter to think more carefully about her behavior, appeared to derive some vicarious pleasure from Christa's precocious eroticism: she would ask Christa to invite Corey over to the house and give them space and time to be alone. Darlene praised Christa for the maturity of her relationship with Corey, despite the fact that the girl's grades were dropping and that she, like Corey, had begun smoking cigarettes. Ray was distraught as he and Christa became more alienated from each other, and he helplessly concluded that his wife was fostering their daughter's decline.

Ray angrily accused Darlene of not setting stricter limits on Christa's relationship with her boyfriend, but Darlene most likely didn't do so precisely because she was privately pleased that Ray was so distressed. Darlene angrily accused Ray of not setting limits on how Ray Jr. treated her and Christa, but Ray most likely didn't do so precisely because he was privately pleased that his son's profanity distressed Darlene.

Both children had been recruited into their parents' respective armies, and were participating in the ongoing oppression, most likely without even being aware of what they were doing. Rather than being free to pursue their own developmental aims, each of them had been unwittingly enlisted as a "soldier of misfortune," entrusted with the lethal mission of psychologically maiming their parent of the opposite sex.

Over the years, I have treated young adults who are somehow able to stave off this kind of recruitment, refuse to be delegated, and escape playing a role in the conflict; through so doing, they may actually promote their parents' marital growth by forcing the two elders to finally address their own conflicts rather than misdirecting them through the children. Most young adults in this situation, however, like Ray Jr. and Christa, have difficulty sidestepping the marital minefield or the gravitational force of the "enlistment." In these families, healthy individuation on the younger generation's part is unlikely to germinate unless and until their parents' unbearable conflict is no longer being rerouted through them.

It is sometimes best for me to work indirectly with conflicted couples—such as by focusing on their coparenting rather than on their relationship itself. So, conjointly with Ray and Darlene, I began by emphasizing the importance of their unifying in the face of their children's worrisome behavior.

I made it clear to Ray that he needed to protect his wife and his daughter from his son's verbal attacks, and to not be afraid to stand up to him and to make it clear that disrespect would not be tolerated. Ray initially defended Ray Jr.'s behavior, noting how "bratty" Christa could be with her brother and how "suffocating" Darlene could be with her son.

But I reminded him that Ray Jr. still needed to learn to control himself. "He doesn't have to like his sister, he doesn't even have to like his mother, but he's not entitled to treat them that way. He apparently thinks that the normal rules of civility don't apply to him," I cautioned.

"But how do I stop him? He's been doing this for years."

"Remember that he's 19. You are not obligated to allow him to live in your house. You have every right to ask him to leave if he can't be respectful toward others. That's a basic rule and he needs to figure that out now."

"You're suggesting I ask him to leave simply because he mouths off to his sister and his mother?"

"He's not just mouthing off—he's speaking terribly inappropriately. And he's too old for that kind of behavior to be tolerated."

Ray squirmed in his chair. "You're pushing me to kick my own son out of the house?"

"I'm pushing you to finish the job of parenting him. Who knows, if he winds up in a bad fight or in legal trouble one day as a result of his not being able to control his mouth, or his hands, I am afraid that you will wish you had taken a firmer stand with him. I'm sure you see people like that all the time in your practice."

I then stressed with Darlene that she needed to exert more influence over Christa and her behavior with her boyfriend, and over her seductive behavior generally.

"You are aware that Christa and her boyfriend are sexually active?"

"Yes, she told me. She confides in me. I'm the only one she can talk to. She can't talk to her father, that's for sure."

"What are your thoughts about her being sexually active at this point in her life?"

"She talked it over with her boyfriend, and they seem very close, and he treats her very well. We've discussed contraception; she's on the pill. I can't exactly stop teenage sexual behavior, you know. The hormones are raging."

"Yes, the hormones are raging, and sexual urges are strong ones, but not every 17-year-old girl is regularly having sex with her boyfriend. I also understand that she's not doing as well in school as she typically does, and that she picked up smoking."

"Look, she's in love, of course her grades are dropping. That happens. Lord knows she hasn't had enough love from her father; why should we be surprised that she's finding it with a boyfriend?"

"And her smoking?"

"I'm not crazy about this, but I'm hoping it's just a phase. I'm hoping she's just into it because her boyfriend's into it."

"So, at this point, are you saying that it's basically okay with you for her to have sex, risk STDs and an unplanned pregnancy, limit her academic and professional options, jeopardize her health and shorten her life? That is, as long as it's all in the name of love?"

Darlene paused, then jabbed her finger in Ray's direction, her face flushed, her eyes on fire.

"Maybe *he* should be talking to her about all of this. Maybe he's the one who should be explaining to her what guys want. Maybe he's the one who lets her brother treat her like dirt so that she has to sleep with a guy to feel good about herself."

"I'd love to talk to her, but you won't let me!" Ray answered loudly. "You close me out, like I'm going to harm her! You have convinced her that I can't be turned to. You have convinced her that she shouldn't take me seriously. You have convinced her that I'm the enemy, not her father!"

"Some father! A father who sleeps with his own clients! That's the kind of father that I want talking to my daughter about responsible sexual behavior? Are you crazy? You're the *last* person I would want instructing her on responsibility!"

"Look, it was wrong, I know. I have apologized for that. I have stopped doing that, but it doesn't mean I can't be a good father. It doesn't mean I can't protect our daughter. And, by the way, do you think she doesn't know about your relationship with your 'work friend'? Do you think she's not reading your text messages?"

"That's beside the point, and, need I remind you, I don't sleep with him. Meanwhile, you don't even protect me from our son! How is it that you're going to protect our daughter from being taken advantage of? You may be a very good lawyer, but you're not much of a role model to our children."

This was an extremely painful conversation, but Ray and Darlene were doing something very important here: they were trying to find a way to talk about how they have hurt each other as spouses and unintentionally neutralized each other as parents. Difficult as it may have been, this was the start of their finding a new point of contact, one that might enable them to heal some of the injuries from the past.

I also couldn't help noticing that they had each started using the word "our": Ray referred to "our daughter" and Darlene referred to "our son." This signified to me that they still saw themselves as connected, at least through their children, which is why I continued to look for ways to help them support each other in more effective parenting.

"Darlene, if Ray is willing to set better limits with Ray Jr. when it comes to how he talks to you, it's important that you make it as easy as possible for him to do this. He has said that you sometimes micromanage your son. For a period of time, could you be more attentive to how you interact with him, and try not to over-supervise him?"

"I get on him because he doesn't take care of what he's supposed to take care of. If he would do what I've asked him to do—and believe me, it's not all that much—I wouldn't have to remind him about everything all the time."

"I'm sure you get very frustrated with him, and I can see why. But while we're in the process of trying to do things differently, I'm simply asking you to be thoughtful about how you speak to him. And if there's something that needs to be done and he's not doing it, you can let Ray know and have him address it with Ray Jr. himself, so you won't have to get so entangled and exasperated."

"Okay, I'll back off for now," Darlene warily agreed.

"And Ray, if you want Darlene to set better limits with Christa, then you have to make it clear to Christa that you are going to be a more involved father."

"I want to be more involved father! It's just that Darlene freezes me out, doesn't let me."

"You are speaking as if Darlene is a warden and you are in jail. There isn't anything stopping you from taking Christa out to dinner and talking with her about relationships between males and females during the adolescent years. Darlene, if Ray told you that he wanted to take Christa out for a discussion, would you stand in the way?"

"Of course not," she said, with a note of hope in her voice. "That would make me very happy. Christa needs her dad right now, she's needed him for a long time, he just hasn't been there."

"Her dad hasn't been there because you haven't allowed him to be there," Ray insisted.

"Well," I emphasized, "we're trying to do things differently now, Ray, and Darlene is saying that she'd welcome your efforts to move a little closer to Christa, so let's assume that she's being genuine. Remember, also, that Christa might resist your sudden desire to institute 'father-daughter time,' but it's important that you begin that process now, because in another couple of years, maybe even sooner at this rate, she may not be living at home and be all that easy to make contact with."

Ray and Darlene approved of the plan, and when they returned, both sounded more optimistic. Darlene told Christa that there would be no more unsupervised time with her boyfriend in the house—essentially meaning that there would be no more sex in the house—and Christa immediately burst into tears and told her mother that she had missed her period and was afraid that she was pregnant. She took a test and it came up negative, but just contemplating this possibility had her, and of course her parents, thinking differently about her sexual activity.

Ray took her out and they had a long talk about the ways in which adolescent males sometimes might be talking about love when they're actually more interested in sex. Christa, who suspected her father's affairs based on having overheard numerous fights between her parents, used this as an opportunity to forthrightly ask Ray about this. He responded candidly, and with great remorse, sharing with her the tremendous shame he felt about the many individuals he had hurt, and his commitment to never acting in this way again.

He also reminded her that his father, a longtime smoker, had died of lung cancer and that he was there to help her stop smoking when she was ready to give it up. They agreed that it would be a good idea for them to continue getting together to talk about these important matters.

Ray took the same tack with Ray Jr. He took him out to dinner, and acknowledged that his son must be very frustrated with his life right now—Ray Jr. had graduated from high school but was not in college, and was working as an attendant at a local skatepark—but that he needed to start growing up and taking more responsibility for his behavior, both in and outside the home.

Ray firmly spelled out that it was okay for Ray Jr. to continue living with them, but that there needed to be changes in how he treated and spoke to his mother and his sister, or he would be asked to leave. The son protested vehemently, illustrating the many ways in which he felt "dissed" by the female members of the family, but his father held fast.

Ray, Darlene, and Ray Jr. then scheduled a couple of family therapy sessions with me to discuss how to help move things forward for him. He confessed to feeling bored and tired of constantly being out of money, and his mother, whose city planning firm had many connections with the construction industry, agreed to work with him to get a job in that field. The opportunity for the two of them to collaborate took the edge off of the tension that had been building between mother and son, and when Ray Jr. was hired as a carpenter's apprentice, paying him twice what he was making at the skatepark, he expressed gratitude to Darlene for her efforts on his behalf, the first display of affection that he had offered her in years.

With both children settling down and behaving better, Ray, Darlene, and I then began a series of couples sessions to determine whether they wanted to work on their marriage or embark on the process of dismantling it in a civil, dignified way. But their recent willingness to team up more effectively as parents appeared to have convinced them that it was worth seeing if they could reclaim some of the attraction that had first drawn them together.

Their marriage had run aground many years before, so it did not turn around overnight, but they worked hard with me in the subsequent months to understand how they had gradually separated into opposing camps and become ever more estranged from each other. I helped them learn to listen better and communicate more effectively, and to uphold more responsibility for their own emotions rather than blaming each other for "causing" what they felt. I counseled them to take the risk of bringing underlying problems and concerns out into the open rather than consigning them to psychological limbo, and to join forces to create a new vision for the relationship they would like to enjoy as they prepared for the next phase of their life together.

In a little more than a year from when we first met, Ray Jr. was continuing to live at home, behave appropriately, and was still working, and he had also begun taking a night course to become certified as a HVAC/R technician (heating, ventilation, air conditioning, and refrigeration). Christa had quit smoking, shifted her focus from flirtatiousness to academics, and was considering becoming a teacher. Ray and Darlene were getting along better and no longer threatening each other with divorce.

And, as I anticipated from my initial appraisal of the family's dynamics, Ray Jr. and Christa started to enjoy a better relationship with each other as well once they were rescued from the river that had been roiling with their parents' divisive undercurrents. Ray Jr. was taking a more protective role toward his younger sister, and Christa was confiding in him more and using him as a resource when it came to her relationships with young men.

Focusing initially on their relationship as coparents launching their young adult children, and proceeding from there to address their relationship as adversarial spouses, freed them from their years of militant ambivalence and paid handsome dividends not only for the two of them, but for the entire family as well.

In these three examples, we have seen some of the ways in which marital and parenting issues remain intertwined, even during the launching phase of family life, and we've looked at how to make the modifications that will provide all family members with more room to grow. The key, as these three couples demonstrated, is finding ways to embody and/or reclaim the qualities that first attracted you to each other while simultaneously discovering original methods of sharing interests and remaining connected to and intrigued by each other.

Here are some additional insights and strategies that couples should keep in mind in their efforts to adapt effectively as the family structure shifts underfoot.

GRIEVING AND FORGIVING

In Chapter Two, we discussed the important role that grief plays in the young adult's evolution—the pain felt at leaving one's childhood behind. But grief also plays an important role in marital evolution, as well.

Every ongoing marriage is destined to be disappointing and disillusioning at various points. After all, we wouldn't become betrothed in the first place unless we had enormously high hopes that we would live "happily ever after," deftly meeting each other's deepest needs and residing blissfully in a state of unalloyed enchantment. But it never takes long for our rosy fantasies to splinter into the dangerously sharp shards of reality: the inevitable loss of idealized love is an agonizing loss indeed.

We always compose a version of the spouse that we believe we need, but she or he will never conform completely to the unblemished image of perfection that we have so painstakingly conceived. We also compose a version of the marriage that we believe we need, and that, too, will prove to be a disappointment, stubbornly refusing to yield to our most cherished wishes. Our marriage is strong enough to handle anything, we tell ourselves at one point, and yet the slightest bump or obstacle seems to send it careening off course, we glumly admit at another. We will keep our love fresh and alive and physically intimate every single day, we passionately promise ourselves early on, and yet we often go for days without any more physical contact than a peck on the cheek and a brush against each other in the bathroom, we sadly concede years later.

So, to avoid remaining grumpily lashed to the hitching post of your painful past, you need to find ways to grieve, and this grief requires the courage for honest, bracing discussions that enable you and your partner to come to terms with the ways in which you have dissatisfied and disheartened each other so that you can begin to satisfy each other anew.

It also requires the courage to forgive. A colleague of mine encourages his patients to be grateful for, rather than annoyed by, their spouse's flaws, imperfections, and idiosyncrasies. "After all, without them," he offers, with a wry smile, "your spouse would have definitely found someone better than you."

Most likely, your partner has not truly meant to hurt or disappoint you any more than you've meant to hurt or disappoint him or her—these processes are unavoidable in an ongoing, intimate relationship. Since we've established that perfection is impossible, the key to a successful marriage lies not in remaining so peripheral or guarded that you are no longer able to wound each other, but in making the small, unmistakable gestures of reconciliation and compromise that are like a salve for the wounds that we inadvertently inflict, to reassure each other of our love so that those wounds can begin to heal in the present, and to make the necessary relational adjustments to avoid wounding one another in the future.

Successful grieving and forgiving of this sort is a liberating process, one that enables spouses to contend with present and future marital challenges while still remaining close and caring.

CONFRONTING UNRESOLVED ISSUES

Every couple finds a way to cloak and obscure their conflicts, but if not fully resolved or acknowledged they invariably reemerge from the depths of a marriage's emotional graveyard, clamoring for attention and resolution.

When I counsel spouses who insist that "everything is fine" and that "nothing is wrong," even after years of marriage, I am usually skeptical and concerned. This kind of assertion generally signifies a problem because it closes off the opportunity for changing things between them, which is in and of itself a bad thing for a marriage. It also puts their children in the position of having to carry out their unresolved business for them, as we have seen in some of the instances above.

It can of course be distressing—at times even excruciating—to revisit matters that we would just as soon forget about, but unless we display an unflinching willingness to bring underlying, unresolved injuries and emotions to the surface, we prevent ourselves from healing and growing. And if you can use your long history with each other to commit to handling problems as they arise, rather than repressing them into the aforementioned psychological cemetery (where nothing unresolved stays buried), then you can inoculate yourselves against a toxic buildup of resentment and the more successful your marriage will be.

ASSUMING RESPONSIBILITY

Each spouse must accept his or her own contribution to their marriage: relying on accusations and denunciations keeps a relationship hopelessly wedged in and forecloses any kind of midlife flowering.

I often ask couples I'm working with to do some version of a two-part assignment. The first part is making a list of things that your spouse could be doing differently that would make things better, and the second part is making a list of things that you could be doing that would make things better. Another project that I'll often assign is for a couple to map out the sequence of individual behaviors that leads to their worst fights.

The point of both assignments, obviously, is to emphasize the reciprocity that is built into any intimate relationship, the ways in which we elicit our partner's behavior, even the very behaviors that we are so angered and frustrated by. When we begin to recognize the reflexive, "autopilot" interactions that take place between us, we become better able to interrupt them and to substitute more productive ones. If we do not awaken from autopilot behavior, we grow increasingly constrained by behavioral patterns that do nothing more than replicate the past—either in our marriage or, at times, in our childhood. These patterns can ultimately become much more powerful than the personalities of the individuals who create them.

One typical pattern is polarization, the ways in which spouses wind up on opposite sides of the fence. Just about every couple I've worked with will conclude that they share the same goals for their marriage and parenting. Problems generally arise when the methods that they each select in an attempt to achieve those goals start to work at cross-purposes and pit the spouses against each other. At these times, both partners must take a step back and slow things down so that they can identify how this happens.

For example, Sam, thinking that his wife, Corinna, is overly strict and punitive with the children, will adopt an overly laid-back and permissive attitude with them, which of course prompts Corinna to feel as if she has to become more draconian to compensate for his laxness, which of course prompts Sam to feel as if he has to be even more lenient, and on and on they go, eliciting the very parental behaviors that they are so troubled by.

In these situations, either partner can make a change that will break both of them out of the cycle: it only takes one person to put a stop to a couple's destructive dance. And if both make changes, they'll break the cycle even more quickly and cocreate a more enticing choreography.

REDEFINING AND REIMAGINING YOUR RELATIONSHIP

I vividly remember the opening lecture of my first graduate course on marital therapy, when our professor announced to the class, "I want to begin by letting you know that I have been married six times." It was as if a silent groan passed through the room. We thought, "This is who is going to be teaching us about building healthy marriages, a man who has been married six times?"

After a brief pause, however, he added, "Fortunately, all six marriages have been to the same fine wife." He went on to explain that any enduring marriage is composed of numerous "marriages," as a couple finds ways to psychologically update their union in response to changing needs, challenges, and expectations.

As young adults launch toward independence, parents must take a good, hard look at their relationship and decide what they want to preserve and what they want to discard, what they want to amplify and what they want to subdue. Being unafraid to do or ask for something different is what infuses a marriage with energy and flexibility, and allows a couple to contend with the loss of child-rearing in preparation for experiencing and enjoying the gains of newly liberated vigor and autonomy.

This is best accomplished in three stages. First, focus not only on what you no longer want from your partner—less criticism, less control, less neglect—but also on what you *do* want—more time together, more affection, more adventure.

Second, be as specific as possible in your requests. For instance, elaborate on "I want more time together" so that you nail down exactly how much time together you want and what you want to be doing during that time together.

Finally, ask yourselves what each of you can do to support your partner in meeting the request. For example, if Tim wants more time together with Linda, then how might he treat Linda in such a way that she naturally wants to spend more time with him? Are there activities that they could pursue together that she might like but that he has tended to avoid? If Linda wants Tim to be less critical, what are some changes she might make that would be less likely to invite his criticism? Is his criticism of her actually an outcome of his feeling underappreciated and taken for granted by her?

The more ways you find to make the terms of your marital arrangement more elastic, the more satisfying that arrangement is likely to remain over time.

COMMUNICATION

Of course, all of these strategies rely on improved communication between you and your spouse so that thoughts and feelings that have long been interred or marginalized are invited back in and allowed to enliven your intimate dialogue. It is no longer adequate to sweep matters under the rug or delicately continue to sidestep them. The launching phase is not only a time for more expansiveness in your discussions with your young adult, as we saw in Chapter Five, but with each other, as well.

None of us can control what life offers us—all we can control is how we *respond* to life's offerings. If we cultivate the capacity to pull together and *talk about* how we will respond, then we will always be better able to negotiate life's challenges and surprises. If not, they will eventually do us in. In other words, intimacy is not really rooted in the events that take place in a marriage, but in how a couple does or does not discuss these events.

With this in mind, couples need to learn to identify their needs clearly and ask directly for them to be met, rather than expecting their partner to read their mind. They need to learn how to express their anger in respectful ways rather than use it to intimidate, manipulate, or obfuscate. But they also need to learn how to recognize the many emotions that often lie beneath anger and that may account for its intensity—sorrow, worry, fear, insecurity—and learn how to express these softer, subtler feelings in coherent ways as well. The key is not anger management, but emotional literacy: a sure grasp of the full bandwidth of feelings that are experienced in the course of a vigorous and lasting relationship. Women are often more finely attuned to gradations of feeling, and they can help the husband learn the vocabulary to express how he feels.

Spouses need to learn how to stand up to each other and fight for what they believe in, but they also have to learn to fight "clean" versus "dirty," avoiding disreputable tactics such as name-calling, preemptive attacks, dredging up any and every issue from the past, The Silent Treatment, and other counterproductive strategies. They need to learn how to give and receive compliments, and to ensure that the ratio of positive comments to negative comments between them is weighted much more heavily toward the positive. They need to learn how to see and talk about their marital "problems" as maladaptive "solutions" to a problem, just as they have (hopefully) learned to do while trying to make sense of their children's problems.

Rather than resorting to time-honored ploys that rely on denial and evasion, they must come up with more thoughtful responses to difficult questions that have not yet been sufficiently answered. Habitually replying "That's water under the bridge" in response to the question "Why didn't you spend more time with the children when they were growing up?" isn't going to pass muster if you no longer want to be troubled by the past. Irritably reiterating "I don't know" in response to "Why have you pulled so far away from me?" isn't going to suffice if you truly want a reinvigorated marriage. As I suggested above, a refreshed relationship is not possible through autopilot behavior.

And, finally (I can't stress this enough), couples need to learn to *listen*—patiently, wholeheartedly, open-mindedly—because it is when we listen that we are the most fully present and able to convey our love to our partners.

SEXUAL RENEWAL

A cartoon depicts a man coming up behind his wife, who is reading a book, and suggesting to her, "Now that the kids are grown and gone, I thought it might be a good time for us to have sex."

Sex can be the most intimate, and conflicted, form of communication between a husband and wife. For that reason, couples often place sex on the back burner during the years when child-rearing and career responsibilities are so consuming. Putting an important part of your relationship on the back burner doesn't have to be a terrible thing, as long as the back burner remains lit. But I find all too often that couples place their sex lives on a back burner that has been snuffed out, and, not surprisingly, things have grown quite cold. Sexual interactions, if they happen at all, seem more exacting than exciting, more episodic than erotic.

Sexuality, which may have been helpful in dissolving tension, now creates tension—rather than discharging the inevitable buildup of stress, it instead becomes yet another source of stress.

But ultimately, a marriage without sex is a marriage in trouble, and it is hard to reawaken marital vitality without some measure of sexual vitality. The launching phase of parenthood can set the stage for sexual renewal if the following challenges are met:

- Men and women must come to terms with their changing bodies, and with the reality that they will not experience desire and respond sexually in exactly the way they did in the past.

- Men and women must overcome negative cultural images of aging, the belief that midlife entails an inexorable decline in romance and passion, and overcome whatever shame they may feel for not meeting an unrealistic societal standard of attractiveness.

- Men and women must examine the seeds of sexual tension that may have been planted long ago whose consequences are still unfolding. How was it established that any physical contact always had to lead to sex? Why was the withholding of sexual interaction used as a tactic or weapon? How were unsatisfying sexual phases understood and talked about between the two of you? (Maybe they were not talked about at all.)

- Men and women must overcome whatever tendencies they may have to neuter or desexualize their marriage, such as through avoidance, hostility, indifference, and unhealthy lifestyles.

- Men and women must break out of the cycles of behavior that have brought them to a deadlocked pattern of sexual frustration and tension, such as a wife's complaint that her husband makes clumsy overtures at inopportune times, which prompts her to withdraw from him, which disposes him to become hurt and critical of her for never initiating, which leads to further withdrawal on her part and even less likelihood of sexual initiation.

- Men and women must reexamine the balance they have established between sexuality and security. Sometimes, by midlife, the pendulum has swung so dramatically in the direction of comfort and companionship that sexuality has receded far into the distance.

A common complaint of couples at this stage in their life is that "sex used to be fun, so why does it now have to be work?" But it does, in fact, require work. Sex may have taken care of itself earlier in your relationship, but now it needs to be taken care of, requiring more consciousness and conscientiousness on both of your parts. There are many ways to care for your intimate bond, and it is always unwise to resign yourself to a sexless marriage when so many sexual problems can be worked out.

Of course, a certain amount of time and privacy is necessary, especially in a situation when your young adults haven't left home, or have returned home for a period of time. In these cases, time and privacy may still have to be assiduously carved out, rather than being left up to chance. But time and privacy won't do the trick unless you've taken the time to discuss your respective anxieties about and wishes for your sex life. The familiarity that the two of you have cultivated may sometimes seem to be an *obstacle* to intimacy, but it can also be a *pathway* to intimacy because it allows you to feel safe about being more honest with each other.

With this in mind, find ways to reassure each other, because that reassurance will be the soil within which a reawakened sexuality can grow. Partners may need reassurance that they're still attractive to each other, that they've still "got it," that they will feel closer to each other when they are more intimate, that by reexamining their amatory life they are not looking to create new battles but to solve old problems and, in the process, reanimate their relationship.

Listen carefully to your partner's concerns and complaints, and make the necessary changes to the pattern of your daily life. The key here is finding ways to express your needs to your partner without coming off as critical or attacking, and finding ways to listen to your partner's needs without feeling defensive or defeated.

Remember, too, that most husbands and wives have kept sexual secrets from each other, either to protect their own or their partner's sensitivities. For example, a wife may not have shared an early experience of being sexually exploited, a husband may not have shared how much pressure he feels to "perform" in bed, or both may collude in keeping private a history of erotic disgruntlement. The more that couples at midlife can talk with candor about their sexual past, the more they will be able to take pleasure in their sexual present and future. Thoughtfully conveying your innermost feelings to your long-term partner can sometimes be the most powerful aphrodisiac of all.

You will also have to take the risk of being more inventive and more adventurous when it comes to breaking long-standing patterns of sexual avoidance or tedium and resuming the pursuit of passion. Whether it's romantic dinners, a weeklong cruise, or a quick afternoon at a nearby hotel, every couple has to find ways to inject a little drama or novelty into their marriage.

Finally . . . relax. Many couples find that the decrease in libido that accompanies our journey into midlife allows for a different and more mature kind of romance, one that is characterized by increased tenderness and gratification, and the opportunity to more finely tune in to each other on both a physical and emotional basis. A reduction in sexual intensity doesn't have to mean a reduction in sexual satisfaction, unless your actions and inactions guarantee this.

An ongoing, active sex life is a great gift not only to each other, but also to your children. Allowing young adults to see that neither ardor nor affection have to evaporate simply because you are no longer youthful will provide them with hope and optimism when it comes to their own sexual journey, and raise the odds that they, can savor sexual pleasure throughout their life span. Plus, it will increase their desire to move on with their lives so that they, too, can ultimately experience the richness of intimacy with a loving partner.

In this chapter, we have focused on the changes that you can make in your marital life that positively influence your young adult's leave-taking. Particularly when you are in the process of trying to launch struggling young adults, you need to exert as much constructive influence as possible, and whether you are aware of it or not, a significant part of that influence originates from within your marriage.

The better the relationship between a husband and wife—as co-parents, as companions, as communicators, as lovers—the better the relationship between parent and child, and the more likely the child will be to climb the ladder of self-sufficiency. There is always a close correlation between a couple's willingness to evolve and their young adult's willingness to evolve.

But there are individual changes that you can each make that have an effect on the launching process, too, changes that we will survey in our next chapter.

CHAPTER EIGHT

LETTING GO, MOVING ON

THE MIDLIFE LAUNCH

"One can only accept in others what one can accept in oneself."

—*James Baldwin*

The Onion, a publication that features satirical takes on contemporary news, once headlined an article: "Astronomer Discovers Center of Universe." The subheadline read, "It is my beautiful 9-year-old son, he says." The astronomer explains with pride and fascination that his son "emits such a powerful field of gravity and significance" that all other persons and objects "take on added significance by virtue of their proximity to him."

In my work with families (and in my own life), I find it helpful to distinguish between personhood and parenthood. When our children are young, our personhood is almost entirely eclipsed by our parenthood: the sheer physical and emotional energy required for nurturing infants, toddlers, and small children is all-consuming, and leaves little room for the exploration and cultivation of the parents' personhood.

However, as children grow, they need to see that we have a personal identity separate from our parental identity: this helps them to get past the narcissism and self-centeredness that are normal components of childhood, and also provides them with something to emulate and strive toward. If we are constantly sacrificing our identities for the sake of perfect parenthood, we are in fact hampering our children's ability to build their own identities, making the eventual leap from the nest more arduous. We need to keep in mind that no child leaves home without some guilt about his departure, however masked it may be. It helps to alleviate young adults' feelings of guilt when they see that their parents are capable of living an enriching, fulfilling life without it having to revolve around their perpetual presence, their "powerful field of significance."

This expansion of our identity, which occurs around midlife for most parents, is clearly easier said than done. Emptying the nest is often romanticized in ways that do not honor the complexity of this process, in ways that make it seem like it's nothing more than the leisurely, logical conclusion to the parenting phase of our lives. In this chapter, we will examine how life—or, better, new life—can indeed begin as you empty your nest, and how that beginning has benefits not only for you, but also for your young adult children as well.

❧   ❧

The cultural idea of midlife, like the idea of young adulthood, is a distinctly modern concept. That is because only over the course of the last one hundred years, when our life span began extending well beyond four or five decades, did the very existence of a "midlife" come about. Of course, when we hear the word "midlife" we almost reflexively associate it with the word "crisis." Here's why . . .

We often resist entering the second half of our lives because acknowledging that there is a second half means we must also accept that there is, in fact, an endpoint. Individual and family crises often result from our doomed desire to fight off the future, to maintain the seductive illusion that nothing is ever going to be different. Midlife crises come about as we struggle against the prospect of mortality that rolls unstoppably toward us, when we willingly succumb to a frenzied panic to achieve eternal life, to stave off aging and remain virile and vigorous forever.

In a society that is as obsessively youth-centric as ours, time is depicted as our enemy and aging has come to be associated with becoming stale and obsolete. This makes it difficult to experience anything but futility and fear as we grow old. Even as I type the phrase "grow old," my initial associations have more to do with words like decline, decay, and deterioration, rather than ascent, ripening, and transformation. We are convinced that once we have lost our youth, we have lost what's most important, that it's "all downhill from here." That is why so many of us are tempted to cling to it long after we have entered midlife. As Woody Allen observed, "I don't want to achieve immortality through my work. I want to achieve it through not dying."

Losing as much as we think we are losing, it is no wonder that we feel "lost" as we cross the threshold into midlife. But just as we have been creating a map to guide adolescents through young adulthood, we need also to chart a course to guide adults through midlife. This map will not only help you to keep your footing and manage some of the confusion that is likely to beset you during this important passage, but also enable you to find some new and interesting landmarks as you journey forth.

Just as we have to shed the skin of childhood to enter young adulthood, we also have to be able to shed the skin of parenthood before we begin midlife. As Carl Jung wrote, "What was true in the morning of life had become in the afternoon a lie." Midlife, be it a time of crisis or opportunity or some of both, is our chance to ferry ourselves and our entire family toward the banks of greater wholeness and authenticity.

This journey has three stages to it:

- Grieving
- Forgiving
- Renewal

Let's spend some time analyzing each of these stages, and follow the path of a patient of mine, Art, as he maneuvers his way through the perils and potentialities of midlife.

GRIEVING

In previous chapters, we have noted how young adults, as well as couples, need to grieve in order to grow. But you must grieve as an individual at midlife, as well. In many ways, parenting young adults seems hauntingly akin to digging your own grave. By preparing your children for departure you are by definition nudging yourself toward your own ultimate departure—the departure from this mortal coil. What you must grieve for has everything to do with reaching the midpoint in your life, the dawning awareness that the end of your existence has suddenly become as real and vivid and close as the beginning. Not only do you think "I'm not getting any younger," but "I'm closer to the end than the start."

At midlife we become more and more surrounded by dramatic reminders of the irreversible passage of time: we may not have actual "near-death" experiences, but we will certainly have nearer-to-death experiences. If your and your mate's parents and older family members have not already passed on, their health is likely diminishing. You and your peers have already passed the pinnacle of your physical prime and are beginning to encounter disquieting ailments and changes that are harbingers of what you will be facing in the years to come. The ages of some of the individuals whose obituaries you read are coming unnervingly close to your own. After having attended funerals sporadically over the past decades, you now encounter them with more and more frequency, and each one that you are present for stirs in you the foreshadowing of your own, try as you might to derail this train of thought. As Philip Roth poignantly writes, it becomes "time to contemplate oblivion."

But even without having to contemplate the conclusion of your life as you reach middle age, you still have to think about the conclusion of your life as a hands-on parent, and that is difficult because we are never more necessary, more relevant, and more important than we are when we are raising children.

When we say good-bye to our children, there is often great pride and relief. But accompanying that farewell is the loss of the part of ourselves that we invested in them, and the feelings of self-worth and self-respect that were intimately bound up with that investment. And when children depart, we not only sing our elegy to parenthood, but to the dreams and wishes that accompanied parenthood: the opportunity to relive our own childhood, to be the nurturer our own parents never were, to be adored and idealized, to execute complete authority and control, to bask in the love of our child. All of this is why midlife is a veritable feast of losses—and why grieving becomes so important.

Grief of this sort, the normal, developmental grief that all of us must engage in if we and our children are going to be free to grow, cannot be easily reduced to a simple formula, but it comprises several key components:

- recognizing what you have lost or are about to lose;
- becoming open to what you may learn and how you may grow even as you come to terms with the inevitability and irretrievability of your loss;
- a growing capacity to appreciate and understand the many strong and complicated emotions aroused by your loss;
- enhanced empathy toward others as you recognize how we are all connected through the shared human experience of loss, how we all remain vulnerable to the finality of life;
- diminished longing for what has been lost and heightened gratitude for what remains;
- a deepened sense of life's meaning and of your purpose in the world.

I refer to "the work of grief" because it is an experience that takes effort, and because our culture does little to support griefwork despite its transformative potential. We live in a feel-good culture, one that encourages us to ignore or circumvent anything that smacks of pain and despair. Grief doesn't make us happy, it's a drag, a bummer. And if we are suffering, then there must be something wrong with us, something inadequate or insufficient, something that needs to be fixed. Grief is not embraced as a universal emotion, but is eschewed as a troublesome divergence from what is supposed to be an everlastingly agreeable existence.

We constantly conflate psychological discomfort with psychiatric disorder and then dash about trying to clinically treat what is often nothing more than the human condition, a condition that is not truly treatable, only livable. It is as if grief were a terrifying snake-haired Medusa's head that we must dodge for fear of being turned into stone—yet by avoiding grief and dodging its healing properties, we ironically end up turning to stone emotionally, or turning to various chemicals and activities that essentially leave us "stoned," estranged from our deeper selves.

Through my practice, after listening carefully to see how different families handle the losses and transitions in their lives and the ways in which they are, or are not, grieving, I have divided them into three categories:

- Active Grievers
- Reluctant Grievers
- Avoidant Grievers

Active grievers are families who intuitively recognize the importance of the grieving process, and who allow grief to carry them to the next stage of their development.

Reluctant grievers are families who are trying to suppress the realities of loss and transfiguration, but who nevertheless recognize that this is impossible and so they grieve somewhat begrudgingly, ultimately seeing grief as a vehicle that transports them forward.

Avoidant grievers are families who counteract the grief process, obstructing the growth of the entire family. When parents don't grieve for the end of hands-on parenthood, they are unable to respond to their children's departure with optimism and equanimity. The inevitable result is a dysfunctional response to their child's effort to separate and differentiate, responses that express themselves as anything from over-protectiveness to rejection, from criticalness to passivity, from withdrawal to scapegoating. By avoiding grief, parents make emptying the nest harder than it has to be, because as long as we can convince ourselves that we need to remain involved as day-to-day parents, we are avoiding the realities of aging, both our children's and our own.

The extent of your grief will of course vary depending on the conditions of your young adult's departure and on the relationship that you have cultivated with him or her over the years. For example, a divorced father who had a very close, peerlike relationship with his 18-year-old son, and who watches him leave home to attend college in another state, will most likely feel something very different from a father in a satisfying marriage whose 18-year-old son has two younger siblings and is still living at home while attending community college.

Another significant factor, of course, is the condition of your own life. A mother whose own parents have died in the past several years and whose job was recently outsourced is more likely to struggle through profound feelings of loss when her daughter finishes college and heads across the continent to attend graduate school than a mother without these outside stresses.

A third factor is what your own departure was like when you left home, because there are always echoes of our childhood experiences in our parenting behavior. Liberating your children means that you have to come to grips with the difficulties that were involved with your own liberation, and now do something other than blindly clone, or thoughtlessly engineer the opposite of, the family dynamic from which you emerged.

But when you willingly take on the grief that is your constant companion during the launching phase of parenthood, you will find that you are more completely and gracefully able to relinquish your attachment to your child, thus facilitating her and your growth and development.

Fifty-five-year-old Art initially consulted with me along with his wife of 27 years, Maggie, due to concerns they were having about their two young adult children. Twenty-year-old Brian, who was living at home and enrolled at a local culinary institute, had wanted to study abroad, or at least in a different state, but was suffering through a seizure disorder that was not being well managed by medication. Because he was prone to frequent and intense seizures and had sustained several mild-to-significant injuries over the last several years as a result of seizure-related falls, both the family and his neurologist had concluded that it simply wasn't safe for him to be living independently, and that he was better off remaining at home until they could get a better handle on his neurological functioning.

Their 18-year-old daughter Chloe was a senior in high school and an excellent artist whose teachers had been encouraging her to attend an art institute after she graduated. But lately she had been procrastinating when it came to putting together her portfolio, an essential part of the application process. She was also beginning to display other worrisome behavior, frequently sneaking out of the house in the middle of the night to get together with friends, and there were hints that she was binge-drinking.

All of this was understandably leaving Art disturbed and perplexed. His wife, Maggie, was concerned as well, but not only about her children.

"I worry about Brian because of his medical condition, and I have no idea what's going on with Chloe right now—I just hope she straightens herself out in time to get her college applications in. But, in a way, Art's the one who's really worrying me. He's just not the same guy these days. He's moody, he's cranky, he almost never smiles—all of the things that people like about him seem to have disappeared."

When I asked him if his wife's concerns were legitimate, Art attempted to sidestep the issue by keeping his focus on the children.

"Look, Brian's seizures just break my heart. I mean, here's a bright, competent guy who could do anything he wants anywhere he wants, and he's stuck at home with us until we figure out a way to get on top of the seizures. And who knows if that's ever going to happen? Is he going to have to live with us forever? And Chloe—well, Chloe was the one we never had to worry about, and now she's starting to tank."

"What about your wife's observations about you? Maggie was saying that she worries about you as much as she worries about Brian and Chloe."

"Oh, that's ridiculous. I'm fine. It's just a little bit of a hard time right now, that's all."

"But Art," Maggie insisted, "we're all noticing it, even the kids: you seem so unhappy, it's like you're always about to blow."

"Well, let's face it, it hasn't been the best of times..."

Art, a former geneticist who was now a high-ranking executive at a biotech firm, went on to explain that the company he worked for was now barely solvent and that his job might be in jeopardy if things didn't turn around soon. Meanwhile, his retirement fund had been decimated by the recent economic downturn, "which means that, at this point, I can't really imagine ever retiring, especially because we don't know what's happening with Brian." They had been hoping to buy a condo in Florida at some point in the next several years, but investments of that sort were now completely out of the question.

In addition, I learned that Art's father was no longer able to take care of his mother, who had Alzheimer's disease, and that he and his two brothers were looking into alternatives, none of which his 84-year-old father seemed amenable to.

With all of these distressing events occurring simultaneously, it wasn't surprising that Art was not his old self. As we spoke, though, I couldn't help but notice the great effort he expended to minimize the grief that he was experiencing as he encountered these profound losses and changes.

"So when I hear about all that is changing in your life, and certainly not all of it for the better, it makes me wonder how you are managing," I offered.

"Oh, pretty well, I guess. I go to work, we go to Brian's doctor's appointments, I try to get Chloe to finish her applications . . . what else is there to do?"

"I would agree that you are managing these complicated matters quite well. But do you spend any time thinking about what it is like to have almost every aspect of your identity—as a father, a son, a professional—in flux right now?"

"Maybe so. But you gotta do what you gotta do, right? No use in whining about it."

"You're right, 'whining about it' is unlikely to be very helpful. But Maggie, who probably knows you better than anyone, is suggesting that you're having a harder time with all of this than you let on, and that you've become a little hard to live with."

"Oh, Maggie, she's such a worrier. There's nothing to worry about with me, hon, it's the kids that we have to worry about. I'll be fine."

Maggie smiled wanly, but didn't seem convinced.

Art's ability to reassure her had further deteriorated by the next time we met when Maggie informed me that his latest physical exam had revealed some problems. Not only were his weight, blood pressure, and cholesterol continuing to escalate, but, for the first time, his liver enzymes were elevated. When I asked him about this, he acknowledged that he had been drinking "a little more than usual" over the past few months.

"I think it's more than 'a little more,' Art," Maggie asserted. "You drink almost every day now, sometimes two or three drinks a day. I think it's a lot more, not a little more."

"Okay, okay, but it's nothing to worry about," he insisted. "I can cut back. It's no big deal."

"What about the blood pressure and cholesterol?" I asked. "What's the plan?"

"He wants to see me again in three months and we'll check them again. Might have been a little temporary spike or something. I just need to lose some weight."

It appeared that Art's effort to quarantine his emotions in the face of such trying circumstances was taking a toll on him not just emotionally, but also physically. Clearly, he was an Avoidant Griever, and would need to be gently, but firmly, pressed forward. With this in mind, he gingerly agreed to meet with me a few times individually (much to his wife's immense relief) to begin tackling some of these concerns more directly.

During our first couple of sessions, I encouraged him to encounter more directly the grief that was weighing on him. Rather than attempting to disregard or deflect the fundamentally changing features of his life, he began to see the importance of becoming better acquainted with them. He began to talk with more honesty about his fears: that neither Brian nor Chloe would ever become self-sufficient, that his father would not manage well once his mother died, that the financial security that he had hoped to establish was now going to be forever beyond his reach, and that now his own health was at risk. We also looked at the role that alcohol was playing in his life, and the ways in which he had begun using it to anesthetize himself against the terrifying feeling that, as he put it, "the walls of my life are closing in on me."

Not surprisingly, as he spoke about these matters, he began to realize how much he had been bottling up, and how much better it felt to release some of the tension.

This release not only enabled him to cut back on his drinking, but it also allowed him to better approach some of these issues. He decided to consult with a new neurologist for Brian, something that he had been thinking about doing for some time. He began speaking with Chloe about her hesitancy to put her portfolio together, and about what was prompting her to sneak out of the house at night. He started to take a closer look at his work situation and assess his future, both individually and within the organization that he had been a part of for almost fifteen years. Further, he arranged to meet his brothers and their father for dinner one evening to discuss their mother's future, rather than relying on sequential email exchanges and "Reply Alls," which weren't leading to any constructive decision-making.

We will pick up with Art again momentarily after we discuss the next important midlife stage.

FORGIVING

Most of us have no clear idea exactly how to forgive, but we all have an intuitive understanding that forgiveness is an immensely valuable act, with profound curative properties and restorative powers. Family forgiveness, the most important of them all, is also the most daunting because of our deep-seated belief that family members should always be loving us rather than hurting us.

You can't truly empty your nest until you have reflected upon forgiveness, both of your young adult and of yourself. We'll begin our discussion with the former.

The idea of forgiving your offspring as she progresses toward self-reliance may at first seem foreign. After all, we tend to think of forgiveness as an act that we invoke when someone has wronged us. But forgiveness is important not only when you have sustained an injury but also when you have experienced a loss. And what is often lost when you are attempting to empty your nest is a sense of fairness, the belief that there can be an even, sustainable balance between what you have given to your children and what you will receive from them.

The emotions that we experience in our close relationships are usually a reliable gauge of how balanced and fair we perceive these relationships to be. For example, we are likely to experience resentment when we're giving more than we're getting in one relationship, and we are likely to experience guilt when we're getting more than we're giving in another relationship. When these imbalances occur, we instinctively try to "right" the relationship, but, depending on how we go about restoring equilibrium, these efforts can be either constructive or destructive.

And when it comes to your relationship with your young adult, the balance is particularly sensitive. After all, the basic, albeit unwritten, parent-child contract goes something like this: "I will make tremendous and enduring sacrifices, investments, and compromises on your behalf, in return for which I expect you to compensate me in a currency that is meaningful to me—in other words, I expect you to become the young adult whom I want you to become." The problem, of course, is that your child never signed this contract, never even knew it existed, and now that he is approaching adulthood he needs to determine who *he* wants to become, not who you want him to become.

So you may have worked two demanding jobs for a decade to send him to a private school so that he might one day qualify for competitive colleges, only to find that he seems to have little interest in attending such institutions. Or you may have invested over a hundred thousand dollars in her private college education, obliterating any retirement plans of your own for at least the next decade, only to find out that she is still unable to make a living without even *more* education. Or you may have put your own career on hold for the past dozen years to be a full-time parent, only to find that you have raised a full-time Fantasy Football League aficionado whose prospects for actual paid employment remain unremittingly bleak.

In these situations forgiveness must enter, releasing both generations from the claws of the unsigned contract. Through this process, our anger and disappointment dissolve and we learn how to love, accept, and let go of our young adult even if he is growing up in ways that we do not completely approve of. If resenting is akin to swallowing poison and expecting the person you resent to die from it, forgiving is the antidote.

In my books *The Good Enough Child* and *The Good Enough Teen*, I hypothesize that every one of our children actually experiences three separate births in our hearts and minds. Before parenthood begins, there is the birth of the Fantasy Child, the child of our dreams whose exquisite perfection leaves us feeling whole and fulfilled. Once we actually enter parenthood, however, there is the birth of the Actual Child, the one who is destined to disappoint and disillusion, to enrage and frustrate us at various points throughout the course of his development. Finally, and hopefully, there is the birth of the Good Enough Child, who is lovable and worthwhile simply for being who he is, rather than who we want him to be. The journey from Fantasy Child to Actual Child to Good Enough Child is a meandering one, but forgiveness is what enables us to reach each successive stage in this journey, and when everyone in the family forgives and is forgiven, the journey generally concludes with a healthy launch.

But forgiveness is not only important when it comes to your relationship with your young adult, but also when it comes to your relationship with yourself. After all, it is difficult to avoid seeing the various milestones in your child's development as some sort of referendum on your parenting, particularly during early adulthood, since this is the penultimate point in time when all of the effort that you have expended is supposed to finally come to fruition and pay off. When it doesn't—and in one way or another, I can guarantee you, it won't—you will scour your past for all of your parental defects and deficiencies, trying desperately to figure out what you might have done differently to have fostered a better outcome.

The reality, of course, is that there are many forces that account for your young adult's particular status at any point in time, only one of which is your child-rearing influence. No matter how loving and attentive you may have been, you cannot count upon a particular outcome, nor can you inoculate your child against distress or misfortune; these are ineradicable components of the panorama of life. So while you have every right, and good reason, to pay close attention to adjustments that might be worth making during the launching phase of parenthood, it will not be productive to lacerate yourself with repeated lashes of your self-persecutory whip in a futile attempt to explain realities that were never completely under your dominion.

And that is where self-forgiveness comes into play, because the loss that we need to forgive *ourselves* for is the loss of our perfection, the acknowledgement that despite our ideal aspirations, we are limited by our clumsy feet of clay. By forgiving ourselves for having broken the promises that we made both to ourselves and to our children regarding the kind of mother or father we wanted to be—promises that we made with all sincerity—we become better able to learn from our experience and do better. And even after our children have left home, it is never too late to do better. Forgiveness doesn't mean brooding over all that we *didn't* do, but opening up to all that we still *can* do as parents, and as people.

How do we forgive? That is a difficult question to answer, but it is worth considering nevertheless. What I have seen in my explorations of forgiveness in the consultation room is that it takes either a spiritual or psychological form, or some hybrid of the two. Since forgiveness is an intrinsic element in every religious tradition, many people find forgiveness through their spiritual self, often through prayer, meditation, or ritual. In the psychological form, when we have grown weary of the burden of resentment that we have been shouldering, we often make an intuitive decision that it's best that we forgive, and actively set about creating and cultivating a forgiving state of mind. So we keep a journal in which we write about forgiveness, or we converse more frankly with individuals whom we want to forgive in an attempt to understand them and their motives better. But however it is pursued, forgiveness is best seen as a process rather than a discrete event.

And either way, spiritual or psychological, our aim to forgive will be truer when we are compassionate with ourselves. We need to examine our actions not with harsh self-criticism but with friendly curiosity and gentle honesty. And when we do this, each generation gains, for we release ourselves from the clutches not only of who we think we ought to be but also of who we think our children ought to be.

The more we learn to be at home in ourselves—with our long history of flaws, fears, and insecurities—the more our children will be at home within themselves, and, as a result, the more likely they will be able to *leave* home with gratitude and an eager appetite for whatever it is that awaits them, the sweet and the bitter. Our relationship with them as young adults will depend intimately on our having a good relationship with ourselves, and this can only result from thoughtfully and tenderly forgiving ourselves.

❧ ❧

Art acknowledged that he had work to do when it came to forgiving himself. But when it came to forgiving his children, he was at first dismissive.

"It's certainly not Brian's fault that he's afflicted with these seizures. And Chloe is just going through a phase."

"Nevertheless," I suggested, "it would be natural for you to feel frustrated and disappointed with both of them. I agree with you completely that Brian's seizures are not his fault, but it's still evidence of his not being perfect, and whenever our children aren't perfect, for whatever reason, whether it's fair or not, resentment can creep in. And that's where forgiveness is useful, to take the edge off of the resentment."

"What about Chloe?" he wondered. "Do I need to forgive her, too?"

"Sure ... after all, she was your 'flawless' daughter until recently, and now she's displaying some flaws as well—not moving ahead with her life, sneaking out of the house at night."

"What do you think that's about?" he asked.

"One thought is she's not really convinced that she's going to be able to leave home out the 'front door,' so she has consigned herself to a back-door escape."

"Why doesn't she think she can leave through the front door? She's got it all—good grades, great artistic talent, a terrific personality ..."

"Perhaps because she sees that her brother hasn't quite left home yet, so she believes that she has to postpone her own leave-taking until he has embarked on his."

"Why would she want to do that? We've never asked her to hold back ..."

"I'm not saying that you did. But siblings often have a certain unspoken loyalty to each other, and Chloe might feel guilty if she were to proceed with a departure before her older brother did. Sort of like the biblical law of primogeniture, the eldest gets 'first rights' to everything, including leaving."

Art agreed to speak with Chloe about this possibility. He was stunned to learn how upset she was about her brother's medical condition and how much she had been secretly worrying about him. He presented our hypothesis to her, and she was relieved to speculate that it wasn't laziness that accounted for her dawdling on her college applications or mere rebelliousness that accounted for her nocturnal excursions, but the depth of her concern for her vulnerable older brother that was most relevant when it came to explaining these behaviors. In addition, though, Art did make it clear to Chloe that they would be supervising her much more carefully and that she would lose driving privileges if they found her sneaking out. This prospective consequence, along with their new understanding of the basis for her behavior, put that problem to rest.

He also followed through with the new neurologist and was heartened to hear that she had recently received a grant to study an innovative surgical technique. The neurologist said Brian would most likely qualify as a participant in the upcoming clinical trials.

When it came to self-forgiveness, Art spoke with great sadness about how busy he had been at work when the children were growing up, and how unavailable he had been, both physically and emotionally. He also disclosed his long-standing, unspoken belief that his side of the family was responsible for Brian's seizures disorder:

"After all," he sadly noted, "my mother's got Alzheimer's, and her father had Alzheimer's, too, and I've got a brother with Tourette syndrome . . . so clearly we're the ones who passed on the bad-brain genes to Brian."

Art and I spent some time assessing the legitimacy of his guilt and holding it up to the light of reason. It was true that he had not been as active and present a father as he would have wanted to be. On the other hand, he had not spent his time on leisure pursuits, but had been fiercely committed to providing well for his family, something that he had accomplished splendidly, and that had enabled his wife to attend more fully to their children.

He agreed with me that, particularly with a son who was medically vulnerable, having money in the bank was of great importance. And to imagine that it was his fault that Brian had seizures was illogical, at best, although we did discuss how it can be more tempting to feel guilty rather than helpless, especially when someone whom we care about deeply is in pain.

But as we pursued our conversations about forgiveness, what Art noticed was that simply *considering* forgiveness—of his children as well as himself—seemed to reduce the intensity of his feelings of both resentment and guilt. And freeing himself of this intensity in turn freed him to be present to his children in a way that served both of them— Brian, from a medical perspective, and Chloe, psychologically—and that made them all feel closer to one another.

RENEWAL

When the shackles of parenthood are untied, when the daily practice of keeping track of children begins to fade, and when we have undergone the intertwined processes of Grieving and Forgiving, a rich personal Renewal is much easier to achieve. After all, remember that the phrase "growing older" implies that growth is embedded in aging. Until relatively recently in human culture, only two stages of life were recognized, childhood and adulthood. But the years that precede self-reliant adulthood are now broken up into various stages: infant, toddler, child, "tween," adolescent, and young adult. So we need to do the same thing when it comes to the 60 or more years that comprise adulthood; the poverty of our single-word vocabulary suggests that we aren't acknowledging the creative possibilities lurking in the decades of postparental life.

But to experience these possibilities, we have to allow ourselves to not just age, but indeed to *grow* old. Growth of this sort can be just as variegated as it was during childhood, adolescence, and early adulthood, and it can be just as disquieting and unpredictable. What once brought us pleasure may now bring us nothing more than frustration, what once was sought after now seems meaningless. Goals for which we strove for so long are, we realize with intensifying twinges of fatality, absolutely unreachable. Personal bargains that we have been making in the service of an idealized future seem to have been a complete waste of time, without any observable payoff now, or possibly ever.

The key to midlife renewal is envisioning the second half of life not as a second childhood or adolescence, which many try to do, but as a midcourse correction that leads us toward a second stage of adult development. It is not that we become free of responsibility when we empty the nest; as I noted in the first chapter, these days it is certainly possible, if not likely, that your young adult will remain financially dependent on you to some extent well into his or her twenties. But even with significant responsibilities in place, the inner voices that have been yearning to be heard but that have been muffled, if not muted altogether, by the pressures of the previous decades can now be listened to with more care and attentiveness.

The crossing of the threshold into midlife is filled not only with endings, but with beginnings, and beginnings are not just part of our children's psychological heritage, but part of our own, as well.

To make this Renewal a reality, here are some emphases to keep in mind:

VISION OVER PLANS

You may have spent your life making plans, but you probably know by now that plans are fragile, because plans depend on the world being exactly the way you want it to be, and the world will never agree to this expectation.

Vision, however, is not fragile—it is sturdy and robust. That is because your Vision is your internal sense of who you are and who you are destined to become, and it will unerringly guide your life, like a compass, toward True North. Relying on Vision requires more persistence and introspection than making plans does but it is the surest path toward Renewal.

QUESTIONS OVER ANSWERS

Answers are reassuring and satisfying in their own way, but a life spent in search of answers doesn't have anything to do with Renewal. Instead, you need to seek out questions—immense, often unanswerable questions, questions that you live with rather than solve, questions that you invite to take up residence within you: What am I doing here? What gives my life meaning? How can I learn to give and receive love more generously?

THE EDGE OVER THE CENTER

We all find it safer to occupy the center of our lives, but the center doesn't provide much room for Renewal. Instead, we need to find a way to move toward the edge of our existence, what we used to think of as the margins, the realms that we are less familiar with, less comfortable with.

Sometimes we will find that life forces us to the edge: we are confronted with adversity that rudely shoves us away from the shelter that the center of life affords us. Sometimes, we will have to move ourselves to the edge, to bravely nudge our main psychological station from the Comfort Zone to the Discomfort Zone and leave what is recognizable behind. This entails taking the risk of experimenting with original ways of thinking and relating, of doing and being. But it's only from the edge that Renewal truly takes flight and carries us toward uncharted horizons.

MISTAKES OVER SUCCESSES

Our victories deserve to be enjoyed and celebrated, but it is our mistakes and failures that connect us both to ourselves and others. By making mistakes and responding to them with open-minded inquisitiveness, you not only learn from your mistakes but also create a home within yourself for Renewal. Remember that if you are not afraid of failure, you greatly increase the odds that you will ultimately succeed.

ACCEPTANCE OVER RESIGNATION

By the time we reach midlife, we have usually begun to recognize that we don't have nearly as much control over the universe as we first imagined we did. There are two ways to respond to this disturbing realization. One is resignation, which usually means passively settling for a pervasive sense of pointlessness and hopelessness: "I might as well submit to my fate, since nothing I can do is apparently going to make any difference, anyway."

Acceptance is the other way, the more active way. When we accept the world as it is, we are activated to do what can be done to make our lives, and the lives of others, better. While resignation leaves us feeling depleted and powerless, acceptance gives us the ability to distinguish between what we do and do not have influence over, and to focus our energies on the former while coming to terms with the latter. Making this distinction clears the path toward Renewal, and enables us to travel it with more courage and joy.

Emphasizing Vision over Plans, Questions over Answers, the Edge over the Center, Mistakes over Successes, and Acceptance over Resignation obviously won't guarantee a midlife Renewal, but will certainly point you in the right direction.

As Art worked his way through Grief and Forgiveness, he began to feel better, both physically and mentally. His spirit had come alive again, and when Maggie rejoined us for a session, she buoyantly portrayed a very different situation.

"It's like I've got the old Art back. He's lighter, he's funnier, and he seems more focused and more directed. He's not this cranky, lost soul wandering through the house like he's in exile."

Indeed, several months after we had first met, things looked much brighter for him. After extensive deliberation, Brian had decided to sign up for the clinical trial of the new neurological device and was going in for surgery at the end of the year to have it implanted. Meanwhile, Chloe had righted herself: she finished up her portfolio, submitted applications to several art institutes, and had stopped sneaking out at night, perhaps as she realized that she was entitled to leave home

the "front door" even while her brother was detained there a
...nger.

Art and his brothers had found a reputable residential facility for
their mother to move into, and they had also been collaboratively able
to sell their father on the idea. Art cut back on his drinking and started
attending martial arts classes three times a week, something that he
hadn't done since he and Brian participated back when Brian was in
middle school.

And, tired of being an executive at a company that was hanging on
by the skin of its teeth, he had begun to explore other professional options. He had recently run into a former graduate school classmate who
invited Art to think about teaching and performing research at a local
medical school. The idea of no longer being held captive by the constraints of product development and returning to academia, his first
love, had breathed new life into him and restored his sense of purpose.

Even though Art had originally contacted me to focus exclusively
on his children's lagging development, his willingness to take a more
careful look at his own psychological state, to Grieve, Forgive, and
Renew, promoted growth that all four family members became the
beneficiaries of.

EXERCISE

As we have just seen, a common missing piece to the launching of your
young adult is your own launch—the launch into a rich and satisfying
midlife. We are often so busy paying attention to our children's evolution, or lack thereof, that we end up neglecting our own.

When I am working with parents to help them empty their nest, I
will often ask them to do the following assignment. For the next two
weeks, I tell them, I would like you to write about your deepest
thoughts and feelings regarding an extremely important emotional
issue that has affected you and your life. Really let go and explore your
innermost landscape with as much candor and inquisitiveness as possible, and do so at least twice a day for at least fifteen minutes at a time.

Individuals who follow through on this invariably find that they instinctively lock onto the personal dilemma or theme that needs to be addressed the most pressingly. They also find that the writing effortlessly opens up perspective, insight, and solutions, all of which galvanize them to leave their own self-limiting nest and create a second half of life filled with revitalized promise and possibility.

CONCLUSION

DANCING TO THE MUSIC OF TIME

THOUGHTS AND REFLECTIONS

A banjo-playing friend told me that banjo players spend half of their time tuning up and the other half playing out of tune. Having been raising children for 23 years now, and having supported countless others in doing the same, it's difficult for me not to see an analogy between parents and banjo players.

We spend tremendous amounts of time reading, thinking, and talking about being effective parents, and a seemingly equal amount of time concluding that we are essentially (and sometimes titanically) ineffective parents. It is extremely difficult to get parental love right, to be certain that we are appropriately "in tune" with our children, no matter their age or stage of development.

And as we have seen during the previous pages, emptying the nest presents unique challenges to contemporary parents, and human development will always be vastly more complex than the relatively simple avian development that inspired the nesting metaphor.

No matter how much we try, we are disturbingly unable to prepare our children for *every* eventuality that they will face. All we can do is hope that we have been "good enough" parents—good enough to stir in our children the capacity to rally their resources, call forth their strengths and overcome their liabilities when life becomes frustrating, difficult or overwhelming, as it inevitably will.

Because my clinical approach to the issue of emptying the nest is not always the standard or conventional one, I would like to close by providing you with some general thoughts and reflections that may be useful as you journey through this crucial phase of child-rearing.

Those of you who have read one or more of my previous books may notice that some of what I have been suggesting and prescribing for this stage of parenthood sounds familiar, and is not altogether different from what I have been suggesting and prescribing for the previous stages of parenthood in *Things Just Haven't Been the Same,* which addressed the opening stages of family life, *The Good Enough Child,* about early and middle childhood, and *The Good Enough Teen* and *When No One Understands,* concerning adolescence.

But as a family psychologist, I have learned that the most anxious and vulnerable stages for individuals generally occur when someone is either entering or leaving their lives, and being that the final stage of parenthood obviously entails a departure, I believe that it has been worth elaborating on some of these original suggestions and prescriptions, as well as supplying the additional ones that we have been discussing.

First, despite the tireless efforts of clinicians and researchers, the mysteries of parent and child development remain endless and elusive, and no amount of education, care or effort is going to inoculate you or your young adult against disappointment and disillusionment, against challenge and complexity. Sometimes, as I examine my own family and the families I work with, I feel as if my years of earnest theorizing have left me no more knowledgeable or sophisticated than a caveman staring up at the night sky, dimly wondering about the origin and essence of stars.

Because of this, it is important to maintain compassion and empathy, both for your children as well as yourself: your goal is not to finish the marathon of parenthood grimly determined to understand what went wrong while insisting on what must go right, but instead to en-counter this very complicated stage of family life with kindness, accept-ance, patience, and, might I add (because you're going to need it), a sense of humor.

Emptying the nest is not to be confused with attaining an ideal state of perfection by smoothing out all remaining rough spots, entirely tying up all of the loose ends and neatly processing and integrating all of the tumult and turbulence that has taken place in the preceding years of family life. It should not be taken on as an exercise in finality or res-olution, a project to complete or a race to win or a battle to fight. It is instead best envisioned as an opportunity to become more acquainted with yourself in your on-going effort to live your life with honesty, meaning, and wholeness.

Emptying the nest is also not to be defined by laying out, with cer-tainty and correctness, a road for your child to compliantly travel. In-stead, it should be defined by your willingness to experience as much wonder during the *psychological* birth of your child's young adult iden-tity as you experienced during the *physical* birth of that same young adult years ago, or during the *welcoming* birth that occurred when your family life began through adoption, foster care, or stepparenthood. Just as you may have been trained during childbirth education classes to see labor pains as "waves that are bringing the baby closer to birth," so you must learn to see the more painful and frustrating parts of the launch-ing process as waves that carry your young adult forward into his new life, and that carry you forward into your new life, as well.

When the nest-emptying process is not going well, your job is to not harden into a position of resentment and indignation, carrying contempt for your young adult, and, unavoidably, for yourself. Instead, you could try to notice how you may have been blocking your heart or closing your mind and, through so doing, permit a larger perspective to emerge. As we have seen, when there is a seemingly intractable family problem it is usually not your failure, nor your offspring's, but a failure of everyone's *imagination*, a collective inability to see the problem as a beacon that can lead the way toward innovative solutions.

And when things are not going well, it's important to remember that no family situation, no matter how dire, is ever hopeless, that every situation is eminently workable. For things to change for the better, there simply needs to *be* a change—sometimes small, sometimes large—in your outlook and approach. I have treated many families over the years, and while I certainly have not batted 1.000, I've done pretty well. Part of the basis for this is my optimistic but clinically well-founded belief that evolution and growth are natural processes, and that if we find ways to remove recent or long-standing obstacles, healthy psychological development will occur quite naturally.

The launching stage of parenthood, just like any other stage, is bound to be frustrating and demoralizing at times, but you can still invite this frustration and demoralization to promote your own development, to continue the process of growing yourself up. Generally, when things go the way we want them to, we may be content for a time, but we tend not to evolve. It is only when our expectations are violated, when the world fails to provide us with what we are so firmly convinced we deserve, that we claim the opportunity to take delight in a deepened understanding of ourselves. The most difficult people and the most humbling situations can be our most powerful, insistent, and influential teachers if we invite them to.

Ultimately, the emptying of the nest can teach us to love ourselves, and our family members, *because of,* not just in *spite* of, our shared flaws and imperfections, our stubborn insufficiencies and frailties. We acquire additional practice through an open-minded engagement in promoting our young adults' separation and liberation, in learning to love them for their *own* sake, rather than because of what they do for us or how well they reflect on us.

While I consistently advocate an empathetic and compassionate outlook, however, that is not to be confused with being exploited or taken advantage of, or with avoiding the necessary struggles and conflicts that are essential nutrients for young adult development. Sometimes the most empathetic and compassionate thing you can do is to draw a line and set a limit with your young adult, and make it clear that you can only tolerate so much, and have simply had "enough." Many parents *reach* the end of their rope; sometimes it's necessary to *stay* at the end of your rope so that you don't capitulate or relent when it comes to line-drawing and limit-setting.

In reality, my approach is not truly about *helping* your young adult to leave home, because once you identify yourself as "helping," you encourage your young adult to see herself as "help*less*"—somehow inadequate and incapable. The key is creating the family scaffolding that encourages and supports your young adult in emancipating *herself*, and sometimes that means doing less rather than more.

Finally, the process of leaving home and moving on is not just about "getting"—"getting a job" or "getting my own place" or "getting out"—but about "giving," as well: giving to one's family, one's community, and to the world at large. Martin Luther King Jr. said it best: "Anybody can be great," he reminded us, "because anybody can serve." Growing up is not just about labor in the commercial workplace, but labor in the *inner* and *communal* workplace, labor that entails the expansion of one's identity, the cultivation of a full and fulfilling life, and the striking of an effective balance between competence and connectedness, between self-care and care for others.

While I am advocating, in the subtitle of this book, a launch toward "success" and "self-reliance," I do not equate the two. Unfortunately, in our culture, we sometimes assume that they are interchangeable— the more successful we are, the less we need others. Success, from my perspective, is ultimately not defined by how much money you have in your bank account, but by how well and gracefully you are able to give and receive love. And no one is truly self-reliant, no matter how prosperous, for the more you acquire, the more burdened you become, and the less you appreciate and value the bonds with others that are what truly nourish and sustain us. In the words of an African proverb, "If you want to go fast, travel alone . . . if you want to go far, travel together."

TREATMENT ISSUES

While I am hopeful that this book has provided you with enough perspective and guidance that you have been able to answer some of the questions and resolve some of the difficulties that led you to read it, it is of course impossible for me to provide the comprehensive cartography necessary to map out the vast landscape of personal and family predicaments that we are all vulnerable to. With this in mind, there may be times when consulting with a professional is worthwhile.

As you may have already gleaned from the numerous case studies presented in the preceding chapters, the therapist's role, from my perspective, is one that hinges entirely on empowering family members to see and do things differently, to acquire tools and design strategies that ultimately render the therapist unnecessary. In this sense, just as I encourage parents to let their children transcend *them*, I encourage my patients to transcend *me*. Promoting a dependency on treatment undercuts the self-reliance that is the precursor for a successfully emptied nest. When they don't need me anymore, then I—or, I should say we— have been successful.

That is why my treatment of young adults and their parents looks carefully at the ecology of the entire family, rather than at any one member's problems or pathology. The basic premise, as I stated in the Introduction, is that no single individual is at fault, but that every individual is responsible for contributing to and creating stuck points, as well as for getting free of them. From my perspective, embracing and cultivating *responsibility* means you are embracing and cultivating *possibility*.

When prospective patients call and ask me if I treat children or adolescents or young adults, I always say "Yes," but the answer is really "No": I don't treat children, adolescents, or young adults—I treat *families*. That is why many of the young adults whom I have taken care of I have never actually met. When open-minded parents are willing to make changes in their behavior, even without their young adult sitting with us in my office, those changes reverberate throughout the family system, and *everyone* winds up changing.

Many of the families that come to me because they're having trouble emptying the nest present their problems as if they have lately arisen, either very recently, during early adulthood, or somewhat recently, such as during late adolescence. However, I usually discover that the genesis extends well into the past, but in a form that was moderate enough that initially it did not present any serious developmental holdups. Only when difficulties with leave-taking are unmistakably presenting themselves do the roots of these difficulties most clearly reveal themselves.

So, some uncovering of the past may be required to understand the basis for the patterns that are in place, but only as much as is necessary to construct useful alterations. It shouldn't take months of work for a skilled therapist to assist you in making tangible progress on this front, so if you and/or your young adult have been working with a clinician for some time without seeing concrete results, it may be time to consider a change.

Also, because (unfortunately) contemporary parents have, from early on, been encouraged to believe that "others" know best when it comes to their child, they often assume that internal and vaguely defined factors (such as "chemical imbalances," "attention deficits," "low self-esteem") wholly account for their young adult's behavior. As a result, they gravely underestimate the potential impact that they themselves can have on their child, even during the leave-taking stage, and they are relegated to being helpless bystanders. As long as every nettlesome separation or liberation problem is reduced to some "medical" or "psychiatric" or "neurological" basis, these problems may remain unsolvable, and healthy autonomy and self-reliance are less likely to be achieved. As a result, I always take an active, problem-solving approach, providing families with specific tactics that are likely to remind them of what they can and need to do to induce change and promote growth.

Many of the parents who consult with me regarding young adult–related issues will at some point ask me exactly how long the process of emptying the nest will take. My answer to this question is always the same: it will take the rest of your life. Separation begins at the moment of birth and evolves into the work of a lifetime. I don't mean this in a pessimistic way, and I certainly don't mean to suggest that you should count on your children being completely dependent on you forever, living in your basement, lounging on your couch, eating your food, squandering your money. Nor am I being facetious.

What I mean, first of all, is that there is never any one point when we are "done" with a relationship as complex, intense, and fraught with worry as parenthood is. There will always be, from our parental perspective, good times and bad times in the lives of our children. It will indeed take most of us our whole life to learn how to create enough room for life to happen—life with all of its triumphs and defeats, all of its joy and anguish—and to do so without leaping into misguided action based on our premature conclusions regarding what is taking place.

What I also mean when I suggest that the launching process is a lifelong process is that we retain, throughout our lives, the capacity to continuously learn and grow, deepen and soften, become more loving and more compassionate, and as long as we are open to this capacity, our relationship with our children (and others, of course) can be worked on and improved upon. That is one of the great gifts of parenthood: it prevents us from ever becoming stagnant and forces us to rise to the persistent, lifelong challenges that child-rearing so munificently offers us.

∽ ∼

I began this chapter with a musical analogy, and I will conclude with one, as well. In many ways, human development resembles to me a most exquisite symphony in that the initial "movement," childhood, establishes the emotional setting for all that follows. Subsequent movements—adolescence, young adulthood, midlife, and late adulthood—will introduce new elements, new themes, new tones and shadings. Some of these may elaborate and build upon the music that was laid out initially, some may establish a melodic counterpoint, but all of the succeeding movements still remain in a vigorously intimate conversation with the orchestral strains that were revealed in the opening movement.

And so life's music unfolds like a symphony, a concerto, striving toward some profound, emotionally powerful resolution—an intertwining of expected and surprising, harmonic and discordant, lovely and painful.

Music represents the composer's effort to structure sound so as to create beauty, and this effort echoes our individual effort to structure our lives so as to create meaning. Our most sublime moments, musically or experientially, speak to our deepest desire to discover the passion and purpose that connect us to one another and that enable us to collectively transcend the terrifying fear that life has no meaning.

I often start off my lectures on the cognitive development of children and adolescents by asking audience members—be they students, parents, clinicians, or instructors—what they believe to be the three most important functions of the brain. Most don't get it right (and it's definitely not "reading, writing, and 'rithmetic"). The remarkable human brain has essentially and ultimately been designed to accomplish three extraordinary tasks: to survive, to reproduce, and to care for those who depend on us. Raising children, our most precious dependents, so that they become independent is life's most meaningful and creative endeavor. And to empty your nest and launch your children upward so that they, too, are able to find meaning and perhaps one day take their own little stab at eternity and raise children of their own— well, that is surely the most extraordinary thing of all.

I hope that this book serves to guide you through this final stage of child-rearing, and that the result is that you and your children find yourselves dancing to a symphony of music—both ancient and timeless—that resounds like love in the most intimate chambers of your family's heart.

Like painted kites, the days and nights, they keep flying by.
—"The Summer Wind," as sung by Frank Sinatra
on "Fridays with Frank"

INDEX